Emigrants and Empire

BRITISH SETTLEMENT IN THE DOMINIONS
BETWEEN THE WARS

edited by Stephen Constantine

**MANCHESTER
UNIVERSITY PRESS**
Manchester and New York

Distributed exclusively in the USA and Canada
by ST. MARTIN'S PRESS

Published by Manchester Univeristy Press
Oxford Road, Manchester M13 9PL, UK
and Room 400, 175 Fifth Avenue,
New York, NY 10010, USA

Distributed exclusively in the USA and Canada
by St. Martin's Press, Inc.,
175 Fifth Avenue, New York, NY 10010, USA

British Library cataloguing in publication data
Constantine, Stephen
  Emigrants and empire : British settlement in the dominions between the wars. ——
  (Studies in imperialism).
  1. Great Britain. Emigration to Commonwealth countries, history. Commonwealth
  countries. Immigration from Great Britain, history
  I. Title II. Series
  304.80941

Library of Congress cataloging in publication data
Emigrants and empire : British settlement in the dominions between the wars / edited by
  Stephen Constantine.
      p. cm. — (Studies in imperialism)
    ISBN 0-7190-3011-0
      1. Great Britain—Emigration and immigration—History—20th century. 2. Great
  Britain—Colonies—Emigration and immigration—History—20th century.
  I. Constantine, Stephen. II. Series: Studies in imperialism (Manchester, England)
  JV7615.E45   1990
  325'.241'09171241—dc20   89-77464

ISBN 0–7190–3011–0 *hardback*

Printed in Great Britain
by Bell & Bain Limited, Glasgow

Photoset in Linotron Trump Mediaeval by
Northern Phototypesetting Co Ltd, Bolton

CONTENTS

GENERAL INTRODUCTION

When the 'Studies in Imperialism' series was founded in 1985, it seemed possible that the study of 'imperial' history was destined to break down into its national components. The titles of both professorial chairs and publishers' series had been converted to the euphemism 'Commonwealth' and the progressive acts of political decolonisation and legal and constitutional repatriation had led to a natural concentration upon the domestic histories of individual territories. But contrary trends were also at work during the 1980s. It became apparent that the effects of Empire upon the United Kingdom had been too little studied; that much remained to be done in the fields of cultural, social and scientific history; and that an integrative and interactive approach to imperial history remained both possible and necessary.

Migration studies provide an excellent example of such work. In the history of the British Empire, there has been a good deal more concentration upon emigration than immigration. Yet migration can only be fully understood in terms of both donor and receiver societies. Viewed in this way, it has an extraordinary capacity to illuminate the social and economic, political and ideological, as well as the cultural and institutional histories of the various states sharing the colonial experience. Attitudes towards migration, and the policies and propaganda in which they were expressed, offer rich insights for the historian in considering the relationship between voluntarism and statism in the twentieth century, approaches to gender, perceptions of social problems and their solution, and the clash of economic and ideological interests.

This work concentrates upon the attempts to promote state-assisted migration in the post-First World War period particularly associated with the Empire Settlement Act of 1922. The various contributions examine the background to these new emigration experiments, the development of plans for both individual and family migration, as well as the specific schemes for the settlement of ex-servicemen and of women, and the varying degrees of encouragement, acquiescence and resistance with which they were received in the dominions. The chapters on Australia, New Zealand, Canada and South Africa set the controversies generated by these policies firmly into the context of the specific political and social strains and economic needs of each of those territories. Thus the research represented here makes a significant contribution to the social histories of these states as well as of the United Kingdom. In charting aspects of post-war reconstruction associated with imperial social engineering, the authors reveal a record of success and failure that casts much adjacent light. The book illustrates what can be achieved when historians from a number of different countries co-operate in the study of significant social planning in a hitherto neglected period.

JMM

LIST OF CONTRIBUTORS

Edna Bradlow graduated from the University of Cape Town, where since 1966 she has been a lecturer in the Department of History. She was awarded her Ph.D. in 1978 for a study of 'Immigration into the Union 1910–1948: Policies and Attitudes'. She is the co-author of *Here Comes the Alabama, Frederick I'Ons, Artist* and *Thomas Bowler of the Cape of Good Hope*, and she has published numerous articles in academic journals.

Stephen Constantine is a graduate of the University of Oxford and is now Senior Lecturer in History at the University of Lancaster, where he has been teaching since 1971. He is the author of several academic articles and of *The Making of British Colonial Development Policy, 1914–1940, Buy and Build: the Advertising Posters of the Empire Marketing Board* and *Unemployment in Britain between the Wars*.

Kent Fedorowich was a student at the University of Saskatchewan where his M.A. thesis dealt with Henry Rider Haggard and the concept of Empire in his adventure fiction. His Ph.D. thesis, completed at the London School of Economics, is called 'Foredoomed to Failure: The Resettlement of British Ex-Servicemen in the Dominions after World War I'. He is now a Lecturer in British Imperial and Commonwealth History at Bristol Polytechnic.

Janice Gothard graduated from the Australian National University, Canberra, taught at Griffith University, Brisbane, and is currently completing her Ph.D. at Murdoch University, Perth, on single female migration from Britain to Australia, 1860–1920. She has contributed to the bicentennial publication *The Australian People*, has published an article on female emigration to Tasmania and is editor of an oral history collection *Across Perth Water: Reminiscences of South Perth*.

Michael Roe was educated at the University of Melbourne and the University of Cambridge and obtained his Ph.D. at the Australian National University. He has taught at the University of Tasmania since 1960, becoming Professor of History in 1977. His publications include

Quest for Authority in Eastern Australia, The Letters and Journal of Captain Charles Bishop, Kenealy and the Tichborne Cause and *Nine Australian Progressives*.

John Schultz graduated from Michigan State University, studied at the University of London and obtained his Ph.D. from Dalhousie University, Nova Scotia. He has taught in the Department of History at Mount Allison University, New Brunswick since 1972. In 1988 he became for two years Professor of Canadian Studies at the University of Tsukuba, Japan. He is the author of several academic articles especially on Canadian immigration.

Keith Williams studied history at the University of York, followed by postgraduate study at the University of London where he completed in 1985 his Ph.D. on 'The British State, Social Imperialism and Emigration from Britain, 1900–22: the Ideology and Antecedents of the Empire Settlement Act'. He is the co-author of an article on women's emigration to South Africa after the Boer War. He is currently employed as a Housing Officer in North London.

CHAPTER ONE

Introduction: Empire migration and imperial harmony

Stephen Constantine

Of course, emigration from the United Kingdom was not a new pheno-menon after the First World War. Rather it constituted another phase in that remarkable exodus of British and other European peoples which, particularly in the nineteenth century, had hugely expanded the number and size of white settler societies overseas and permanently changed the economic, political and cultural geography of the world. Over 16 million British people left the United Kingdom between 1815 and 1914.[1] Most, but not all, intended to settle abroad; exact numbers are difficult to establish because emigrants were only specifically identified among passengers and counted separately from 1913. Some historians have assumed that emigration was much lower after the First World War, but this is to echo those contemporaries who misleadingly compared post-war emigration figures with pre-war passenger figures. Assuming the same ratio existed between outward passengers and out-ward migrants as during the decade 1920–29, a total of 1,816,618 British emigrants may be calculated for the decade 1901–10. Figures then rose sharply to a peak of 389,394 in 1913. Post-war averages were certainly lower than that, but they remained substantial. There were 1,811,553 recorded emigrants in 1920–29. It must be conceded, however, that the figure for 1930–38 was reduced to a mere 334,467.[2] Net emigration was as always significantly lower than gross, amounting to 1,185,952 in 1920–29. More remarkably there was even a net immigration of 151,641 between 1930 and 1938.[3] Revival after the Second World War led to a net extra-European emigration of United Kingdom citizens of around 652,000 in the 1950s.[4] Gallup polls suggest a persistent interest in emigration: between 1948 and 1975 usually 30–40 per cent of respondents expressed a wish to settle in another country.[5] The inter-war years did not then witness simply the last gasp of a nineteenth-century experience, but were part of a story indicative of a continuing, though variable, propensity to emigrate among British people.

The Gallup polls also produced some notable answers to the question of which country would potential emigrants choose as their destination. In March 1948, of the 42 per cent of respondents interested in emigrating, 9 per cent selected Australia, 9 per cent South Africa, 8 per cent New Zealand, 6 per cent Canada and only 4 per cent opted for the United States of America.[6] The charm of a new life in the white Commonwealth was much more a characteristic of the twentieth century than of the nineteenth century. In the 1880s and 1890s less than one-third of British emigrants had sailed to Empire destinations; most of the rest had headed for the USA. A redirection is discernible thereafter, with nearly half the emigrants travelling to the dominions between 1901 and 1910 and two-thirds in 1911 and 1912.[7] In the 1920s over 65 per cent chose homes in the dominions. Even in the difficult depressed years of the 1930s this was the choice of nearly 47 per cent of British emigrants.[8] The preference for Empire was therefore one of the important characteristics of the inter-war experience.

Another distinctive feature of the period was the Imperial government's practical encouragement for emigration specifically to Empire destinations. This element is one of the main themes selected for emphasis in the chapters which follow. There were precedents for the involvement of the Imperial authorities in the processes of emigration. Indeed, some of those most enthusiastic about state-supported Empire migration between the wars took inspiration from eighteenth- and early nineteenth-century mercantilist concerns to achieve by state management a proper distribution of manpower within the old imperial economic system.[9] After the Napoleonic wars, in circumstances not too dissimilar from those experienced after the First World War, there were several attempts to settle emigrants in South Africa and British North America.[10] The Poor Law Amendment Act of 1834 also allowed Boards of Guardians to assist the emigration of those in need, accounting for the departure by 1860 of nearly 26,000 people, mainly agricultural labourers.[11]

These policies, however, were increasingly condemned in the United Kingdom and overseas as 'shovelling out paupers', and as expensive and ineffective practices which neither eased domestic British problems nor satisfied colonial demands for independent respectable immigrants. Colonial requirements were initially better met by the Colonial Land and Emigration Commissioners appointed by the Imperial government in 1840 to sell crown lands in the colonies and to use profits to subsidise the passages of emigrant labourers. Over 370,000 had been assisted by 1869.[12] But white settler societies, emboldened from mid-century with self-governing powers, preferred to take over responsibility for such operations themselves, and the consequent diminution in the Commissioners' responsibilities virtually terminated Imperial government assistance for emigrants. The official mind of the British government, reflecting the dominant liberal economic thinking of the nineteenth century and encouraged by the country's apparently secure domination of world and not just Empire markets, was reluctant to intervene. A free movement of labour in and out of the United Kingdom and impartiality towards the destinations chosen by British emigrants were its guiding principles. The recruiting, transport, reception and settlement of British emigrants became henceforth primarily the responsibility of the emigrants themselves, or of trade unions, philanthropic bodies, overseas land companies and shipping agents, or especially of overseas governments.[13] Most of the remaining responsibilities of the British government extended only to ensuring that passengers were transported safely and in tolerable conditions, and that they were not grossly misled about opportunities overseas by persuasive emigration agents and passage brokers. This last concern was largely the brief guiding the activities of the Emigrants' Information Office, established in 1886. It disappointed those who by this time were agitating for a more encouraging and imperial-minded state agency. It offered largely only factual information about opportunities overseas, not exclusively in imperial properties, and it issued warnings about adverse overseas conditions, even in the colonies.[14] Not until the turn of the century did British authorities become marginally more involved in the encouragement of emigration and then only for a selected range of clients. The Local Government Board revived the use of the emigration clause of the Poor Law between 1880 and 1913, mainly to send children to Canada. The Home Office likewise dispatched some unfortunate children abroad initially under the Reformatory and Industrial Schools Act of 1891 and later the Children's Act of 1908. In addition, the Unemployed Workmen's Act of 1905 allowed for the funding of assisted emigration.[15]

None of this matches the commitment to state-assisted emigration specifically to Empire destinations spectacularly demonstrated by the Imperial government after the First World War. The first novelty was the establishment in 1919 of the Oversea Settlement Committee (OSC); its advisory functions were taken over by the Oversea Settlement Board (OSB) in 1936. It was chaired usually by the Parliamentary Under-Secretary at the Colonial Office (from 1926 at the Dominions Office), and manned by representatives from the Colonial (or Dominions) Office and from other government departments, for example, the Ministry of Labour, Board of Trade, Ministry of Health, War Office, Ministry of Agriculture and the Treasury. Selected non-officials with a known interest in Empire, emigration or labour questions were also appointed. Its secretariat and administrative staff constituted the Oversea Settlement Office, later Department (OSD), of the Colonial Office (later Dominions Office). It also included from 1920 as its women's branch the Society for the Oversea Settlement of British Women (SOSBW), formed out of various women's emigration organisations. The OSC was responsible for recommending policy to the Secretary of State and for the administration of government initiatives. In the process it authorised prominent publicity campaigns encouraging Empire settlement, developed intimate links with philanthropic bodies, shipping companies and other interest groups at home and in the Empire, and aimed to form close contacts with dominion governments, not least by the appointment of its own British Migration Representative in Australia and in the dispatch of several missions of inquiry around the Empire.[16]

Its first major responsibility was the launch in 1919 of the Imperial government's plan for settling ex-service personnel and their families or next of kin in the dominions. The scheme was kept open until March 1923, and it involved the Imperial government in a sizeable cash commitment to provide free passages for approved emigrants. This programme proved to be only the preliminary to a more substantial statement of the Imperial government's new convictions, the Empire Settlement Act of 1922. Initially framed to last fifteen years, it authorised an expenditure of up to £3 million a year to encourage Empire migration with land settlement schemes, assisted passages, training courses or other methods, in co-operation with Empire governments or with public or private bodies in the United Kingdom or overseas (see Appendix). The commitment was renewed in 1937 for a further fifteen years on a less ambitious financial basis, up to £1.5 million per year, and it was repeated at regular five-year intervals from 1952 to the 1970s as a modest facilitating measure.[17]

The novelty of these remarkable inter-war innovations attracted their first historians. In 1929 W. A. Carrothers used official reports to chronicle their origins and recent operations in a chapter of his *Emigration from the British Isles, with Special Reference to the Development of the Overseas Dominions*, and a similar contemporary concern and comparable sources informed A. G. Scholes's still valuable *Education for Empire Settlement: a Study of Juvenile Migration*, published in 1932. G. F. Plant's *Oversea Settlement: Migration from the United Kingdom to the Dominions*, 1951, has become virtually the official history. It was written by the man who had served until 1937 in the key post of Secretary to the OSC and OSB. Though remaining essential for its information and the author's rueful observations on the inter-war experience, it inevitably reflects largely official perceptions. This is true also of his short record of the origins and operations of the *SOSBW: A*

Survey of Voluntary Effort in Women's Empire Migration, 1950, and indeed of another official history, U. B. Monk, *New Horizons: a Hundred Years of Women's Migration*, 1963, rich in information, but short in interpretation. W. K. Hancock, in his magisterial *Survey of British Commonwealth Affairs*, 1940, was predictably the first to place inter-war Empire migration into a wider political and economic context, albeit briefly. That approach is also attempted in S. Wertimer's unpublished 1952 doctoral thesis, 'Migration from the United Kingdom to the Dominions in the Inter-war Period, with Special Reference to the Empire Settlement Act of 1922', which drew exhaustively on the published reports. All these studies were, however, at least in part consciously concerned with what at the time of writing was still a lively contemporary issue, the merits or otherwise of existing or prospective Imperial government emigration schemes. The withering of public concern thereafter was followed by a lapse in academic attention until Professor Drummond's two pioneering studies, *British Economic Policy and the Empire 1919–1939*, 1972, and *Imperial Economic Policy 1917–1939*, 1974, helped to revive interest in Empire migration and other aspects of inter-war imperial economic history.[18] The considerable merits of these two volumes include a critical academic detachment from their subject and their employment of a much wider range of official sources, particularly British Cabinet and departmental records, supplemented by some private papers, making possible a more exhaustive and convincing appraisal of the processes of official policy-making and of the operation of the schemes.[19] All subsequent studies of Empire migration are indebted to this work. It has encouraged deeper explanations and interpretations of central themes in Imperial government policy-making. These are exemplified by the first three chapters in this book.

What emerges from such reassessment is the need to set the policy and practices of inter-war Empire migration into a longer chronological framework and into a deeper ideological context. This is made particularly clear in Keith Williams's analysis of the long-term ideological roots and short-term political origins of the Empire Settlement Act and also in Kent Fedorowich's study of the imperial ex-servicemen's scheme. The strategy indicated by these initiatives was a response to anxieties frequently expressed in the United Kingdom by social and political commentators, philanthropists and some politicans from as far back as the 1880s and with renewed vigour during the First World War and in the subsequent depression. Externally, economic, political and military challenges were generating doubts about the security of overseas markets, trade routes, the formal Empire and even the United Kingdom. Moreover, adequate responses were impaired, it seemed, because internally, too, there were problems. Investigations partly provoked by social unrest and peaks of unemployment appeared to expose debilitating inadequacies in industrial and social conditions: the efficiency of labour, the physical health of the British people, their standards of nutrition, their income levels, their security of employment, their housing conditions, their education and, even, their political reliability. These phenomena were often explained as alarming but inevitable consequences of an unbalanced national economy made vulnerable by free trade and excessive urbanisation.

In retrospect we can identify two parallel reforming responses.[20] The first emphasised primarily domestic solutions to Britain's economic and social difficulties. New Liberalism before the First World War and 'middle opinion' between the wars encouraged, on the one hand, state domestic demand management, economic planning and the mixed economy, and, on the other, such state-run domestic welfare services as national health and unemployment insurance, pensions and council housing. This much is widely recognised in the secondary literature exploring the history of government economic policy and the founding of the welfare state.[21] But there was an alternative, imperial strategy which also attracted considerable support in the years up to the Second World War and which also aimed at the goals of security, prosperity, welfare and social order. Solutions were sought within a more united, re-energised, mutually supportive and consequently more buoyant imperial economic system. Most attention was undoubtedly drawn to schemes for tariff protection with imperial preferences, particularly after 1903; only rather modest results were achieved, including the creation in 1926 of the Empire Marketing Board as a non-tariff substitute, until economic crisis brought in the mixed blessing of protection and the Ottawa agreements in 1932. There were also partially implemented plans to direct fructifying capital investment into imperial destinations either via state colonial development programmes or by channelling private investment after 1931 within the almost coterminous sterling area. In addition and of allied importance there was much support for the idea of Empire migration and settlement. State-aided programmes should stem the haemorrhage of British manpower draining away to foreign destinations, stimulate instead the markets and production of the dominions, and strengthen thereby British resistance to her external and internal dangers.[22]

It is important to recognise that after the First World War each step developing the domestic programmes for economic and social security was for a while paralleled by an imperial initiative. Cabinets wrestling with council housing, the out-of-work donation for ex-servicemen and the rising costs of unemployment insurance were also engineering ex-servicemen emigration to the dominions and the Empire Settlement Act. In the 1920s Cabinet unemployment committees kept domestic and overseas imperial options under constant review. Typical, too, was the report of the government's Industrial Transference Board in 1928 which urged the assisted movement of workers deemed surplus in the depressed areas of north and west Britain either to the more buoyant regions of the British economy or to fresh opportunities in the dominions.[23]

The emigration strategy was based upon a cluster of assumptions about Empire which hindsight and the chapters in this book make clear. Centrally it was assumed by many in the United Kingdom, and by supporters in the dominions, that the Empire and particularly the United Kingdom and the white settler societies were united by a natural harmony. The needs and interests of the metropolitan centre and those of the Empire overseas appeared to be complementary and capable of mutual satisfaction. Economically the parts should form a coherent whole. The United Kingdom was regarded essentially as the supplier to the dominions of industrial products and the provider of financial and other services. But the United Kingdom lacked sufficient domestic resources of food and raw materials needed to feed its urban population and insatiable industries. However, the dominions should gear their economies largely to supplying the British market and satisfying those needs, earning thereby the income to meet their own imports of mainly British products and to maintain their own high standards of living. Dominion economies had grown rapidly from the 1880s, essentially conforming to this model, and in the 1920s a further realisation of their potential to produce for the United Kingdom and absorb from the United Kingdom was confidently expected, at least in the United Kingdom.

Such sustained growth appeared to depend, however, on the import of further factors of production, certainly of capital but also of labour. Here, too, other fortunate complementary interests appeared to exist, between the contrasting demographic needs of the United Kingdom and the dominions. The United Kingdom's overcrowded islands could be contrasted with the sparse population per square mile in the dominions. Moreover, since many of the United Kingdom's domestic problems seemed to stem from the over-concentration of people in towns, a transfer of population from urban Britain to the supposedly rural societies of the dominions would be exceptionally rewarding, enhancing the health and moral welfare of those who left and those who remained. The assumed cohesion between kith and kin of the same racial or national stock allowed such population shifts to be viewed as no more a loss of manpower, for economic or if need be for military purposes, than if the movement had been strictly internal, say from Lancashire to Middlesex. It was also known that the dominion authorities were taking exceptional pains to prevent the entry into their territories of people of non-European stock: immigration controls helped to preserve what was still frequently regarded as at heart an Anglo-Saxon Empire.[24] As Keith Williams and Kent Fedorowich demonstrate, such considerations at a time of demobilisation, unemployment and social unrest did much to inspire the new official Empire migration policies.

Assumptions about gender were also involved, as Janice Gothard indicates. The need for female emigration, particularly of single women, had been widely canvassed since the mid-nineteenth century, driven by two contemporary claims. The first was that in a society like that in the United Kingdom in which women numerically outnumbered men, unmarried women constituted surplus stock and therefore a social problem. The second was that the efficient running of households and decent standards of living required the labour of female domestic servants. Perfect opportunities therefore lay readily to hand in the overseas Empire where it was believed that men continued to outnumber women and domestic help was scarce. The export of the United Kingdom's surplus women would spread harmony, encourage domesticity, foster civilisation, increase marriage rates and promote population growth. It is striking how many of these nineteenth-century perceptions survived the First World War, in spite of British women's supposed newly earned political and social status, in spite of their wider work experiences during the war and in spite of the agitation on their behalf for more challenging employment opportunities by, for example, the formidable Lady Londonderry, head of the Women's Legion.[25] In practice, the openings for women in the dominions were not substantially broader than they were at home. Neither the British nor especially the dominion authorities encouraged migrants to raise their expectations. Instead, much was made of the openings for servants and, discretely, of the chances for marriage. The claimed benefits of female migration were therefore essentially conservative: the confirmation of women's traditional roles and the satisfaction of masculine needs, the preservation of British cultural and political predominance in the dominions by the breeding of new generations from fresh British stock, and the sustaining of economic production and prosperity through the stimulus of more marriage, higher birth rates, population growth and larger markets.

Research on an allied topic remains incomplete, but the theme deserves identification here. Child and juvenile emigration to the dominions retained much of the appeal it had shown since the later nineteenth century and, like female emigration, for similarly conservative social and economic reasons.[26] Before 1914 major philanthropists like Dr Barnardo and minor ones like T. E. Sedgwick with his scheme for putting *Town Lads on Imperial Farms*, the title of his 1913 report, had shared a common perception that the United Kingdom's urban society generated exceptional difficulties for particular cohorts of working-class children, frequently orphans but more numerously those from poor homes or with 'inadequate' parents. The longer such children remained deprived of proper protection within the urban environment, the more they would be corrupted physically and morally. Philanthropists, church organisations and some Boards of Guardians had responded by trying to save children before it was too late. Protection might be guaranteed by fostering or through institutional care in the United Kingdom, but there were thought to be particular advantages in dispersing children overseas. For one thing, such transfers left room in institutions for newly rescued 'waifs and strays'. In addition, there appeared to be a demand in the dominions for the labour of such children, even young ones. Youngsters were also assumed to be more adaptable to the novel conditions they would find overseas and therefore easier to assimilate as settlers. It was expected that these children would grow up physically and morally stronger in the rural societies of the dominions where they would be trained for the robust rural trades apparently awaiting them.

It is true that serious doubts about the disposal overseas of young children under the age of fourteen had been fuelled by stories of child abuse and by changing professional concepts of child care. Opposition after the First World War became particularly strong in Canada where most child migrants had been sent. The emigration to Canada of children below school-leaving age without their parents was therefore largely abandoned following an inquiry in 1924 headed by the Labour Minister Margaret Bondfield.[27] But the OSC continued to approve of the general philosophy.[28] Demand for child migrants appeared to be growing elsewhere, especially in Australia. Children were still transported by charities to orphanages and farm schools overseas, and special efforts were made to encourage juvenile migration, for example, via the Boy Scouts Association and Australia's Big Brother Movement.[29] Such measures survived even the depression of the 1930s and were reinvigorated after the Second World War with, as we now know, sometimes traumatic consequences for individual children.[30] The last Dr Barnardo's party left for Australia in 1967. Their story indicates that philanthropic organisations dealing with children, as with single women, did not abandon their activities between the wars. Instead we see their pre-war lobbying being substantially satisfied. They entered into a partnership with the state, obtaining thereby state subsidies for their operations. State social reform did not necessarily squeeze out philanthropic organisations but could sustain their functions.

The attraction of Empire migration and settlement as part of a greater imperial economic and welfare strategy therefore remained self-evident to many commentators in the United Kingdom between the wars. But it was never possible for such a programme simply to be imposed on the dominions. One primary purpose of this book and particularly of its four territorial studies is to analyse dominion responses to Imperial government policy-making on migration matters and to explode any lingering notions that the Imperial government could dictate terms to the governments of the dominions. After all, the British authorities had effectively left them to do their own recruiting of settlers by the mid-nineteenth century in free competition with each other, the United States of America and elsewhere, and they had by 1919 long since devised mechanisms for the attraction, selection and settlement of such new state-assisted recruits as they wanted, if any, and they were hardly likely to abandon such marks of sovereignty in the face of a re-assertion of Imperial authority during and after the First World War. Indeed, it could appear that the Imperial government had rather capitulated to the pressures for imperial support from some of the dominions, especially Australia. The new-found willingness of the Imperial government to encourage and even pay for emigrants to the Empire may have delighted some dominion governments, but it was still improbable that in a flush of gratitude they would abandon their controls over the selection of assisted migrants and the annual volume they wished to absorb. Australia, too, was particularly anxious to tie increased migration to easier access to British sources of capital for development. Decisions on these matters, moreover, were not determined simply by negotiation between dominion and Imperial governments. Rather they were consequent also on circumstances and debates internal to each territory. The dominions were complex societies, each divided by class, interests and ethnic origins. Whether and on what terms a dominion would co-operate with imperial projects was consequent largely on internal dialogues.

For example, Michael Roe's study of Australian responses to British plans for assisted passages and land settlement in the Empire reveals how many divisions such proposals exposed within Australian society. Rural and industrial interests expressed different needs, labour and capital likewise, and such conflicts could be further inflamed by religious and ethnic distinctions, roughly those between Anglo-Saxon Protestants and Catholic Irish. Such disputes took on vivid political colouring through the lobbying of, for example, the Country Party and especially the Labour Party, and they could be elevated via the federal system into disputes at a higher level, straining the relationship between the governments of the states and the Commonwealth of Australia. Opportunities for varied and contradictory responses to Empire migration were already legion enough in the 1920s without the later impact of economic crisis. Moreover, even Hughes and Bruce, perhaps Imperial Britain's closest sympathisers, nevertheless translated the imperial vision of Empire migration into the rather different language of Australian immigration and development.

The chapter on New Zealand immigration recognises that economic cycles and geographical and climatic realities significantly determined the volume and type of assisted immigrants selected and the absence of any Imperial-government supported land settlement schemes. But immigration policy-making and administration in New Zealand were also swayed by the balance of power between rival domestic interest groups with their alternative visions for New Zealand's future. The issue fired up the hostility between organised labour and employers. Tension can also be discerned between the conservative interests in immigration of most farmers and the newer and more aggressive aspirations of New Zealand manufacturers. The problem for New Zealand governments was to negotiate a politically acceptable strategy between those lobbies. Such navigation removed any chance of New Zealand merely conforming to the wishes of the United Kingdom, even before economic depression and subsequently a Labour government presented further obstacles.

The work of John A. Schultz on Canada identifies an additional complication. There were, it is true, economic lobbies especially in the western provinces anxious to increase their rural populations by encouraging immigration. But efforts to satisfy those requirements led before and after the First World War to significant recruiting from Eastern and Southern Europe. To some observers the cure was worse than the complaint. Such immigrants apparently threatened the predominance of British cultural and political values in a Dominion of Canada always conscious since its creation of domestic ethnic divisions and rivalry. Not surprisingly, representatives of Anglo-Saxon Protestanism were especially insistent that the Canadian government should seize the opportunity presented by the Imperial government's offers to increase the volume of the immigration from the United Kingdom. But there were countervailing prejudices against assisted immigrants derived especially from the pre-war operations of philanthropic organisations and Boards of Guardians, particularly the belief that immigrants requiring help were of suspect quality. Between Empire enthusiasts on the one hand and anti-immigrant and some anti-imperial sentiment on the other, Mackenzie King's policy tacked and weaved, aiming more to preserve the political pre-eminence of its helmsman than to steer towards the imperial vision of British ideologues.

The problem of ethnic conflicts was, of course, manifestly more severe in South Africa, as Edna Bradlow's chapter demonstrates. The impotence of the Imperial government to affect South African policy and the pre-eminence of internal dynamics to an explanation of South African immigration policy explain the choice of 1910 and 1948 as the proper terminal dates for this study. From the time of the Union the white population and their government were anxious to secure white racial dominance by increasing their numbers. While such a strategy made state encouragement of European immigration superficially attractive, it was, however, countered by another assumption – that black workers must remain the principal source of unskilled labour. In turn, this focused concern on the problem of 'poor whites' and discouraged the mass immigration of people of limited means and skills. The strategy was also frustrated by Afrikaner suspicions, not altogether unwarranted, that the British community intended immigration from the United Kingdom to secure British numerical and, hence, political predominance over Afrikaners. This tangle of suspicion and the growing power of Afrikaner nationalism effectively prevented official co-operation with imperial migration initiatives. Not until Afrikaner anxieties to preserve white predominance outweighed their suspicion of the British in South Africa after the Second World War were more positive attempts made to recruit white immigrants, and only then on specifically South African and not imperial terms.

Ultimately, during the 1930s, the high hopes expressed by enthusiastic supporters of Empire migration, in and out of office, in the United Kingdom and overseas, were to be frustrated.[31] Optimism largely evaporated in economic depression, which as in the past demonstrated that most migrants could be pulled in only by prosperity overseas and would not be expelled merely by distress at home. The disappointment demanded a more circumspect study of that natural harmony which was supposedly sufficient, with a nudge from assisted passages and land settlement schemes, to send a flow of British migrants overseas. A sequence of inquiries followed.

For one thing, economic complementarity was apparently flawed. The share of British overseas commerce with the Empire was undoubtedly higher in the 1930s than ever before (albeit as a percentage of a lower volume), but over 50 per cent of British exports were still heading for foreign destinations.[32] The United Kingdom needed more than Empire markets, and therefore had to accept more than Empire suppliers, as the twenty bilateral trade pacts with foreign countries signed in the 1930s after the Ottawa agreements appear to indicate.[33]

The dominions, too, were becoming anxious about their reliance on the British market. There was no guarantee that the growth of the British population and the increasing affluence of the British people would bring a proportionate increase in demand for basic foodstuffs and simple raw materials. Rising living standards alter patterns of demand to the disadvantage of primary producers, and in any case the population of the United Kingdom was growing less rapidly than in the past.[34] In the 1930s, a glut in world supplies of many primary products and the ensuing lower prices and a fierce competition with foreign producers for access to the British market were hardly conditions to encourage settlers on the land. Moreover, dominion producers were rudely reminded by a more articulate lobby of British farmers, who had the ear of the Conservative Party, that the United Kingdom was not carpeted from coast to coast with wall-to-wall factories. One New Zealand commentator was obliged to remind his countrymen that there were, in fact, more workers on the land in the United Kingdom than in any single dominion.[35] Reconciling the interests of the Empire at home with the Empire overseas would never be easy, as negotiations at Ottawa in 1932 too clearly revealed.

This became even more true when some dominion economies themselves became more diverse. So long as their home markets boomed and absorbed their locally made manufactured goods plus a full complement of British imports, most dominion suppliers could remain reasonably content; but in tighter economic conditions their attempts to promote dominion products in dominion markets potentially at the expense of British imports could only cause anxiety in the United Kingdom. This shift then affected attitudes to migration. It was recognised by now that many British immigrants drifted anyway into urban employment, but the prospect of the dominions setting out to develop more balanced economies by selective immigration for industrial and not just for rural employment was bound to generate some misgivings in the United Kingdom. The movement of skilled workers to the Empire could not be regarded as necessarily benign.[36]

In addition, it was also becoming recognised by the 1930s that the opportunities for demographic engineering were much more limited than once imagined; the complementarity between the population needs of the United Kingdom and of the dominions was getting weaker. In the first place, disillusionment with the pace of Empire migration focused attention on those geographical and climatic conditions which in truth explained the sparsely populated territories of the Australian deserts, the New Zealand Alps and the Canadian Arctic. Lack of suitable territory for fresh settlement largely limited the opportunities to shift much of the urban population of the United Kingdom to the rural

Empire.[37] The capacity to absorb immigrants in order to equalise the population densities of mother and daughter societies also depended upon the balance locally between the supply and demand for labour. However, immigration was losing the centrality it had once had as the principal source of new labour. Natural increase, the excess nationally of births over deaths, inevitably became a more fruitful cause of demographic growth with the passage of time and the expansion of each dominion's population base. What was true first in Canada and Australia became clearer between the wars even in late-settled New Zealand. It was also evident that the imbalance of sex ratios characteristic of newly settled societies, which according to supporters of Empire migration was an anomaly needing correction by imperial manipulation, was being adjusted anyway. The more dominion populations grew through natural increase and the less, proportionately, through immigration, the more sex ratios balanced.[38]

It was true that birth rates were declining in the dominions between the wars, and this suggested the need to accelerate immigration in order to maintain population growth. But the birth rate was also falling in the United Kingdom. This diminished the claim that the overpopulated United Kingdom needed Empire migration as a vent for the surplus. Indeed, by the 1930s there was serious talk of British population growth either ceasing or actually going into reverse, with incalculable but alarming economic, social and military consequences. A fall in the birth rate, especially at a time of increasing life expectancy, presaged an ageing population, increasing the burden of dependants supported by the labour force and adding to the cares and costs of the social services. A relative decline in the most healthy, energetic, adaptable and fecund sector of the population suggested that the United Kingdom could ill afford to lose a percentage of such stock even to the dominions.[39] Far from there being a harmony of interests between the United Kingdom and the Empire, mother and daughter societies appeared to be competing for the affections of the next generation. By the 1930s several commentators concluded that any future increase in dominion immigration would have to draw upon sources outside the United Kingdom.[40]

For one other reason confidence in Empire migration and settlement as a solution to British economic and social problems began to wane. In spite of the extraordinary efforts made between the wars to penetrate popular culture with imperial ideas,[41] the British people seemed to many observers regrettably unwilling to seize the opportunities presented by Empire. There seemed a reluctance to emigrate.[42] Some detected a decline in pioneering spirit, no doubt a product of urbanisation with its baleful moral and cultural consequences. The labour movement had also helped to shift expectations and the political agenda by its variable but generally sceptical and sometimes hostile attitude to emigration and by its insistence upon domestic social reform.[43] Indeed, there was a suspicion that the alternative domestic strategy for easing social distress was already having a sapping effect. The development of welfare services was perhaps providing such social security that it discouraged emigration. Concern was sufficient to persuade Leo Amery as Secretary of State for the Colonies to launch an inquiry in 1925 which concluded that social insurance was certainly one disincentive to emigration:

> These schemes have an effect in discouraging migration, both directly as a result of the sense of security they induce, and indirectly in that they raise the standards of living in this country, and so counteract to an appreciable extent the attraction of the life of independence offered in the Dominions.

The lack of harmony between social provision in the United Kingdom and in the overseas Empire made migration risky.[44] This conclusion was endorsed by the OSB in 1938:

> Unemployment and health insurance, improved public assistance, contributory old age, widows' and orphans' pensions, improved educational and medical facilities, have all served to create a sense of social security and stability which in itself militates against the inclination to migrate.[45]

This was unlikely to have been the major explanation for the disappointing volume of Empire migration, particularly in the 1930s, but the more persistent public emphasis by then on domestic social reform and domestic economic planning and management is indicative of the disillusionment with emigration which had set in among policy-makers and commentators. The Empire Settlement Act survived and was renewed without enthusiasm in 1937,[46] but its centrality to programmes for economic and social welfare was lost and its devotees marginalised. One sceptic concluded in 1937 that 'emigration can do almost nothing to solve any general problem in Britain'.[47] In reality, a strategy devised primarily in the late nineteenth century had become anachronistic shortly after its official adoption.

The commitment made by the Imperial government and some of the dominions had nevertheless been real enough. The scheme to emigrate ex-service personnel and their families cost the British taxpayer £2,418,263 and assisted the departure of 86,027 people.[48] As Kent Fedorowich shows, they were distributed unevenly around the Empire, and constituted a modest 12 per cent or so of the total number of British emigrants settling in the Empire between 1919 and 1922. Annual spending by the Imperial government under the Empire Settlement Act was much less than the maximum finance available, peaking at only £1,282,906 in 1927–8, but totalling a not inconsiderable net expenditure of £6,099,046 by March 1936. This outlay had by then supported the emigration of 405,230 people. Distribution was hugely unequal: 186,524 to Canada, 172,735 to Australia, 44,745 to New Zealand and a mere 1,226 to South Africa.[49] Assisted migrants made up a substantial 36 per cent of the total volume of Empire migration,[50] but how many would have departed anyway for the Empire without financial assistance remains a complex and unanswered question. Of 346,319 classified between 1923 and 1932, 123,349 were males aged over twelve, 103,792 females over twelve and 122,178 young children.[51] This remarkably even split compared with the traditional predominance of adult males among emigrants suggests that the special support for the migration of women, children and families may have had some effect.

There is much we still do not know about Empire migrants. Questions remain about their social and occupational background, about their motives for migration and about their choice of destination.[52] There is room for study of the unofficial agencies often involved in their transfer, for example the charitable organisations like the Salvation Army and the Child Emigration Society. Shipping companies, whose interest in the migrant trade was often second to none, also deserve examination. In addition, we need some consideration of reception arrangements in the dominions, whether run by the state or voluntary bodies, and about the problems of assimilation and the impact of these newcomers on their host society.[53] Most of all, perhaps, we need to hear the voices of Empire migrants. The oral records and personal letters used by some of the contributors to this book indicate how further research may enable us to comprehend better the life experiences of those who settled and stayed, and of those who remained restless and returned. Such a programme of research suggests the value of further academic collaboration between historians working in the former dominions and those in once Imperial Britain.

Acknowledgements

My research on Empire migration in the United Kingdom and New Zealand was made possible by generous awards from the British Academy's Small Grants Research Fund in the Humanities and from the University of Lancaster, which also allowed me a period of study leave. I was also enormously assisted by staff in archives, libraries and organisations in both countries, and I welcome this opportunity to thank them for allowing me to use and to quote from material in their care. As a temporary migrant in New Zealand I much appreciated the help and hospitality of Professor David Hamer and his collegues at the Victoria

University of Wellington. I have learnt a great deal from my fellow contributors to this book; for their advice and support I am grateful.

Appendix

The Empire Settlement Act, 1922 (12 & 13 Geo. 5 ch. 13) An Act to make better provision for furthering British settlement in His Majesty's Oversea Dominions

Be it enacted by the King's most Excellent Majesty, by and with the advice and consent of the Lords Spiritual and Temporal, and Commons, in this present Parliament assembled, and by the authority of the same, as follows:

1. (1) It shall be lawful for the Secretary of State, in association with the government of any part of His Majesty's Dominions, or with public authorities or public or private organisations either in the United Kingdom or in any part of such Dominions, to formulate and co-operate in carrying out agreed schemes for affording joint assistance to suitable persons in the United Kingdom who intend to settle in any part of His Majesty's Oversea Dominions.

   (2) An agreed scheme under this Act may be either:
      (a) a development or a land settlement scheme; or
      (b) a scheme for facilitating settlement in or migration to any part of His Majesty's Oversea Dominions by assistance with passages, initial allowances, training or otherwise;

   and shall make provision with respect to the contributions to be made, either by way of grant or by way of loan or otherwise, by the parties to the agreed scheme towards the expenses of the scheme.

   (3) The Secretary of State shall have all such powers as may be necessary for carrying out his obligations under any scheme made in pursuance of this Act:

   Provided that:
      (a) the Secretary of State shall not agree to any scheme without the consent of the Treasury, who shall be satisfied that the contributions of the government, authority, or organisation with whom the scheme is agreed towards the expenses of the scheme bear a proper relation to the contribution of the Secretary of State; and
      (b) the contribution of the Secretary of State shall not in any case exceed half the expenses of the scheme; and
      (c) the liability of the Secretary of State to make contributions under the scheme shall not extend beyond a period of fifteen years after the passing of this Act.

   (4) Any expenses of the Secretary of State under this Act shall be paid out of moneys provided by Parliament:

   Provided that the aggregate amount expended by the Secretary of State under any scheme or schemes under this Act shall not exceed one million five hundred thousand pounds in the financial year current at the date of the passing of this Act, or three million pounds in any subsequent financial year, exclusive of the amount of any sums received by way of interest on or repayment of advances previously made.

2. His Majesty may by Order in Council direct that this Act shall apply to any territory which is under His Majesty's protection, or in respect of which a mandate is being exercised by the government of any part of His Majesty's Dominions as if that territory were a part of His Majesty's Dominions, and, on the making of any such Order, this Act shall, subject to the provision of the Order, have effect accordingly.

3. This Act may be cited as the Empire Settlement Act, 1922.

Notes

1 Precise figures are not available but outward passenger figures from the United Kingdom to extra-European destinations 1815–1914, excluding aliens from 1853, total 16,857,367: calculated from N. H. Carrier and J. A. Jeffery, *External Migration: a Study of the Available Statistics*, HMSO, London, pp. 90–1.

2 *Ibid.* and G. F. Plant, *Oversea Settlement*, Oxford, 1951, pp. 174–5.

3 *Ibid.*

4 Calculated from B. R. Mitchell, *British Historical Statistics*, Cambridge, 1988, p. 83.

5 G. H. Gallup, *The Gallup International Public Opinion Polls: Great Britain 1937–1975*, New York, 1976.

6 *Ibid.* Thereafter the only signficant change was a sharp drop in the preference for South Africa to the advantage of other Commonwealth countries.

7 W. A. Carrothers, *Emigration from the British Isles*, London, 1929, pp. 308–9: emigration here equated with outward passenger movement.

8 Calculated from S. Wertimer, 'Migration from the United Kingdom to the Dominions in the Inter-war Period with Special Reference to the Empire Settlement Act of 1922', Ph.D. thesis, University of London, 1952, Table XXVII. The total number of emigrants to the dominions in 1920–29 was 1,179,986 and in 1930–38 it was 157,015.

9 See, for example, L. S. Amery, *National and Imperial Economics*, Westminster, 2nd ed., 1924, pp. 47–9.

10 H. J. M. Johnston, *British Emigration Policy 1815–1830*, Oxford, 1972.

11 W. S. Shepperson, *British Emigration to North America*, Oxford, 1957, p. 48.

12 F. H. Hitchins, *The Colonial Land and Emigration Commission*, Philadelphia, 1931, especially pp. 207, 211; D. V. Glass and P. A. M. Taylor, *Population and Emigration*, Dublin, 1976, pp. 69–84.

13 For examples, see R. M. Dalziel, *The Origins of New Zealand Diplomacy: the Agent-General in London 1870–1905*, Wellington, 1975, pp. 34–52; P. Horn, 'Agricultural trade unionism and emigration, 1872–1881', *Historical Journal*, 15, 1972, pp. 87–102; A. J. Hammerton, *Emigrant Gentlewomen: Genteel Poverty and Female Emigration, 1830–1914*, London, 1979; G. Wagner, *Children of the Empire*, London, 1982; B. Trescatheric, 'The Furness Colony: the History of an Emigration Society in Great Britain and Minnesota from 1872 to 1882', M.Litt. thesis, University of Lancaster, 1981.

14 *Memorandum on the History and Functions of the Emigrants' Information Office*, British Parliamentary Papers, Cd. 3407, LXVIII, 1907; Glass and Taylor, *Population and Emigration*, pp. 84–8.

15 A. G. Scholes, *Education for Empire Settlement: a Study of Juvenile Migration*, London, 1932, p. 28; J. Harris, *Unemployment and Politics*, Oxford, 1972, pp. 184–7; K. I. Williams, 'The British State, Social Imperialism and Emigration 1900–1922: the Ideology and Antecedents of the Empire Settlement Act of 1922', Ph.D. thesis, University of London, 1985, pp. 87–94, 282–5.

16 For membership and functions of the OSC, OSB and OSD see the annual *Colonial Office List*, the annual report of the OSC in British Parliamentary Papers and Plant, *Oversea Settlement*, pp. 66–8, 77–80.

17 There were Commonwealth Settlement Acts in 1952, 1957, 1962 and 1967, the last expiring in 1972.

18 London is the place of publication for all titles.

19 Although see M. Beloff, 'The political blind spot of economists', *Government and Opposition*, 10, 1975, pp. 107–12.

20 While much of what follows derives from the essay by Keith Williams and his Ph.D. thesis, see also Stephen Constantine, *Unemployment in Britain between the Wars*, London, 1980, pp. 45–76 and 'Empire migration and social reform, 1880–1950', in C. G. Pooley and I. Whyte (eds), *Emigrants, Migrants and Immigrants: a Social History of Migration*, London, forthcoming.

21 For example, G. C. Peden, *British Economic and Social Policy: Lloyd George to Margaret Thatcher*, Oxford, 1985; and P. Thane, *The Foundations of the Welfare State*, London, 1982.

22 In addition to the works of Hancock and Drummond already cited, see I. M. Drummond, *The Floating Pound and the Sterling Area 1931–1919*, Cambridge, 1981; J. M. Tomlinson, *Problems of British Economic Policy 1870–1945*, London, 1981, chs. 3 and 7; Stephen Constantine, *The Making of British Colonial Development Policy 1914–1940*, London, 1984, *Buy and Build: the Advertising Posters of the Empire Marketing Board*, London, 1986, and 'Bringing the Empire alive: the Empire Marketing Board and imperial propaganda 1926–33', in J. M. MacKenzie (ed.), *Imperialism and Popular Culture*, Manchester, 1986. See also the memoirs of L. S. Amery, *My Political Life*, London, 1953–55.

23 *Report of the Industrial Transference Board*, Cmd. 3156, X, 1928.

24 R. A. Huttenback, *Racism and Empire: White Settlers and Colored Immigrants in the British Self-Governing Colonies 1830–1910*, Ithaca and London, 1976.

25 For Lady Londonderry see Public Record Office, London, CO 532/118/CO58056, minute by Macnaghten, 28 November 1918.

26 Scholes, *Education for Empire Settlement*; J. Parr, *Labouring Children: British Immigrant Apprentices to Canada, 1869–1924*, London, 1980; K. Bagnell, *The Little Immigrants: the Orphans Who Came to Canada*, Toronto, 1980; Wagner, *Children of the Empire*; R. A. Parker, 'The Emigration of Unaccompanied British Children to Canada 1867–1917', ESRC End-of-Grant Report, London, 1982; P. T. Rooke and R. L. Schnell, 'Imperial philanthropy and colonial response: British juvenile emigration to Canada 1896–1930', *The Historian*, 46, 1983, pp. 56–77.

27 *British Oversea Settlement Delegation to Canada*, Cmd. 2285, XV, 1924–25.

28 See also the endorsement in the *Report to the Secretary of State for the Dominions of the Inter-Departmental Committee on Migration Policy*, Cmd. 4689, X, 1933–34, pp. 45–9.

29 For the former, see migration records in the Scout Association Archives in London, especially files TC/27 and TC/215 and *The Call of Empire*; for the latter, see G. Sherington, *The Dreadnought Boys*, privately published.

30 P. Harrison, *The Home Children: their Personal Stories*, Winnipeg, 1979; P. Bean and J. Melville, *Lost Children of the Empire*, London, 1989.

31 Late enthusiasts remained, for example, House of Commons Empire Development and Settlement Research Committee, *The Redistribution of the Population of the British Empire*, 1933, copy in the Malcolm MacDonald papers, University of Durham; A. G. B. West, *Empire Settlement and Unemployment*, London, 1934; Commissioner D. Lamb, 'Migration problems of the Empire', in H. E. Harper (ed.), *Empire Problems*, London, 1939, pp. 12–33.

32 Drummond, *British Economic Policy and the Empire*, p. 19; see also Economic Advisory Council, *Committee on Empire Migration Report*, Cmd. 4075, IX, 1931–32, pp. 23–4.

33 S. Pollard, *The Development of the British Economy, 1914–1980*, London, p. 123.

34 For a contemporary recognition of the implications see D. Christie Tait, 'Migration

and settlement in Australia, New Zealand and Canada', *International Labour Review*, 34, 1935, p. 58.

35 A. Fraser, *A Case for Immigration*, Wellington, 1936, p. 38.

36 'Empire migration', *The Round Table*, 25, 1934, pp. 72–3; PRO, DO 114/90, Minutes of the Oversea Settlement Board, 9 March and 4 May 1939; the emigration of industrial workers from Britain to the dominions was suggested by Tait, 'Migration and settlement'. The general dilemma is well analysed in R. F. Holland, 'The end of an imperial economy: Anglo-Canadian disengagement in the 1930s', *Journal of Imperial and Commonwealth History*, 11, 1983, pp. 159–74.

37 See I. Bowman (ed.), *Limits of Land Settlement: a Report on Present-Day Possibilities*, New York, 1937; W. D. Forsyth, *The Myth of Open Spaces*, Melbourne, 1942.

38 This conclusion is generally supported by the figures in *Committee on Empire Migration Report*, pp. 78–9 and B. R. Mitchell, *International Historical Statistics: the Americas and Australasia*, London, 1983, pp. 47, 53, 57, 77–9.

39 The debate is described in S. Glynn and J. Oxborrow, *Interwar Britain: a Social and Economic History*, London, 1976, pp. 202–8; see also 'Empire migration', pp. 64–6; *Committee on Empire Migration Report*, pp. 11–12; *Report of the Oversea Settlement Board May 1936 to June 1938*, Cmd. 5766, XIV, 1937–38, pp. 13–15; Carrier and Jeffery, *External Migration*, p. 11.

40 *Report of the Oversea Settlement Board*, p. 16; W. D. Borrie, 'Immigration to New Zealand Since 1854', University of Otago thesis, 1939, Preface and p. 404.

41 J. M. MacKenzie, *Propaganda and Empire*, Manchester, 1984 and MacKenzie (ed.), *Imperialism and Popular Culture*.

42 See the results of inquiries in the late 1930s reported in Forsyth, *Myth of Open Spaces*, pp. 161–2.

43 P. S. Gupta, *Imperialism and the British Labour Movement, 1914–1964*, London, 1975, pp. 86–90; Wertimer, 'Migration from the United Kingdom', pp. 192–211, 347.

44 *Report of the Inter-Departmental Committee appointed to consider the Effect on Migration of Schemes of Social Insurance*, Cmd. 2608, X, 1926, p. 25; for an anxious contemporary response see Sir John A. R. Marriott, *Empire Settlement*, London, 1927, pp. 108–11.

45 *Report of the Oversea Settlement Board*, p. 11.

46 Compare the debates on the 1922 Empire Settlement Bill with, for example, the second reading debate on the 1937 Bill, Hansard, *Parliamentary Debates*, House of Commons, vol. 319, cols 595–708, 25 January 1937. Operations resumed on a small scale from 1938, Wertimer, 'Migration from the United Kingdom', p. 349.

47 W. D. Reddaway, 'Migration from the British point of view', in W. G. K. Duncan and C. V. Janes (eds), *The Future of Immigration into Australia and New Zealand*, Sydney, 1937, p. 61.

48 Hansard, *Parliamentary Debates*, vol. 173, cols 2560–1, 23 May 1924.

49 *Ibid.*, vol. 304, col. 1244, 18 July 1935 and vol. 318, col. 214, 24 November 1936; for destinations and totals by year see *Report of the Oversea Settlement Committee for the period 1 April 1935 to 31 March 1936*, Cmd. 5200, XIV, 1935–36, p. 8. It is interesting to speculate on why the OSC's figures for each dominion differ from those compiled by dominion Immigration Departments and cited in later chapters.

50 Plant, *Oversea Settlement*, p. 75; for annual percentages see Wertimer, 'Migration from the United Kingdom', Table LII.

51 *Ibid.*, Tables XXII and LIV, based on OSC annual reports.

52 Analyses so far lack the sophistication of D. Baines, *Migration in a Mature Economy; Emigration and International Migration in England and Wales 1861–1900*, Cambridge, 1985, but see Wertimer 'Migration from the United Kingdom', pp. 272–301 and two econometric exercises, D. Pope, 'Empire migration to Canada, Australia and New Zealand, 1910–29', *Australian Economic Papers*, 7, 1968, pp. 166–88 and W. L. Marr, 'The United Kingdom's international migration in the inter-war period: theoretical considerations and empirical testing', *Population Studies*, 31, 1977, pp. 571–9.

53 Some unfortunates were deported, see H. F. Drystek, 'The simplest and cheapest mode of dealing with them: deportation from Canada before World War II', *Histoire Sociale –*

Social History, 15, 1982, pp. 407–41, and B. Roberts, 'Shovelling out the mutinous: political deportation from Canada before 1936', *Labour – Le Travail*, 18, 1986, pp. 77–110.

CHAPTER TWO

'A way out of our troubles': the politics of Empire settlement, 1900–1922

Keith Williams

After the First World War there was a striking reorientation of state policy on emigration from the United Kingdom. A state-assisted emigration scheme for ex-servicemen and ex-servicewomen, operating from 1919 to 1922, was followed by an Empire Settlement Act, passed in 1922, which made significant British state funding available for assisted emigration and overseas land settlement in British Empire countries. The Empire settlement programme which followed consolidated the historic legacy of British settlement in Canada, the antipodes and southern Africa as perhaps the most striking monuments to the reality of an Empire of migration. Until then, for all its impact on the shape of the modern world, British colonisation of territories outside Europe had had a remarkably chequered history. Nineteenth-century efforts to establish planned migration and an organised process of settlement were sporadic and often ineffective, especially those sponsored by the imperial authorities. The celebrated colonisation schemes of the 1820s, such as the Albany Settlement at the Cape of Good Hope, the Swan River settlement in Western Australia and assisted-passage schemes to Canada, were exceptional and not entirely successful. The considerable volume of British emigration in the nineteenth century owed more to individual or family initiative than to state planning or directive.[1]

In the 1880s recession and social unrest in the United Kingdom stimulated the most vigorous campaign since the 1820s to secure state assistance and to promote land settlement within the Empire, but this agitation came to precious little and the demands for state aid were rejected by the Commons Select Committee on Colonisation which sat from 1889 to 1891.[2] However, after 1900 the economies of the self-governing dominions, especially Canada, Australia and New Zealand, expanded dramatically while the United Kingdom continued to experience cyclical unemployment problems and social unrest.

Dominion governments and British emigration agencies now intervened more vigorously in the recruitment and assistance of Empire settlers; even the British government adopted initiatives for the emigration of the unemployed and pauper children. Moreover, the South African War, and the fierce ideological struggle over its significance in the United Kingdom itself, generated an amalgam of imperialist and social Darwinist concerns, prompting the emergence of a revitalised movement for state-aided migration within the British Empire which paralleled the campaign for imperial trade preference and other favoured leitmotifs of Edwardian imperialism.

In the troubled years before the First World War a cohesive lobby of imperialists and philanthropic emigrationists in the United Kingdom and expansionist dominion interests overseas forced the emigration issue onto the political agenda. The war itself provided the opportunity to push home the ideological case for British state aid for Empire settlement. After the war, despite a general mood of retrenchment, imperialists succeeded in pressing the case for state financial support for schemes of assisted migration and land settlement within the Empire. Between 1919 and 1922 conflicting departmental views, the sensitivities of the dominions to any threat of a mass transportation of British paupers and the vagaries of a Parliament which had rejected an earlier Emigration Bill in 1918 were all overcome. With the aid of the adroit political skills of Leo Amery, the case for a British financial commitment to the 'Empire settlement' of British migrants in the dominions was finally made. The 1922 Empire Settlement Act represented a major political achievement for the imperialist lobby which this chapter sets out to explain.

'Good Britishers all'[3]: emigration and the struggle for 'Greater Britain', 1900–14

As Bernard Semmel and other historians have shown,[4] between 1880 and 1914 British society was under a dual challenge. Externally the challenge of American and German industrial productivity signalled the erosion of British industrial competitiveness. In the United Kingdom itself significant periods of social unrest and the emergence of an organised labour movement posed a direct challenge to the metropolitan bourgeoisie. One of the most radical responses to these perceived challenges was represented by the strands of 'social imperial' ideology which offered both an acerbic critique of the prevailing liberal orthodoxy in government, economy and society, and a persuasive alternative blueprint – corporatist, statist and imperialist.

In the context of the dual challenge and the social imperialist prescription, the issue of British emigration became politically charged and ideologically fought over.[5] For the social imperialists who advocated systematic Empire development and close colonial political and economic ties with the 'mother country', the redirection of the bulk of British emigration to Empire countries was a matter of profound symbolic importance which also addressed in practical terms both aspects of the challenge facing the British ruling class.

By 1900 state management of British emigration was limited and piecemeal. A number of government departments held responsibilities over aspects of emigration. The Board of Trade was responsible for passenger shipping, including emigrant ships, supervised the operations of passenger agents and collected the limited official statistics on passenger traffic. The Local Government Board administered the emigration of families and of unaccompanied children under the Poor Law and from 1905 of unemployed adults and their families under the Unemployed Workmen's Act. The Home Office oversaw the small-scale emigration of children from industrial and reformatory schools. As one official put it: '[The state's] interest is really a Distress or Poor Law or Unemployed interest in emigration'.[6]

The Colonial Office held no direct brief in respect of emigration beyond the provision of information and advice to emigrants through its Emigrants' Information Office (EIO), established in 1886; it was nevertheless for historical reasons regarded as the policy-making department in this area. Policy, however, was determined by traditional Gladstonian liberal principles reaffirmed in the 1880s; the ebb and flow of what permanent officials called 'natural emigration' were best determined by market forces with the minium of interference by state bodies. Where emigration was to be encouraged or assisted, it should be left to private initiative, whether philanthropic or capitalist. Moreover, the EIO was not supposed to promote the advantages of the dominions over other destinations for British emigrants. The liberal orthodoxy here was that any attempts to impose upon the office an obligation to encourage specifically Empire emigration, for political reasons rather than on the merits of individual countries, 'would be fatal to the usefulness of the office' in its prime duty to offer impartial advice.[7] But in practice its officers argued that the familiarity of social and political institutions, advantages of language, the availability of land and 'blood' ties made the dominions the best possible destination for the discerning emigrant.[8] The EIO advised emigrants to choose a 'British' country 'simply because they offer better openings'.[9]

Not surprisingly, the limited efforts of the EIO fell far short of the definitive state-aided programme of Empire settlement sought by many emigrationists and imperialists in the face of external threats to British interests. They argued that the vital national asset of human resources should be recognised and that emigration from the United Kingdom should be openly and systematically channelled to Empire countries for reasons of racial solidarity, imperial political unity, imperial defence and Empire economic development. The white colonies would be provided with the British population (and white labour) they sought, while ties between the 'mother country' and the 'Greater Britain' overseas would be maintained and developed. Moreover, in conjunction with a policy of Empire trade preference, the dominions populated by British settlers would guarantee sources of raw materials for the United Kingdom and expanding markets for its industrial goods.

This notion of a 'Greater Britain' of Empire settlement had immense implications for the significance of emigration from the United Kingdom. In *The Expansion of England*, published in 1883, the influential imperialist J. R. Seeley argued that it was British colonisation overseas which had effectively extended the boundaries of the British state.[10] Seeley's conception of 'Greater Britain' was a key ideological construction which fed into the self-image of the British as an imperial race. The racial definition of an imperial ruling caste, reinforced by scientific racism and the social Darwinism of contemporary pseudo-anthropology, became increasingly sharp. It was the white kith and kin of the self-governing dominions who were ideologically selected as the imperial Britons, while the non-white masses of the British Empire were not so privileged. Indeed, it was exactly this expression of an organic nationality, transcending the immediate territorial confines of nationhood without jeopardising the blood purity of the Anglo-Saxon 'race', which allowed the negotiation of the potential contradiction between nation and Empire.

In this ideological context imperialist literature suggested a clear distinction between emigration to foreign countries – 'that is, wandering out of the Empire . . .'[11] – and migration within the boundaries of the Empire. The loaded semantic distinction between 'Empire settlement', 'oversea settlement', 'Empire migration', all acceptable terms, and 'emigration' which was 'by many people regarded almost as synonymous with exile'[12] was regularly underlined. As Leo Amery, the leading political spokesman of the Empire settlement movement after 1918, told the House of Commons,

I shall be glad if the word 'emigration' with its implied suggestion of expatriation of the individual and of loss on the part of the community which he leaves, could be habitually confined to migration to foreign countries. Change of residence to another part of the empire, is . . . more appropriately described by some such term as 'oversea settlement'.[13]

The idea that a consolidated overseas Empire of British settlement would serve as a crucial outlet for dangerous social tensions at the heart of the Empire, in the United Kingdom, itself, was intrinsic to imperialist cosmology. In the perception of imperialists, political and social turbulence at the centre was as great a threat to the longevity of Empire as 'centrifugal forces' on the periphery. Class struggle in the United Kingdom represented a serious challenge to the imperial schema, yet the 'Greater British' state itself preferred the means of defusing class conflict in the metropole. By providing protected markets for British goods, by guaranteeing supplies of food and raw materials, and by offering an outlet for population growth and surplus labour the British Empire, conceived as a protected, complementary satellite of the British economy, could counteract the effect of foreign competition on the United Kingdom's industrial and trading position, guarantee the living standards of British workers and provide the necessary surplus for domestic social reform. Furthermore the argument could be stood about; in the social Darwinist struggle between nations it was essential for eugenic reasons that the imperial 'race' of 'Greater Britain' should be a healthy, competitive and dynamic breed. According to Amery in the 1920s, Empire settlement was 'simply social reform writ large and dealing with the whole problem of national life on a wider scale'.[14]

The notion of Empire settlement as a species of social reform undoubtedly gained ideological appeal in periods of trade downturn such as the mid-1880s, 1903–05, 1908–09 and in the 1920s, when unemployment, pauperism and distress fuelled socialist agitation and occasioned intense middle-class unease. For the Salvation Army leader, General William Booth, what was required

> would be a bridge across the seas as it were, to some land of plenty over which there should constantly be passing . . . our surplus population, instead of its melancholy gravitation, as at present, down to the filthy slums, the hated workhouses, the cruel casual wards, the hopeless prisons and the like.[15]

The prospect of emigration creating a 'bridge' from the corrupted metropole to 'the England beyond the sea' was a recurring metaphor in imperialist literature and was adopted with some enthusiasm by organised charity in the United Kingdom. Between 1860 and 1900 many of the most famous British charities were established; many of these both promoted and practised emigration in the ethical struggle for spiritual redemption and social salvation. To voluntary emigration societies like the East End Emigration Fund or Dr Barnardo's and the numerous other children's societies engaged in child migration, Empire emigration represented an alluring form of social rescue work. It offered solutions at an individual level and as a collective vent 'for the alleviation of the congested condition of our over-populated country'.[16]

Petty-bourgeois self-help ideology, with its emphasis on self-reliance and thrift, was a further powerful ideological current which lent appeal to the emigration safety-valve. The representation of the British dominions as being lands of fresh opportunity, social equality and advancement, morally untainted by the corruption and degradation of city life in the metropole, was a feature of imperialist rhetoric and dear to the self-image of the white colonies themselves.[17] Naturally, in the self-governing dominions there was considerable antipathy to the notion of the United Kingdom 'shovelling out' its paupers, but the contradiction was masked by the increasingly emphatic if optimistic stress on the potential of British migrants as land settlers essential to the rural development of the 'open spaces' of the Empire. Indeed, the land settlement dimension in Empire settlement ideology was critical to its presentation, both in the dominions and in the United Kingdom itself. The important place of rustic inconography in the English self-image and ideas about Englishness is now widely recognised.[18] In modern society the myth of urban degeneration and of rural revitalisation offers a collective asylum from the traumas of industrialisation and the uncertainties of social change. Between 1880 and 1914 misgivings about the decline of rural society and the social and political costs of urbanisation were acutely felt in the United Kingdom. In this context the dominions were the rural metaphor writ large. The ideological representation of the colonial landscape as 'wide open spaces' – the *Lebensraum* of the British race – provided an agrarian psychological counterpoise to the industrial metropole and a field for the recreation of the British yeomanry within the frontiers of 'Greater Britain'.[19]

Land settlement was therefore at the heart of the cause of 'Greater Britain' as a response to perceived external and internal dangers. However, in practice the attempts of social engineers to implement programmes of rural settlement of British migrants on undeveloped colonial land demonstrated just how wide could be the gap between the aspirations of ideological discourse and the realities of effective settlement and agricultural production. The most celebrated trial of the principles involved between 1880 and 1914 was the reconstruction scheme of agricultural colonisation introduced in the annexed Afrikaner republics – the Transvaal and the Orange River Colony – after the end of the South African War in 1902. The programme of anglicisation through which the British authorities hoped to secure political hegemony in South Africa depended on the creation of a 'loyal' electoral majority through British immigration.[20] Between 1902 and 1905 1,200 settlers were allocated almost 2 million acres of crown land in South

Africa, but by 1912 few of the settlers remained. Yet despite the high costs and disappointing results of the South Africa schemes the relative failure of the project did not inhibit the development of the imperial land settlement lobby. On the contrary the post-war anglicisation policies fanned a major resurgence of the movement for state-aided Empire settlement.

In 1904 there was a major initiative involving the Rhodes Trustees, the Salvation Army and the agrarian enthusiast, Henry Rider Haggard. At the prompting of Earl Grey, a founding director of the British South Africa Company and the Governor-General of Canada between 1904 and 1911, Haggard was commissioned to report on the Salvation Army's rural training colonies in the United States of America; the investigation was surprisingly granted official status although the cost was to be borne by the Trustees.[21] Haggard's report was published in 1905 under the suggestive title *The Poor and the Land*.[22] It glossed over the many inadequacies in Salvation Army settlement methods, while Haggard put forward his own 'Scheme of National Land Settlement'; the state-aided emigration of the United Kingdom's surplus urban population and its settlement overseas would, he claimed, 'counteract at least to some extent that tendency towards race ruin . . . the end of which must be a progressive national weakening and depletion which if unchecked, may well bring about national defeat at the hand of those ruder peoples of the world that remain land dwelling and agricultural'.[23] Haggard was 'in great hopes that a big thing may result'.[24] However, it was never plausible that the British state would over-turn its emigration policy on the basis of his unconvincing report. In deference to Haggard and the Rhodes Trustees a departmental committee under Lord Tennyson, lately Governor-General of Australia, was appointed to consider Haggard's proposals, but its report gave short shrift to his scheme and to the case for overseas land settlement generally. Nevertheless, the Tennyson Committee accepted that emigration could offer 'a partial relief' from unemployment and other social problems and advocated more liberal use of the facilities for state assistance that already existed. The committee proposed further discussions on Empire migration with dominion governments at the forthcoming Colonial Conference.[25]

For their part, dominion governments were predictably determined to resist the dumping of the United Kingdom's 'social wreckage' upon them. However, the Australian government was anxious to increase the volume of immigration, and it perceived British state aid as a means of redressing the geographical disadvantage Australia perpetually suffered in competition with Canada to attract British emigrants; to that extent its officials were generally prepared to indulge the excesses of Empire settlement rhetoric and to make common ground with the imperialist lobby. At the 1907 Colonial Conference the Australian government seized on the Tennyson Committee's proposals and tabled a resolution calling for the United Kingdom 'to co-operate with any colonies desiring immigrants in assisting suitable persons to emigrate'.[26]

British officials were alarmed by the Australian resolution and the underlying appeal for British state aid. At the conference John Burns, President of the Local Government Board, defended the British state's limited role in the promotion and direction of British emigration with what proved to be the definitive public statement of official policy between 1906 and 1914. His case was that, first, since all colonies were competing for British migrants, it was difficult to assist emigration without appearing to choose between colonies and arousing the hostility of those not favoured. The British government should be seen to occupy a neutral position, restricting its role to the provision of accurate and unbiased information to prospective emigrants. Secondly, vigorous government intervention would interfere with the useful work of voluntary emigration societies. Thirdly, emigration from the United Kingdom to the Empire was proceeding anyway at a level which was as great as the United Kingdom could bear and the dominions could comfortably assimilate.[27] The British government would support only a general resolution that it was 'desirable to encourage British emigrants to proceed to British colonies rather than to foreign countries'.[28]

Between 1907 and the next Imperial (formerly 'Colonial') Conference in 1911 there was a further shift of British emigration in favour of the white dominions. As John Burns pointed out in 1911 when the issue was again raised by Australia, emigration from the United Kingdom was now approaching 300,000 annually and 'the stream . . . has been diverted from foreign countries to the Empire'. A further increase would be demographically disastrous in the long term since 'with a diminishing birth rate and with an increasing emigration of fertile people, the Mother Country cannot safely go beyond 300,000 a year . . . Crowded emigrant ships are no compensation for empty cradles in any country in the British Empire'. Burns advised the conference 'to let well alone'.[29]

With the exception of Australia's Andrew Fisher, dominion leaders accepted the United Kingdom's assurances that emigrants were already being strongly encouraged to choose Empire countries for settlement and its reservations that a policy of full-blown state assistance would prejudice future Empire migration. More auspicious for the future prospects of Empire settlement was the conference's decision to recommend the appointment of a Royal Commission to report on 'all matters connected with trade, commerce, production and intercourse'.[30] The Dominions Royal Commission would not issue its Final Report until 1917, but its report on migration was to prove a significant contribution to the widening debate about the state's role in emigration.

In the meantime the Empire settlement lobby in the United Kingdom was lent a more unified voice by the establishment in 1910 of a Standing Emigration Committee of the Royal Colonial Institute (RCI). The committee represented the emigration societies and imperialist organisations which had attended a conference on emigration organised by the RCI. Between 1910 and 1914 it provided an effective and articulate lobby for British emigrationists and proved a forceful advocate of the case for Empire settlement. With separate sub-committees concerned with child migration and the emigration of single women, the RCI committee pressed British and dominion governments on detailed issues in these specialised fields of emigration work with some success. Although the RCI failed to obtain the extended discussion of emigration it hoped to see at the 1911 Imperial Conference, its lobbying secured the inclusion of 'migration' in the terms of reference of the Dominions Royal Commission.[31] When the commission took evidence from British emigration societies and dominion emigration agents in London in 1912, the RCI organised a virtual consensus of views around its own submission which emphasised the common interests of the United Kingdom and the self-governing dominions in encouraging Empire migration and the need for a new official body to co-ordinate the work of the voluntary societies. This central body should be equipped to advise on all emigration questions, to supervise voluntary efforts and to deal with dominion representatives. Moreover, it should be empowered by statute to make advances to the societies to assist their emigration work. The RCI singled out women and children as sections of the British population whose emigration ought to be especially encouraged.[32]

By 1914 the Empire settlement movement was well organised and vociferous. It could claim with justification to speak for all those active in British emigration work and could rely on the patronage of the imperial zealots of the *haute bourgeoisie*. Some dominion politicians and officials, particularly Australians, subscribed to the cause of Empire settlement, but, critically, support in the British Parliament was limited. Moreover, the liberal orthodoxy of state departments, including the Colonial Office, remained largely intact; despite the Australian interventions and the hopes pinned on the Dominions Royal Commission, the struggle for state aid was a long way from being won.

The wartime debate, 1914–18: reconstruction and Empire land settlement

The expansion of state control was a ubiquitous consequence of organising society for 'total war'. It touched all aspects of life and by the end of

1916 had transformed dramatically the political arena in the United Kingdom, opening up new possibilities for the emigration lobby. While emigration itself fell off, the ideological struggle over British emigration intensified in the nationality-conscious climate of the war years, and the possibility of a significant redirection of state policy began to emerge.

Social imperialist politics found a new lease on life during the war and by 1917 had all but captured the discourses of state policy-making in key areas.[33] The threat from industrial militancy and a disaffected working class, the perception of wartime disruption as an opportunity for radical change and the central place of imperial solidarity in the ideology of the British war effort all situated social imperial radicalism as an especially apposite response to the problems which beset the British state in the crisis mid-war years. In particular, there was enormous concern about the problems of demobilisation and reconversion, particularly large-scale unemployment, which seemed certain to follow the peace. From 1916 onwards the demands of 'reconstruction' – 'the larger and worthier ideal of a better world after the war'[34] – were taken up by state departments in earnest. This vision of a reconstructed United Kingdom was also designed to win the support of labour and shared the assumptions of social imperialist thought – statism, protectionism and the demand for 'efficiency' in all areas of national life. These dramatic new circumstances created the conditions for a more effective challenge to established British policy on emigration and for a persuasive presentation of the case for Empire settlement.

Within weeks of the outbreak of war the Empire settlement lobby was petitioning the Colonial Office to secure a commitment to post-war emigration and settlement. Major schemes involving British loans for land settlement in Australia were submitted. One of these was enthusiastically backed by Earl Grey, now president of the RCI, but the official response was cool: no pledges could be made and enquiries were referred to the Dominions Royal Commission.[35] In March 1915 the RCI Council approved the establishment of a new committee to press the case for land settlement facilities for ex-servicemen both in the United Kingdom and overseas. Besides Grey, Rider Haggard and emigrationists from the Salvation Army and the Naval and Military Emigration League, a number of dominion officials and businessmen joined the After the War Empire Settlement and Rural Employment Committee. The committee dispatched a deputation to the Colonial Office in July 1915. The RCI representatives stressed the importance of adopting a rural settlement policy 'before we have men in thousands upon us'. This was a matter for state action, it was impossible for the institute 'or for any other private body to deal with a matter so urgent and complex'.[36]

While the Secretary of State for the Colonies, Bonar Law, and the Minister of Agriculture, Lord Selborne, expressed their personal sympathy with the aims of the RCI Committee, in private permanent officials were dismissive of the institute's efforts to commit the British government to assisted schemes for ex-servicemen and scathing about the suggestion from Sir John Taverner, the Agent-General for Western Australia, that Rider Haggard should be commissioned to tour the dominions seeking their co-operation in an Empire-wide scheme of rural settlement for ex-servicemen.[37] However, the right-wing press latched on to this proposal, and *The Times* reported that dominion governments would welcome the opportunity to discuss land settlement plans with a British commissioner.[38] Encouraged by this, in October 1915 the RCI's Empire Land Settlement Committee (the former After the War Committee) resolved to send Haggard on a fact-finding mission on its own account. Financed by donations from shipping lines and dominion commercial interests, chiefly Australian, in February 1916 Haggard sailed for Cape Town.

Haggard was unable to secure any commitment from the government in South Africa, but in Australia all the state governments made some pledge to consider British ex-servicemen alongside their own returning troops; in reality most of the offers depended on the ability of state governments to raise development loans (with the implication that these should be underwritten by the British Treasury). New Zealand also offered assistance 'as a duty to the Empire', and in Canada, too, Haggard was well received and repeatedly assured of support. For the RCI's agitation on behalf of ex-servicemen, Haggard's tour was an unexpected and spectacular success. The RCI emissary was back in London by August 1916, and his report to the institute was published at the end of the month. Acclaimed by the imperialist press, Haggard's conclusion that 'everwhere there is now an open door for British ex-servicemen'[39] seemed to give the lie to the official insistence that the dominions would not take British troops and to presage real movement in the Empire settlement cause.

By late 1916 the 'wait and see' approach of Colonial Office officials was increasingly out of step not only with the views of the imperialist lobby and many dominion politicians and officials but also with the policy deliberations of other British government departments. The Ministry of Labour told the Colonial Office that for many British troops emigration would be preferable to 'the dull ways of peace' and might 'relieve our own market of what is likely to be a serious incumbrance'.[40] When the Board of Agriculture's Departmental Committee on Land Settlement reported in June it also argued that the likelihood of post-war emigration needed to be faced and that some co-ordination of British policy with that of the dominions was becoming imperative. Whereas in early 1916 the Colonial Office had been able to dismiss speculation about British ex-servicemen taking up dominion land schemes as 'only so much hot air',[41] by the summer the possibility could no longer be ignored. Haggard's successes in Australia and the pledges by New Zealand and Canada to give consideration to British ex-servicemen undermined the Colonial Office's prevarication. As the Board of Agriculture pointed out, the danger was that if the British government failed to implement its own rural settlement programme in concert with the land development plans of the dominions the pick of the British forces would be lured overseas.[42]

When the Dominions Royal Commission issued its Final Report in March 1917 it, too, drew attention to 'the past lack of method in recruiting migrants in the Mother Country . . . and the urgent necessity for reforming the existing system'. There was a need for more vigorous forms of state regulation of emigration. The key to the government's supervisory role would be the establishment of a 'Central Emigration Authority' to centralise the functions of British government departments and to exercise far greater control over the commercial activities of passenger agents, which voluntary emigration societies and the Emigrants' Information Office had been demanding for many years. The commission was ambivalent about large-scale emigration of young men after the war in the light of war losses, but the case for assisted emigration and Empire settlement of British women and children was considered unassailable.[43]

While the Royal Commission's report circulated government departments, the new Secretary of State for the Colonies, Walter Long, appointed a further committee to recommend a framework for the assistance of soldier settlement after the war and for the constitution of a central authority to supervise this. Lord Tennyson agreed to chair this Empire Settlement Committee, which included representatives of all the dominion governments (including all six Australian and seven Canadian Agents-General) and a number of British departmental officials as well as several individuals including Haggard. The Colonial Office would not allow the RCI to be directly represented, but its ideological perspective on British emigration was shared by many members of the committee. The report of the Empire Settlement Committee issued in August 1917 echoed the institute's imperialist rhetoric:

> if opportunities are lacking at home, the Home Government should help, not hinder, [British migrants] on their way to other parts of the Empire. So too, the Dominions should not desire to pursue a policy calculated to denude the Mother Country of the population which she needs. But they will welcome those whom she is able to spare, and give them every chance

of success in a new and wider life. Particularly . . . will they rejoice to receive the men who have fought the Empire's battles in this war, who are the best of the British race. No settlers could be more desirable both as regards themselves, and their progeny, which may well be of priceless worth in the now unpeopled districts of the Empire overseas.[44]

In the face of the increasingly assertive imperialist and dominion lobby the Colonial Office was divided. Some officials remained sceptical about dominion governments' intentions and concerned about the consequences for the United Kingdom of excessive post-war emigration. Others were ready to concede that it was 'doubtful whether HMG or the Governments of the Self-Governing Dominions . . . will be satisfied with the maintenance of the old system'.[45] The politicians meanwhile opted for a course 'midway between an untenable laissez-faire and equally untenable wildcat schemes'.[46] Long was still opposed to state aid for overseas land settlement, but he was now prepared to consider that 'where men and women desire to leave this country and start afresh in one of our Dominions, every possible assistance, including even, in some cases, pecuniary help, should be given to them'.[47]

Accordingly, by the autumn of 1917 the British government was keen to arm itself with the legislative powers proposed by the Dominions Royal Commission and the Empire Settlement Committee before the widely anticipated spate of post-war emigration materialised. Both reports had favoured the establishment of an emigration authority which would combine the existing functions of state departments and tighten state control over emigration from the United Kingdom, providing financial assistance to approved categories of emigrants or 'overseas settlers' where appropriate. The creation of such an authority was the main intention of the Emigration Bill which was brought before Parliament in May 1918. The powers of the new authority would be extensive. It would supervise through a reformed licensing system the passage-broking activities not only of shipping companies and their agents but also of the voluntary emigration societies and even of the dominion governments' emigration agencies. Moreover, relatively punitive fines were proposed for breaches of the new regulations.

The 1918 Emigration Bill found few friends. Through its emphasis on bureaucratic regulation it succeeded in offending all interested parties. It was attacked by Members of Parliament for 'savouring too much of continental methods, of German notions of colonizing', and by representatives of the powerful Shipowners Parliamentary Committee for intending 'to substitute Government control for the old freedom of action, introducing unnecessary expenditure' and 'tyrannous regulations'.[48] Outside Parliament, Australian Agents-General petitioned the Colonial Office for exemption and told a meeting at the RCI that the bill 'ought to be described as one for the discouragement of emigration within the Empire'.[49] The RCI's Empire settlement zealots agreed that it was wholly unsatisfactory.

The bill went on to be savaged by dominion leaders at the 1918 Imperial War Conference before becoming humiliatingly becalmed in Grand Committee. In October 1918 a demoralised Long had to report to the War Cabinet that the government could not command a majority for the bill and it was abandoned. The Emigration Bill fell fatally between two stools. It pleased neither proponents nor opponents of emigration and promised only an intensification of state control. The vested interests of the emigration industry – shipowners and passenger agents, emigration societies and dominion governments – were not prepared to see such rigid powers bestowed on the state bureaucracy without a much clearer indication of what government policy on emigration would be. Conversely, radical and Labour MPs suspected that the purpose of the bill was to institutionalise the emigration safety-valve, while some employers feared the consequences for the labour market.

Attempts to revive the Emigration Bill in early 1919 came to nothing. Indeed, already by 1918 the imperialism and statism of 1916 and 1917 were being thrown-back on to the ideological defensive; the counter-attack of *laissez-faire* forces was under way and the failure of the Emigration Bill was an indication of the likely fate of reconstruction measures which threatened powerful interests. However, after the Armistice and the khaki election of late 1918, a new team was appointed to the Colonial Office, Lord Milner as Secretary of State and L. S. Amery as Under-Secretary. The commitment to imperial unity of Milner and Amery was well known. Under their direction state policy took a decisive turn towards the imperialist conception of British emigration.

'A way out of our troubles':[50] Oversea Settlement and the post-war unemployment crisis, 1918–22

Unquestionably the appointment of Milner and Amery to the Colonial Office in 1919 was of immense significance for Empire settlement. Milner was an established figurehead of the imperialist movement, but it was Amery, as Under-Secretary of State for the Colonies (1919–21), Parliamentary and Financial Secretary at the Admiralty (1921–22), First Lord of the Admiralty (1922–24) and Secretary of State for the Colonies (1924–29), who was the driving force behind the Empire settlement policy of the 1920s. Amery adopted the ideas of Grey, Haggard and other Empire migration zealots and brought a degree of political skill, even opportunism, to the Empire settlement lobby which it had not previously commanded. Amery's imperialism was forged in the South

African crucible of social imperialist thinking, informed by the political ideology of Chamberlain, Milner and the 'kindergarten' imperialists. His commitment to the causes of tariff reform and 'Empire development' was perhaps even stronger than his espousal of Empire settlement.[51] However, it was Empire migration which offered the immediate prospect of state patronage, and Amery's contribution was to make explicit the extent to which an organised programme of Empire settlement might help to relieve the unemployment situation in the United Kingdom. It was this aspect of the project which enabled him to mobilise support at Cabinet level and overcome the obstructionism of the Treasury.

As many emigration enthusiasts had feared, despite the lengthy wartime deliberations the end of hostilities found the British government without a settled policy or the machinery to direct emigration. Conservative peers in the House of Lords called it 'not only a misfortune . . . but almost a scandal', and demanded the establishment of a provisional supervisory body pending the reintroduction of the Emigration Bill.[52] Within a few days the Colonial Office appointed a 'Government Emigration Committee' representing government departments and the shipping industry along with one or two unofficial nominees; neither the RCI nor any of the voluntary emigration societies was represented on the new non-statutory committee, which assumed all the functions proposed by the Dominions Royal Commission which did not require legislation. In a press statement, however, the government announced its intention to 'undertake closer responsibility in connection with emigration than they have exercised in the past'.[53]

After inconclusive soundings on the state of the British labour market, the efforts of the new committee – which was chaired by Amery and soon re-christened the Oversea Settlement Committee (OSC) – were largely devoted during 1919 to the promotion of emigration by ex-servicemen and single women, areas of potential state assistance identified as particularly deserving by the wartime reports. Under the aegis of the OSC the principal women's emigration societies were reorganised in July 1919 as the Society for the Oversea Settlement of British Women (SOSBW). The SOSBW received a substantial Treasury grant and was officially recognised as the women's branch of the OSC in 1920. It remained the central agency for state mediation of women's emigration throughout the inter-war period. The OSC also pressed the case for assistance to ex-servicemen. It proposed to the Cabinet in February 1919 that 'those who fought for the Empire should be entitled to take their reward in any part of the Empire'. The provision of free ocean passages from the United Kingdom to acceptable Empire destinations by British ex-servicemen and women who were approved by dominion governments was agreed by the Cabinet and announced in April 1919. In the transition from the statist reports of the war period to state supervision and finance of emigration after the war, the importance of the ex-servicemen's free-passage scheme is manifest. However, the scheme was one of emigration rather than overseas land settlement. Moreover, from the British perspective the financial outlay, less than £2.5 million between 1919–22, was small compared to the £20 million cost of the domestic land settlement programme.[54]

By 1920 the state's role in British emigration had been significantly recast since the end of the war. The Emigration Bill had been wrecked by the passenger shipping lobby, but a non-statutory central body was substituted, and under its direction state assistance was made available to emigrating ex-servicemen and ex-servicewomen and their families. However, all these arrangements were explicitly transitional. The OSC was envisaged as a temporary body and the ex-servicemen's scheme was to be of limited duration. Furthermore, all the state financial assistance was directed towards the provision of passages for emigration rather than dominion land settlement. As the RCI put it, 'such a scheme can only be regarded as a makeshift, and does not constitute a policy of organised Migration and Settlement'.[55] It remained the task of the Empire settlement lobby to consolidate the temporary commitment to state assistance for ex-servicemen into a more permanent and generously funded programme of imperial co-operation in overseas settlement; in this task the decisive factor proved to be the growth of mass unemployment in the United Kingdom.

During 1919 and 1920 the OSC proceeded cautiously where the question of a broader scheme of state assistance was concerned. According to Cabinet figures, unemployment in the United Kingdom fell from 1 million in April 1919 to less than 100,000 by April 1920. Against this background the Ministry of Labour opposed further measures to encourage emigration, and the Treasury, although sanctioning the ex-servicemen's scheme, remained suspicious of open-ended commitments and intervened to restrict OSC expenditure wherever possible. The persistence of wartime travel conditions – the shortage of shipping and the priority of repatriating dominion troops – continued to limit the volume of emigration well into 1920. Attempts to convert the Emigration Bill into an Oversea Settlement Bill failed to enthuse the Prime Minister, Lloyd George.

Cabinet approval for new schemes of Empire settlement came out of the blue. In April 1920 the employment cycle turned downwards decisively. The level of national unemployment rose from below 1 per cent in April to more than 7 per cent by November.[56] The upward trend continued into 1921, alarming the government and creating a far more favourable climate for the consideration of Empire settlement. In August 1920 a new Cabinet Unemployment Committee was established. The committee focused on the short-term unemployment problem of the winter of 1920–21. In this context, a memorandum to the Cabinet from Lord Milner seeking the extension of the free-passage scheme, drew attention to the efficacy of assisted emigration in relieving unemployment and reducing the cost of the government's housing programme. In the absence of other initiatives, the Cabinet Unemployment Committee accepted the expediency of 'encouraging overseas settlement as a means of relieving abnormal unemployment'. The committee proposed the extension of the free-passage scheme and temporary funding for the OSC to assist the emigration of the unemployed. More significant still, the committee called on the Colonial Office to 'formulate a scheme of assisted emigration on a large scale' in co-operation with dominion governments.[57] The full Cabinet agreed these proposals in December 1920; the Cabinet decision was a milestone in emigration policy and set the scene for the reformulation of state emigration policy in 1921.

The new British commitment to Empire migration rested on the perception that a state-aided programme could relieve unemployment in the United Kingdom, forestall class conflict and save state expenditure. Yet to dominion leaders and public opinion this was close to anathema; dominion governments would not countenance a return to the discredited policy of 'shovelling out paupers'. However, the linking of Empire settlement to an extensive programme of rural development in the dominions made it possible to juggle the apparently conflicting interests of British social policy and the dominion demand for high-quality settlers. The settlement and development of marginal areas were attractive to commercial interests in the dominions as a stimulus to economic growth, especially if they could be financed by cheap development loans raised on the London capital market and underwritten by the British government. For the British the development of the Empire's primary resources indulged their notion of a complementary imperial economy and promised the realisation of agrarianist and social Darwinist imperatives.

Dominion representatives attended a conference at the Colonial Office in early 1921 to draw up a joint scheme of Empire settlement to put before the 1921 Imperial Conference. It was agreed that any British Empire migration policy had to focus on land settlement and provision for rural development. Other opportunities for British migrants in trades, manufacturing and the service industries would depend on a dramatic increase in the number of 'primary producers'. Milner and Amery put forward a British initiative: Britain would co-operate with dominion governments in a 'comprehensive policy of Empire Land Settlement and Empire-directed Migration', and would contribute £2 million each year for assisted passages and other schemes. Half of the British funds would be for land settlement in the form of repayable loans of up to £300 per settler, to be administered by 'oversea governments' or private organisations. The balance would be assigned to assisted passages, including outfitting and landing allowances; only half of this would be repayable. With few modifications these proposals became the basic principles of the Empire Settlement Act.

The British proposals were accepted by the dominion representatives and went forward to the Imperial Conference in July. The Cabinet authorised negotiations 'on the understanding that caution should be exercised with regard to any immediate expenditure'.[58] For their parts Australian and New Zealander Ministers tied their participation in any scheme to their ability to raise development loans in London, and demanded an unequivocal commitment by the British 'to make clear that the policy of co-operation now adopted is intended to be permanent': this would require legislation. To no-one's surprise the South African government would not participate in a general scheme of Empire settlement 'due to the limited field for white labour'.[59]

Despite the endorsement of the 1921 Imperial Conference, the OSC's Empire settlement programme still had to weather Treasury antipathy to new financial commitments. The Geddes Committee on National Expenditure was appointed in August 1921 and demanded severe reductions in state expenditure, the orthodox response to economic recession. It set the seal on the prevailing mood of retrenchment. Moreover, the interventions of Australian politicians, with their talk of massively expensive development projects, did nothing to improve the prospects of reaching a financial settlement with the Treasury, where any expenditure on oversea settlement was already regarded as the thin end of a wedge which would draw the British exchequer into disastrous involvements with huge and uncontrollable Empire development schemes.[60] Once again, however, the unemployment situation came to the rescue of Empire settlement. In the winter of 1921-22 the high level of unemployment posed a serious challenge to government. There were few departmental initiatives in the pipeline. Worried officials and politicians clutched at straws. Particularly keen to embrace Empire settlement was Sir Alfred Mond, the Minister of Health, who called for 'liberal assistance from public funds here and overseas' for Empire settlement, and who invited Amery to raise emigration at the Cabinet Unemployment Committee, which Mond chaired.[61] Seizing his chance Amery proposed the allocation of £5 million a year to emigration to help to relieve the 'permanent and prolonged shortage of employment' which was likely to last for a decade or more: 'The key to the employment situation is the shifting of British population from Great Britain to the Dominions, and from industry to agriculture. What is needed is a policy of Empire Migration and Empire land Settlement carried out on a large scale.'[62]

By the end of 1921 Treasury resistance to the principle of oversea settlement was crumbling, although it determined to so limit expenditure that the United Kingdom could not be drawn into financial entanglements with Australian development schemes. When the Geddes Committee reported in February 1922 it reduced the sum allocated to the remaining few months of the ex-servicemen's free-passage scheme, but there was no wholesale attack on oversea settlement. In March the 'Cabinet Oversea Settlement Committee' met to thrash out the remaining differences between Amery and the Treasury. Amery advanced Empire settlement as 'the best cure for the industrial situation and for the serious overcrowding in this country'. He was supported by Mond, and the new chancellor, Sir Robert Horne, compromised on the financial question; £1.5 million would be available in 1922–23 and £3 million each subsequent year. Amery considered this enough for a 'fair beginning'.[63] Moreover, the OSC were to be allowed to negotiate interest-sharing collaborations with the dominions for land settlement and development schemes, provided the British commitment did not exceed the general financial provisions.[64] A week later the Empire Settlement Bill was laid before Parliament. It was not finally approved by the full cabinet, only by the Home Affairs Committee which accepted Amery's plea to get the bill into Parliament before the Easter recess.[65]

On 7 April 1922 the government introduced into the Commons a bill 'to make better provision for furthering British settlement in His Majesty's Overseas Dominions'. Amery's Empire Settlement Bill was notable, according to him, for its 'elasticity'.[66] It lacked the regulatory clauses of the 1918 Emigration Bill and made no attempt to interfere with the business of passenger agents or the work of emigration societies. In these areas it was a tactical retreat from the vigorous state role enshrined in the 1918 bill. In financial terms, however, the Empire Settlement Bill was a radical departure. It empowered the Secretary of State to conclude schemes of co-operation with public or private bodies in either the United Kingdom or the dominions for the assistance of 'suitable persons' intending migration within the Empire. Eligible schemes under the bill could be either land settlement or development schemes, or for the assistance of migration and settlement through passage allowances, outfitting grants, initial maintenance or agricultural training. The British contribution to a scheme was not to exceed half the total cost and each scheme was subject to Treasury approval. The legislation would apply not only to schemes in the dominions but to all colonies, protectorates and mandated territories.

The Empire Settlement Bill passed through Parliament with little debate and little opposition; it received the royal assent on 31 May 1922. The Act was welcomed by the shipping companies who anticipated commercial gain from the new policy; indeed they were to prove the principal financial beneficiaries of the Empire settlement programme.[67] Dominion governments were also much happier with the 1922 measure. This was not surprising since it promised to attract British funds to the development and settlement of their territories. Much more important to its acceptance by the British Parliament and public opinion, however, was its relationship with the acute problem of British unemployment.

Unemployment averaged nearly 17 per cent of the insured workforce in 1921 and thereafter never fell below 9 per cent throughout the inter-war period. It was against the socially divisive background of an unemployment crisis of grave proportions that Amery and the OSC launched their Whitehall initiative to secure the principle of state financial aid to Empire settlement. Other government departments, especially those directly involved in employment and social welfare policy, were glad to accept the OSC's contention that emigration could be a palliative for unemployment. It is questionable whether Amery's ministerial allies shared his deep conviction that Empire settlement could provide a long-term solution to endemic domestic problems of unemployment, poverty and social unrest, and to the external challenges from rival foreign powers. However, in the circumstances of 1921–22 they were prepared to entertain oversea settlement as a counter-cyclical expedient which did at least have an air of finality about it. Moreover, in a period of retrenchment the sheer financial strain of unemployment benefits and relief works troubled the Treasury and diluted their resistance to Amery's social imperialism. The United Kingdom adopted a programme of Empire settlement in 1922, apparently against the prevailing emphasis during the depression on economy in public expenditure, because in the absence of other adequate initiatives, state-aided Empire settlement offered itself as a relatively inexpensive and ideologically precocious policy.

After 1900 social imperialist ideas challenged orthodox liberal political economy with increasing authority. The debate about emigration was bound up with fears of pauperism, physical and moral deterioration, the political threat from 'the dangerous classes' and the challenge of foreign competition. Emigrationists and imperialist ideologues presented Empire settlement as a palliative for class conflict in the

United Kingdom and an instrument of imperial organic unity. The encroaching statism characteristic of wartime politics between 1914 and 1918 and the post-war unemployment crisis in the early 1920s created the conditions for a dramatic revaluation of emigration within state departments. When the Dominions Royal Commission reported in 1917, it effectively condemned the pre-war emigration system. However, the attempt to erect a new framework based on the commission's own recommendations failed with the demise of the 1918 Emigration Bill. In the event the post-war government improvised, and this allowed Leo Amery with considerable backing from vociferous Australian interests, gradually to extend the state's commitment to Empire settlement, finally securing Treasury and Cabinet approval for the introduction of an Empire Settlement Bill which promised a dramatic new era of imperial co-operation in migration policy in the simplest of legislative formulations. The inter-war Empire settlement programme, explored in detail by the other essays in this volume, was perhaps the most far-reaching achievement of the social imperialist politics in the United Kingdom during the early twentieth century.

Acknowledgements

I am glad to have this opportunity to express my gratitude to Professor Shula Marks of the Institute of Commonwealth Studies, London, without whose support and encouragement the research on which this essay is based would not have been possible.

Notes

1 C. Erickson, *Emigration from Europe, 1815–1914*, London, 1976, p. 9.
2 H. L. Malchow, *Population Pressures: Emigration and Government in Late Nineteenth-century Britain*, Palo Alto, Calif., 1979.
3 T. E. Sedgwick describing the people of New Zealand in a letter to the first of his parties of 'town lads' sailing for New Zealand in October 1910; Sedgwick Papers, vol. 1, Royal Commonwealth Society Archives.
4 B. Semmel, *Imperialism and Social Reform: English Social Imperial Thought, 1895–1914*, London, 1960; see also G. Stedman Jones, *Outcast London: a study in the Relationship Between Classes in Victorian Society*, Harmondsworth, 1984.
5 For a detailed exploration of these themes see K. I. Williams, 'The British State, Social Imperialism and Emigration from Britain, 1900–22: the Ideology and Antecedents of the Empire Settlement Act', Ph.D. thesis, University of London, 1985.
6 Minute by H. Lambert, 18 July 1911, Public Record Office, London (hereafter PRO) CO 532/34/25188.
7 Minute by H. Lambert, 24 September 1907, PRO, CO 532/3/8611.
8 *Memorandum on the History and Functions of Emigrants' Information Office*, British Parliamentary Papers, Cd. 3407, LXVIII, 1907, p. 4.
9 Minute by C. P. Lucas, 27 April 1911, PRO CO 532/31/11242.
10 J. R. Seeley, *The Expansion of England*, London, 1883, pp. 8–9.
11 J. Saxon Mills, 'Sir Rider Haggard's great tour', *United Empire*, 7, September 1916, p.

613.

12 Hansard, *Parliamentary Debates*, House of Commons, vol. 97, col. 1000, 14 August 1917.

13 *Ibid.*, vol. 134, col. 220, 2 November 1920.

14 *Ibid.*, vol. 174, col. 570, 28 May 1924.

15 General William Booth, 'Our emigration plans', *Proceedings of the Royal Colonial Institute*, 37, 1905–06, pp. 142–3.

16 Lord Brabazon, *State-Directed Colonisation: its Necessity*, London, 1886, p. 17.

17 See, for example, H. Gullett, 'The empty places', *United Empire*, 2, November 1916, pp. 781–3; on the development of a distinct cultural identity in one dominion see R. White, *Inventing Australia: Images and Identity, 1688–1980*, Sydney, 1981, pp. 110–43.

18 Alun Howkins, 'The discovery of rural England', in R. Colls and P. Dodd, (eds), *Englishness; Politics and Culture, 1880–1920*, London, 1986, pp. 62–88; J. Marsh, *Back to the Land: the Pastoral Impulse in England from 1880 to 1914*, London, 1982; M. Wiener, *English Culture and the Decline of the Industrial Spirit, 1850–1980*, Cambridge, 1981.

19 Willaims, 'The British State, Social Imperialism and Emigration', pp. 60–7; W. D. Forsyth, *The Myth of Open Spaces*, Melbourne, 1942, p. 54.

20 M. Streak, *Lord Milner's Immigration Policy for the Transvaal 1897–1905*, Johannesburg, 1970; J. J. van Helten and K. Williams, ' "The crying need of South Africa": the emigration of single British women to the Transvaal, 1901–10', *Journal of Southern African Studies*, 10, 1983, pp. 17–38.

21 Colonial Office correspondence, October–November 1904, PRO, CO 417/406/36293, 38215, 39834.

22 H. R. Haggard, *The Poor and the Land: Being a Report on the Salvation Army Colonies in the United States and at Hadleigh, with Scheme of National Land Settlement*, London, 1905.

23 *Ibid.*, p. 23.

24 Haggard to Grey, 8 May 1905, Grey Papers, Department of Palaeography and Diplomatic, University of Durham.

25 *Report of the Departmental Committee Appointed to Consider Mr Rider Haggard's Report on Agricultural Settlements in British Colonies*, Cd. 2978, LXXVI, 1906, pp. 14–19.

26 Colonial Conference 1907, *Minutes of Proceedings*, Cd. 3523, LV, 1907, p. 160.

27 *Ibid.*, pp. 168–71.

28 *Ibid.*, pp. 155–78.

29 Imperial Conference 1911, *Minutes of Proceedings*, Cd. 5745, LIV, 1911, pp. 200–1.

30 *Ibid.*, p. 343.

31 T. Reese, *The History of the Royal Commonwealth Society, 1868–1968*, London, 1968, p. 163; records of the RCI emigration committee are available in the Royal Commonwealth Society Archives. For the history of the Dominions Royal Commission, see Sir Keith Hancock, *Survey of British Commonwealth Affairs*, vol. II, *Problems of Economic Policy, 1918–39*, pt. 1, London, 1940, pp. 98–106.

32 Dominions Royal Commission, *First Interim Report*, Cd. 6516, XVI, 1912–13, 'Report of the Standing Committee', pp. 200–4.

33 R. J. Scally, *The Origins of the Lloyd George Coalition: the Politics of Social Imperialism, 1900–18*, Princeton, 1975.

34 Ministry of Reconstruction, *The Aims of Reconstruction*, pamphlet, p. 4.

35 See the correspondence in PRO, CO 532/76/31807, 48673, CO 532/82/2090.

36 Grey to Asquith, 13 May 1915, PRO, CO 532/83/23437,

37 Report of the RCI delegation, 22 July 1915, PRO, CO 532/82/34937.

38 *The Times*, 26 July 1915, cutting enclosed in PRO, CO 532/82/34937.

39 H. R. Haggard, *The After-War Settlement and Employment of Ex-Service Men in the Overseas Dominions: Report to the Royal Colonial Institute*, London, 1916, p. 37.

40 G. H. Young to T. C. Macnaghten, 28 October 1916, PRO, CO 532/89/51794.

41 Minute by T. C. Macnaghten, 25 February 1916, PRO, CO 532/88/9153.

42 Board of Agriculture to Colonial Office, 29 May 1916, PRO, CO 532/89/26194 and 5 August 1916, PRO, CO 532/89/37065.
43 Dominions Royal Commission, *Final Report*, Cd. 8642, X, 1917–18, pp. 202–63.
44 *Report of the Empire Settlement Committee*, Cd. 8672, X, 1917–18, p. 2.
45 Memo by Macnaghten, 20 February 1917, PRO, CO 532/98/28638.
46 Minute by A. Steel-Maitland, PRO, CO 532/98/28638.
47 Minute by W. H. Long, 16 March 1917, PRO, CO 532/98/28638.
48 *Parliamentary Debates*, House of Commons, 31 November 1918, vol. 106, cols 1136–40, 1143, 1158.
49 *The Daily Telegraph*, 21 June 1918, cutting in PRO, CO 532/113/30293.
50 F. Fox, 'A way out of our troubles: empire re-settlement', *National Review*, June 1922, pp. 562–7.
51 On Amery's imperialism see L. S. Amery, *My Political Life*, vol. 2, London, 1953, pp. 182–8, 335–70; S. Constantine, *The Making of British Colonial Development Policy, 1914–40*, London, 1984.
52 *Parliamentary Debates*, House of Lords, 19 November 1918, Vol. 32, cols 238–42.
53 Draft press statement, PRO, CO 532/135/575.
54 G. F. Plant, *Oversea Settlement: Migration from the United Kingdom to the Dominions*, London, 1951, p. 73; on the British land settlement programme see C. S. Orwin and W. F. Darke, *Back to the Land*, London, 1935, pp. 29–34.
55 Memo from the RCI Empire Migration Committee to the Secretary of State for the Colonies, 20 June 1921, RCS Archives.
56 Figures from the 'Special Weekly Report on Unemployment for the Week ending 29 November 1920', PRO, Cabinet Paper, 24/75/CP2195.
57 Extract from the Second Interim Report of the Cabinet Unemployment Committee, p. 8, PRO, CO 532/159/62517; I. M. Drummond, *Imperial Economic Policy, 1917–39: Studies in Expansion and Protection*, London, 1974, pp. 63–4.
58 Minutes of the Cabinet meeting, 16 June 1921, PRO, CO 532/196/29438.
59 Imperial Conference 1921, *Summary of Proceedings and Documents*, Cmd. 1474, XIV, 1921, p. 8.
60 Drummond, *Imperial Economic Policy*, p. 74.
61 Ministry of Health to Colonial Office, 20 October 1921, PRO, CO 532/199/152/52299; Drummond, *Imperial Economic Policy*, p. 79.
62 Memo by L. S. Amery, 'Unemployment and Empire Settlement', 12 December 1921, PRO, CO 532/181/269.
63 J. Barnes and D. Nicholson (eds), *The Leo Amery Diaries, Vol. 1, 1896–1929*, London, 1980, p. 283.
64 Cabinet Committee on Oversea Settlement, Minutes and Memoranda, PRO, CAB 27/174.
65 Extract from Committee of Home Affairs, 4 April 1922, p. 4, PRO, CO 532/224/17745.
66 *Parliamentary Debates*, House of Commons, 26 April 1922, vol. 153, col. 582.
67 C. Newbury, 'Labour migration in the imperial phase: an essay in interpretation', *Journal of Commonwealth and Imperial History*, 3, 1975, pp. 244–5.

CHAPTER THREE

The assisted emigration of British ex-servicemen to the dominions, 1914–1922

Kent Fedorowich

For many in the British Empire, the long struggle in Europe between 1914 and 1918 demonstrated the importance of imperial co-operation, unity and self-sufficiency, goals which became increasingly emphasised as the war intensified. The war presented the opportunity for governments to shed older, established conventions, proceed along new paths and experiment with new ideas. Some of the new ideas were directed towards social planning and reconstruction, some towards 'constructive imperialism: a renewed determination to invigorate the Empire as a bastion of British ideals and a bulwark of democracy'.[1] The majority of these high-minded imperial projects either did not survive the war or never left the drawing board. However, there were a few achievements. Foremost amongst them was the free-passage scheme for ex-servicemen and women which operated between 1919 and 1922 under the auspices of the Oversea Settlement Committee (OSC), established in January 1919 and itself a creation of wartime imperial co-operation. This chapter is concerned, first, to explore and explain the origins of the scheme within the ideological and political context analysed in the previous chapter by Keith Williams; and, secondly, to trace and assess its implementation and achievements.

The origins of assisted emigration for ex-servicemen

The ex-servicemen's scheme was, in part, a response to the emotional outpouring generated by the war which led the government to reward its fighting men for the sacrifices they endured for 'king and country'. But it would be an over-simplification to state that free passage was granted merely on the basis of services rendered. Its inauguration must also be seen in the light of the United Kingdom's wartime anxieties, its turbulent domestic political scene after 1918 and the Imperial government's attempts to grapple with the complex problems of demobilisation, veterans' discontent, industrial regeneration and chronic unemployment.

The outbreak of war effectively ended imperial migration for five years. 'Of course everything here is all war and excitement, and consequently the matter of emigration has fallen very far into the background', reported W. W. Cory, Canada's Deputy Minister of the Interior in August 1914.[2] W. D. Scott, Superintendent of Immigration in Ottawa, agreed. Policy discussions had been 'totally eclipsed by the war'. Conditions were so 'abnormal', he explained, that I scarcely know what to recommend'.[3] The Colonial Office used stronger imagery. Emigration was 'at present virtually dead and shows no signs of early revival'.[4] It emphasised that all emigration would be actively discouraged for the duration of the war, particularly in cases of persons of military age. '*All* emigration of persons capable of [war] work should be stopped', insisted Arthur Steel-Maitland, Parliamentary Under-Secretary for the Colonies, in 1915. Bonar Law, the Canadian-born Secretary of State, strenuously agreed.[5] Subsequently, all dominion governments dutifully adhered to the policy of disallowing the entry of British immigrants eligible for war work or military service.

Post-war imperial migration was not regarded as a major issue by the Imperial government until the summer of 1916, but thereafter its close association with post-war reconstruction made it an increasingly important matter. The pressure for positive state intervention in the resettlement, rehabilitation and retraining of British ex-servicemen, including a state-aided free-passage scheme to the dominions, came from two sources. One was the Royal Colonial Institute (RCI) which initiated and led the campaign during the war. The other resulted from the failure of the Board of Agriculture and the fledgling Ministry of Reconstruction to formulate an appealing and large-scale domestic colonisation scheme between 1915 and 1920.

Imperial migration had always been a prominent issue on the agenda of the RCI, but after the Boer War, and especially after the formation in 1910 of the Standing Emigration Committee representing voluntary emigration agencies and organisations, the RCI assumed a leading public role. It set out to raise public awareness of the advantages of redirecting British emigrants to destinations within rather than outside the Empire and to press upon government the value of a state-aided imperial migration policy.[6] It was not deterred from its purpose by the oubreak of war. As early as November 1914 the Standing Emigration Committee requested permission to send an official deputation to Lewis Harcourt, Bonar Law's predecessor as Secretary of State for the Colonies, to discuss the employment and emigration of ex-servicemen after the war.[7] This was the first time the issue was broached with

British government officials during the war. However, it was not an issue without precedent. Since 1820 several small-scale experiments had been carried out involving state assistance for ex-service migrants desirous of settling in Canada, New Zealand and South Africa, the most recent example being the British government's failed reconstruction policy in the conquered Boer republics after the Boer War.[8]

The Colonial Office promptly poured cold water on this initiative by playing down the importance of post-war emigration in general. Officials were certain that the Imperial government would not commit itself to any policy pronouncements until the final recommendations of the Dominions Royal Commision (DRC) had been tabled. 'An additional reason for going slow', minuted one official, 'is that no one can now foresee whether it will be desirable to encourage in any way the emigration of men after the war'.[9] Emigration, another Colonial Office official remarked, was not one of the first but one of the last expedients the government should implement. The nation could not afford to bleed itself of vital manpower during reconstruction. And soldier resettlement was 'only a small fractional part of the huge and infinitely more complex problem' of imperial post-war population adjustment. What was certain was that the RCI initiative could not be sanctioned, and it was condemned by the bureaucrats as premature, inopportune and mischievous.[10]

Preoccupied with the immediate demands of the war, it was obvious that the Colonial Office had not the time, inclination or enthusiasm for such an issue. It maintained that the Imperial government had given no indication of changing its pre-war policy of 'neither encouraging [nor] discouraging emigration' after the war.[11] In fact, the Colonial Office was unsure whether post-war emigration even fell within its jurisdiction. The Board of Trade, it suggested, with its network of 400 employment exchanges nationwide, was better suited to undertake administrative responsibility once the government had chosen a policy. Officials of the Board of Trade were inclined to agree.[12]

Undeterred, the RCI pushed ahead for an audience. Its President at this crucial juncture, the fourth Earl Grey, threw his customary energy and determination into the fray. An ardent social reformer with a keen personal interest in emigration and a passionate disciple of imperial unity, Grey provided the RCI with strong leadership and unquestioned prestige during his five years in office (1912–17).[13] He was deeply concerned about the potential threat posed by large numbers of idle, restless, unemployed ex-servicemen on the nation's social and political stability after the war. Alarmed by recent political developments in the United Kingdom since the turn of the century, in particular the rise of socialism, Grey found a receptive audience at the RCI who shared the same deep concerns over the 'organic' nature of British society and Empire. He and his RCI colleagues feared that demobilisation would bring unacceptably high levels of unemployment and ensuing political unrest which would accelerate socialism to the detriment of the status quo: 'It is obvious that when the war is over there will be thousands of ex-soldiers and sailors out of employment; industrious, disciplined men who if left to themselves may become a social and political menace.'[14] Like many others, he was convinced that the outdoor experience of British troops in the trenches would inculcate a strong spirit of adventure which 'will have taken so strong a hold as to make them most reluctant to return to the humdrum conditions of their old life'.[15] To harness this constructive but potentially dangerous energy and avert post-war political and social unrest, he advocated large-scale overseas soldier settlement projects which would guarantee work and a future for returning soldiers.

Reluctantly the government partially relented. Bonar Law, who had recently succeeded Harcourt as Secretary of State, and Lord Selborne, President of the Board of Agriculture, agreed to meet an RCI deputation on 22 July 1915, although the permanent officials at the Colonial Office thought it a complete waste of time.[16] The deputation was made up largely of members of the reconstituted Standing Emigration Committee, which had been given the very unmanageable title of the After the War Empire Land Settlement and Rural Employment Committee. Formed in early 1915 and chaired by Earl Grey, the new committee was given the task of redrafting and re-invigorating Grey's earlier proposals into a new platform from which to carry on the fight for positive intervention in the migration field.

Bonar Law appeared somewhat sympathetic to the deputation's entreaties. However, he made it very clear from the outset that he would make no commitment nor issue any policy statement. Privately, however, he supported the general Colonial Office tenet that the RCIs efforts were hasty, untimely and inappropriate. His carefully worded response was a masterful display of official intransigence sugared in a coating of public courtesy. Moreover, the discussion of overseas settlement was deflected by his emphasis on the Board of Agriculture's investigation of domestic soldier colonisation.[17] The RCI went away empty handed.

Undaunted, the RCI persevered and kept post-war emigration and land settlement and particularly the needs of ex-servicemen in the forefront of the public's attention. On 10 February 1916 they dispatched Rider Haggard, imperial adventure novelist, agricultural reformer and active RCI member, on a fact-finding mission to the dominions to investigate their opinions of plans to assist ex-servicemen to settle in the overseas Empire after the war. The impact of Haggard's mission and the overwhelming response he received in most of the dominions far exceeded even the most optimistic RCI expectations. The Colonial Office was also surprised by its success.[18] Immediately upon Haggard's return in late July, the RCI began marshalling its forces for another assault on the government. Another deputation was formed and presented its views to Bonar Law and Lord Crawford, the President of the Board of Agriculture, on 10 August 1916. The deputation, led by the intrepid Earl Grey, applauded and endorsed the British government's examination of domestic soldier settlement, but repeated its previous demand for the establishment of an Imperial Migration and Land Settlement Board and reiterated the importance of assisting those British ex-servicemen and their families who wanted to migrate to imperial destinations after the war. According to Grey, land settlement was receiving growing support as an instrument of repatriation and post-war reconstruction not only in the United Kingdom but throughout the Empire. Therefore it was time to formulate an imperial policy. Once again Bonar Law's reply was warm and polite but guarded.[19]

Almost simultaneously, the Reconstruction Committee, created in March 1916, requested the views of seven government departments, including the Colonial Office, on the specific issue of ex-service migration, and whether the government should encourage any form of emigration after the war.[20] The departments concerned unanimously accepted that if emigration was going to be encouraged it must go to the dominions, but they could agree on neither the principle itself nor the degree and type of assistance.[21] As for the Colonial Office, Terence Macnaghten, Chairman of the Emigrants' Information Office, acknowledged the importance that the Reconstruction Committee and the Board of Trade attached to post-war emigration, but he remained sceptical: 'We are still ignorant of what the post-war conditions will be', he commented in June 1916, 'and whether it will be right to encourage or discourage emigration, or simply to pursue the neutral policy of the period before the war.'[22] By August, however, he was more hesitant: 'I am not at all clear what our policy in this Office is towards emigration, and I have no notion what the policy of H.M.G. is likely to be.'[23] At least he now accepted that it was logical and 'safest for the Gov't to take the matter in hand, and guide such emigration . . . into the best channels'.[24]

Pressure from both inside and outside government to formulate some kind of policy became so intense during the summer of 1916 that the Colonial Office could no longer maintain its customary disdain for so-called amateur and uninformed opinion which had allowed it to evade the issue. In September 1916 Bonar Law finally decided that it was time to take some practical steps to deal with post-war ex-service migration.

He emphasised the need to find openings at home for the largest number of British ex-servicemen. However, he admitted that some would emigrate no matter what kind of domestic arrangements were prepared. In order to ensure that they did not drift outside the imperial sphere 'from want of guidance and knowledge of the opportunities available to them in the Dominions', the first priority was the creation of a central authority complete with dominion representation to 'formulate plans and co-ordinate efforts'. Moreover, what he specifically wanted from the dominions was concrete and immediate information on the nature of their own land settlement and employment schemes for ex-servicemen.[25] The permanent officials at the Colonial Office, however, remained circumspect and demonstrated their intense hostility to organised emigration by a determined rearguard action throughout the rest of 1916. While promising to establish a central body they plotted against attempts by the RCI to seek representation on it or to influence policy-making.[26] Attempts to cirumvent the RCI failed, however, when political events overtook the Colonial Office's departmental machinations.

In December 1916 Walter Long replaced Bonar Law as Secretary of State for the Colonies when Lloyd George became Prime Minister. Unlike his predecessor, Long was truly interested in the emigration issue and proved eager to forge ahead. Reminding the dominions of the urgency of the ex-service migration question, he prodded them (except New Zealand) for a response to Bonar Law's September telegram. The Canadian government promised an answer after the Provincial Premiers' Conference in early January 1917. The Duke of Devonshire, Governor-General of Canada, reported that while the conference was interesting, revealing and provided a useful exchange of ideas, it had not arrived at any definite conclusions.[27] Australia, which was discussing the subject at an inter-state conference when Long's reminder arrived, also delayed its reply until January. It was more positive. British veterans would be granted unconditionally the same soldier settlement facilities as Australians. On the other hand, South Africa had not come to a decision and indications were that when it did it would be polite, non-committal and strictly limited to helping South African veterans. The idea of a central authority to co-ordinate post-war ex-service migration, however, fell on indifferent ears.[28]

Meanwhile, Long demanded the early formation of a consultative committee which would consider ex-servicemen and post-war migration, and he insisted that it should contain knowledgeable individuals from outside government.[29] To prepare for this Long appointed the emigration enthusiast Lord Tennyson as chairman of the Empire Settlement Committee. The committee that consequently took shape in early 1917 originally comprised twenty-five members, later expanded to thirty-three, representing a cross-section of British, dominion, state and provincial governments. Several outside interests, including the Salvation Army, were nominated to the committee.[30] The RCI was successfully denied official representation by the Colonial Office. However, indirect representation was achieved by the inclusion of Rider Haggard as a committee member.

The committee's brief was to make recommendations as to the steps the British government should take in constituting the central body to facilitate the supervision and assistance of post-war emigration, to collate information that might be useful to intending emigrants and report on the necessary measures to be taken for settling ex-servicemen in the Empire. Long had it in mind that, as he told Tennyson, the central body would probably emerge from his committee using the existing committee members.[31] The Tennyson committee agreed with the recommendations of the DRC's Final Report, published in March, but went one step further. The DRC supported the establishment of special machinery to assist ex-servicemen to select, purchase and settle on land in the overseas dominions. It did not, however, mention free passage as part of the package.[32] The Tennyson committee, however, supported the principle of free passage to the dominions for ex-servicemen and the provision of development capital for the various land settlement schemes.[33]

Aware of the Tennyson committee's opinions and with the findings of the DRC before it, the Imperial War Cabinet, with little discussion, approved the New Zealand resolution that intending British emigrants be offered inducements to settle within the Empire.[34] The pronouncement was significant for at last the British government officially endorsed the need for limited state intervention in imperial migration matters. However, it was a general statement of principle and made no specific reference to free passages for British ex-servicemen. The British Cabinet was content to let the Colonial Office get on with drafting a post-war emigration policy based on the recommendations of the DRC and Tennyson committee reports. The permanent officials were, however, still convinced that British stock was needed at home. They regarded the development of post-war Britain as more important than overseas development, and they opposed any propaganda enticing ex-servicemen to emigrate to the dominions. Instead, Macnaghten argued, priority should be given to 'an attractive land settlement and general development programme in the UK'.[35] This is precisely what happened. The issue of free-passage and overseas development assistance for British ex-servicemen after the war became submerged after April 1917 in the British government's pursuit of a domestic colonisation scheme and the Colonial Office's preoccupation with casting an all-encompassing Emigration Bill in 1918.

Indeed, home colonisation proved popular with British agricultural reformers and politicians alike.[36] Naturally, patriotism permeated the demands for a domestic soldier settlement scheme. Many believed that small-scale farming operations offered returning veterans the best opportunity of leading a healthy, fulfilling and productive life. Patriotism aside, there were also important strategic, social and economic arguments for resettling British ex-servicemen on smallholdings, such as increased agricultural self-sufficiency, enhanced revival of British agriculture, fortification of the social fabric against revolution and reinforced political stability. Landholding ex-servicemen, trained with the necessary agricultural skills, would prove a welcome addition to the long and noble tradition of the British yeoman, representative and defender of a healthy, stable rural society.

Domestic settlement nevertheless proved an utter failure. Despite detailed and exhaustive examinations from as early as May 1915 by the Board of Agriculture and the Ministry of Reconstruction, other ministries chose to ignore the issue. Wartime inflation, speculation, limited resources and the Treasury's freeze on local spending made it extremely difficult for county councils to meet the demand for smallholdings from returned veterans.[37] The sudden ending of the war on 11 November 1918 therefore caught the British government by surprise and without a home or overseas soldier settlement policy. The government was forced to provide an emergency grant of £20 million to the county councils for the acquisition of land and equipment. Further delays threatened when a general election was announced the day after the Armistice. R. E. Prothero, President of the Board of Agriculture, became deeply concerned that a number of candidates attempted to make political capital out of the issue which they knew little or nothing about. Worse still, he feared that strong pressure from an ill-informed public would force Lloyd George to endorse a misconceived policy on grounds of political expediency. Of Lloyd George's six major campaigns speeches the first three dealt with domestic reconstruction in which agricultural reform and veteran resettlement were increasingly emphasised. Combined with the new housing policy, it was calculated to woo the veteran vote.[38]

As an electoral tactic, Lloyd George's appeal to the British public as a friend of the returned soldier was a shrewd piece of politicking. At the same time, it demonstrated that he was to some degree sensitive to veterans' problems. Nevertheless, the government was unprepared, despite continual warnings from the reconstructionists led by Prothero and Addison, Minister of Reconstruction, to deal quickly and effectively with the demands of its ex-servicemen. The charge of political expediency must also be examined in the larger context of the events and atmosphere surrounding the 1918 election and its aftermath. The British government in the latter part of 1918 and the first six months of 1919 was confronted with widespread discontent in the armed forces. In part, military discontent was fuelled by the chaotic demobilisation procedure. Confronted with growing unrest and impatience within the armed forces over the slowness of the demobilisation procedure, senior army officers in both France and the United Kingdom were faced with increasingly violent outbreaks of indiscipline. Similarly, it was reported that the Navy was in danger of open mutiny.[39] Initially preoccupied with the general election most politicians ignored these problems. However, as the disturbances escalated and intensified, a growing number of politicians and Ministers grew sensitive to veterans' issues, in particular domestic, and then overseas, soldier settlement. It was these domestic constraints which revitalised the apparently moribund plans to assist ex-servicemen to emigrate.

According to some government Ministers, indiscipline and mutiny were symptoms of a larger, more menacing and socially destructive disease – Bolshevism. 'There is undoubtedly, in this country', reported Sir Alfred Mond, the First Commissioner of Works, in November 1918, 'a certain fever of revolutionary Bolshevist ideas.'[40] The Russian Revolution had stimulated the growth of radical and revolutionary movements in the United Kingdom. Trade unionism, influenced by and supportive of the Russian Revolution, had grown during the war as well. So, too, had the British government's domestic intelligence surveillance unit which monitored a variety of 'red', 'socialist' and 'anti-government' individuals and associations, including a number of ex-servicemen's organisations.[41] For the most part, veterans' leaders were level-headed and pragmatic individuals who sought legitimate redress of grievances using constitutional methods through established institutions and forms of protest. The National Union of Ex-Service Men (NUX) and the International Union of Ex-Service Men (IUX) were the exceptions. The Special Branch reported that James Cox, the National Secretary of the IUX, rejected constitutional action and that the IUX was 'an out and out revolutionary socialist organisation seeking to establish an industrial republic'. However, it was unemployment, lack of proper housing and grievances over pension gratuities which fuelled the fires of most veteran discontent.[42] After a new and more acceptable demobilisation scheme was introduced in late January 1919 and soldiers were absorbed into the labour market, the unrest soon subsided. With hindsight, this challenge to authority may not have been critical, 'but it was unnerving'.[43]

The period between 1919 and 1922 proved to be a crucial one for constructive imperialists throughout the Empire. Their hopes were initially raised by the appointment in January 1919 of Lord Milner, the embodiment of the social imperial creed, as Secretary of State for the Colonies, and his disciple and close confidant, Leo Amery, as Under-Secretary. Stressing the need for 'a complete change' in the Colonial Office, determined to impose their will over the permanent officials and assert their authority, the new leadership eagerly launched itself into its responsibilities convinced 'that we must in time give it a new "orientation" '.[44] The distinguishing feature of the Milner-Amery partnership was that they possessed a clear set of imperial objectives.[45] Leading the list of priorities was an aggressive Empire migration policy.

The task of assisting ex-servicemen was a completely separate matter, according to Amery when he first took office in January: 'I had already at the [Oversea Settlement] committee hammered at any rate one point, namely that the treatment of ex-Service men is one of an award they are entitled to and has nothing to do with general emigration policy.'[46] Amery envisaged the free-passage scheme as a limited venture restricted to a maximum of three years. However, there was an important qualification: 'In order . . . to avoid a mere stimulation of emigration in an undesirable form, this privilege should be strictly confined to *bona fide* settlers on the land, or those who can prove that they have a definite offer of other suitable employment.' As far as Amery was concerned the 'problem of the emigration of ex-service men is very largely an agricultural one'.[47] Indeed, permanent officials at the Colonial Office were unenthusiastic and seemed to regard the free-passage scheme as the responsibility of another department such as the Ministry of Labour or the War Office.[48] Similarly, they acknowledged that some ex-servicemen would leave the United Kingdom no matter what the government's attitude or policy, but so far as they were concerned the free-passage scheme was not an emigration scheme proper and therefore outside its jurisdiction or interest. Nor did they regard it as having any economic significance. It was simply a humanitarian gesture designed to lessen the financial burden of those wanting to make a new life for themselves and their families in the overseas Empire.[49]

Amery's more immediate aim was to frame a new emigration bill which would enhance imperial unity, contribute to the economic well-being of the Empire and offset the fiasco of Long's ill-conceived 1918 Emigration Bill. Despite his optimism, he encountered only delay, disappointment and frustration from a confused and divided Cabinet between January and March 1919. He complained to Milner, who was in Paris at the peace talks, that he badly needed his support in the Cabinet. Until Milner returned, the emigration bill would be 'left in the air'.[50]

The majority of the Cabinet were convinced that the nation would shortly experience an intense period of prosperity and a tremendous shortage of labour. To promote emigration would therefore exacerbate the shortage, delay prosperity and hamper reconstruction. The Ministry of Labour strongly concurred. Milner and Amery were, however, equally convinced that if a new emigration bill were not forthcoming immediately the country would face serious economic and social distress, and Sir Auckland Geddes, Minister of National Service, agreed.[51] The Cabinet ignored the argument. Amery struggled constantly to get his emigration bill discussed in Cabinet. On 7 February he saw Bonar Law, Lord Privy Seal, and ascertained that Empire migration was to be included in the King's Speech. Four days later Amery went down to Parliament to hear the speech. To his disappointment, Lloyd George had struck out its reference at the last moment. At a stormy Cabinet meeting two weeks later the Prime Minister continued to vacillate, being sceptical about the entire issue. Meanwhile, Amery was being asked questions on emigration in Parliament of which he had to give 'evasive answers'. Growing impatient, he pressed Bonar Law in early March once again to put Empire migration on the Cabinet agenda and sent an additional note to the Prime Minister to prod him into action. Milner, who had returned from the peace talks, saw Amery several days later and reported that Lloyd George was 'still very sticky about the Overseas Settlement business'. After this further display of the Prime Minister's irresolution, they chose to concentrate on getting the finances for the more immediate task of assisting the emigration of ex-servicemen. The broader overseas settlement legislation would have to wait.[52]

Suddenly at the end of March, the War Cabinet decided to take up the question of assisting ex-servicemen to emigrate overseas, catching Amery off balance. Although he had prepared the necessary drafts complete with arguments, he had not supplied Milner with them. None the less, the Cabinet was eager to push ahead and on 31 March it accepted, subject to Lloyd George's approval, the recommendations on free passage outlined by Amery in February.[53] Why the sudden rush to implement a policy which most of the Cabinet had recently been content to ignore? Unemployment had become the government's main problem. In March 1919 over 300,000 veterans were receiving unemployment benefits, and this was a factor in Lloyd George's sudden desire to implement Amery's free-passage scheme.[54] Furthermore, the Cabinet feared the revolutionary spirit which was apparently sweeping the country and in particular ex-servicemen. Assisted emigration could diffuse the situation.

Amery wanted the government's offer of free passage to be open for three years beginning 1 January 1920. This allowed ex-servicemen ample time to choose between employment opportunities in the United Kingdom or the overseas Empire. It was also designed to give the dominions time to establish the necessary administrative machinery, prevent a rush of applications swamping the Oversea Settlement Office and 'to meet the possible charge that we wish to hustle people out of the country'.[55] It was estimated that a three-year programme would assist no less than 405,000 ex-servicemen and their families at a cost of just over £6 million.[56] But three years was too long to promise, argued the Treasury. Austen Chamberlain, Chancellor of the Exchequer, thought it better to limit free passage to one year and reconsider its extension in light of the experience gained. On 8 April Amery stood before Parliament during question time and announced the government's one-year free-passage grant for ex-servicemen and women which would begin on 1 January 1920. Pleased with the accomplishment, he realised that enormous difficulties yet lay ahead.[57] Its implementation would require the creation of an effective administrative structure and the willing co-operation of dominion authorities.

Sustained unemployment among British ex-servicemen provided the impetus for the extension of the ex-servicemen's free-passage scheme. As unemployment intensified in the latter part of 1920 Milner and Amery were determined to get it extended for another year. In October Amery appeared before the newly formed Cabinet Committee on Unemployment, chaired by Sir L. Worthington-Evans, to argue for the scheme's extension as 'a means of relieving abnormal unemployment during the coming winter'. Milner reiterated the point to the Cabinet two weeks later. Money spent on assisted passages, he argued, also saved the Exchequer from the sustained burden of crippling unemployment benefits.[58] The Treasury nevertheless remained hostile to any suggestion of increased expenditure, particularly for the extension of the ex-servicemen's free-passage scheme. As winter tightened its grip and unemployment rose, however, even a reluctant Treasury had to admit the need for limited action. In November the Cabinet agreed with Milner's October memorandum, and the Treasury sanctioned a one-year extension of the free-passage scheme. 'I am clear', wrote Chamberlain, 'that if the original policy was right this extension is still more right.'[59] The financial provisions of the scheme were not extended past December 1921 because of plans to introduce the broader Empire Settlement Act in early 1922. However, successful applicants were given until 31 December 1922 to make their sailing. The deadline was further extended until March 1923 for those few who had delayed their departure because of illness or bureaucratic problems.

The implementation of the assisted-passage scheme

What were the mechanics of the free-passage scheme? Ex-servicemen and women who had enlisted for active duty and whose service began before 1 January 1920 were eligible under the scheme but not those who had served solely with dominion, colonial or Indian army units. Women were required to have served for not less than six months in a corps administered by a British government department. This not only included the women's branches of the armed forces but a variety of nursing services, the Women's Land Army, the Forage Corps and the Forestry Corps. All concerned could obtain free third-class passages for themselves and their dependants to the nearest convenient port of the dominion or colony of their choice. The same privilege was extended to the widows and dependants of fallen ex-servicemen provided they fulfilled the criteria above and were drawing a pension from the Imperial government.[60] The British government through the local officials of the fledgling Ministries of Labour and Pensions established the eligibility of applicants. Then, properly screened, applications were forwarded to the representative of the dominion or colony in which the candidate concerned wanted to settle. The onus was placed squarely on the dominions to evaluate each case individually and to judge whether the candidate was medically fit and properly suited for employment opportunities overseas.[61] Only when the OSC had received dominion approval would a third-class passage warrant be issued. However, using a variety of advertising techniques the OSC worked hard to inform returning ex-servicemen of its services, the benefits of the free-passage scheme and the employment opportunities which existed overseas. It seemed straightforward, but in fact it was far from being so.[62]

The reaction and response of the dominions to the free-passage scheme varied. The antagonism between the two white communities in South Africa made the emigration issue extremely sensitive and politically divisive. In January 1919 the South African government informed the Colonial Office that it was not in a position to undertake any state-aided immigration of British ex-servicemen to South Africa. It was busy investigating what could be done for its own ex-servicemen, there was no organised government resettlement scheme and the government was not making any special appeals to other than its own. Therefore South Africa could not encourage the emigration of British ex-soldiers unless they had substantial financial means or solid offers of guaranteed employment.[63] For men like Milner and Amery the news was disappointing but not unexpected. Instead, private enterprise took the initiative in South Africa during and after the war, and was enthusiastically encouraged by Milner and Amery. One organisation founded in 1920, the 1820 Memorial Settlers' Association, proved instrumental as a promoter of British emigration to South Africa, particularly among the ex-officer class. Despite the association's valiant efforts, South Africa received the fewest number of British ex-servicemen and their families. Of the final total of 86,027 who participated in the free-passage scheme, South Africa received only 6,064 or 7 per cent.[64]

New Zealand proved equally disappointing but for different reasons. The most patriotic and 'British' of the dominions, New Zealand was the first dominion to initiate and enact soldier settlement legislation in 1915.[65] However, the granting of equal treatment to ex-imperials was limited by two key factors. Crown land suitable for agricultural development was scattered, isolated and scarce. Prime Minister W. F. Massey's government, forced to buy private land at prices inflated by wartime speculation, committed itself to reserving its meagre land resources for New Zealand veterans. Only after these claims had been honoured was the New Zealand government willing to consider applications from British veterans. During the Haggard mission, Massey reiterated this point. Haggard recorded that Massey was most sympathetic and generally eager to help but far from definite on the form or substance of the assistance.[66] When hostilities ended and the free-passage scheme was formulated the New Zealand government once again stressed its desire to help British ex-servicemen settle in New Zealand on the same terms as New Zealand veterans, but only after New Zealand claims had been satisfied. Furthermore, it would not allow the conveyance of British ex-servicemen to New Zealand until all New Zealand troops had been repatriated. And at that point, it warned there was a strong possibility that there would be no government land available beyond the needs of domestic requirements.[67]

A shortage of shipping throughout 1920–21 further aggravated a frustrating situation for prospective British ex-service migrants and a dominion keen on restocking its Anglo-Saxon heritage. There was another, even more serious problem: a severe housing shortage in 1920 that threatened to stifle any and all British migration to the dominion. The problem became more acute in 1921 as the world's economy slumped, inflation spiralled and unemployment sharply increased. In March 1921 the Massey government informed the OSC that after examining New Zealand's commercial, industrial and financial outlook in relation to the depressed labour market, the free-passage schemes would have to be curtailed. The OSC was instructed 'that no approved Imperial Overseas Settlement applicant, whether single or married, be allowed to proceed to New Zealand unless employment and accommodation await him on arrival'.[68] This was a critical blow to those who advocated an unrestricted 'white' immigration policy. There was unrelenting hostility in some sections of New Zealand society, including elements of the New Zealand Returned Soldiers Association (NZRSA), towards the entry and influx of 'Asiatics'. And equally strident warnings from the same quarters that from a racial and strategic viewpoint to limit the flow of immigrants from the United Kingdom was extremely dangerous, unnecessary and unpatriotic.[69] Cooler heads prevailed, however. After a vigorous debate at the 1922 NZRSA annual conference the association agreed to support the government's temporary restriction of the free-passage scheme. The recent dumping of hundreds of unemployed, homeless and destitute ex-imperials in Auckland emphasised the necessity for such action. Confident that the economic downturn was a passing phase, the NZRSA endorsed the government's policy.[70] At the conclusion of the free-passage scheme New Zealand had received 15.5 per cent or 13,349 British ex-servicemen and their families.[71]

The Canadian response to the free-passage scheme was one of cautious enthusiasm. The senior dominion was quite proud of its immigration machinery, the success of which over the years was the envy of its sister dominions. Assisted passage, however, was not a policy favoured by Canadian immigration officials or appreciated by the general public.[72] 'Canada will always welcome the man who can pay his own way, and stand on his own feet, but the man in Canada who requires "public assistance" is regarded as a failure.'[73] The special assistance given to British settlers, reported Sir William Clark, Britain's first High Commissioner to Canada, was resented by many Canadians who had carved their homesteads out of the wilderness without any government assistance whatsoever. They had worked hard, made good and could not understand the reason for all the 'mollycoddling'.[74] Canadian authorities were confident that their vast immigration network, extensive experience and advantageous geographical position would prove as effective in attracting British emigrants to Canada after the war as it had before the outbreak of hostilities and that emigration would therefore resume even without government subsidies.[75] None the less, the granting of free passages to British ex-servicemen and women who had unselfishly defended the Empire in its hour of need was a well-deserved exception to the general rule.

Before 1914 Canada's national immigration policy was based on an economic strategy designed to develop its primary resource sector. The emphasis on agriculture and the federal government's firm control over all aspects of immigration, colonisation and settlement ensured the pursuit of a consistent economic development policy. The settlement on the land of its own ex-soldiers was a logical extension of this national strategy. It was not simply an emotional response which acknowledged the sacrifices of Canada's fighting men and rewarded them for their suffering. Rather, it was a calculated plan designed to open up vast new areas of land, expand agricultural production, enrich the social fabric and increase national wealth under the paternalistic control of the federal government. First introduced in 1917, Canada's soldier settlement legislation was overhauled and expanded on a very generous and liberal footing in 1919.[76] However, the returned soldier was not regarded as just a national but also as an imperial matter. The extension of the soldier settlement benefits to British veterans, discussed by Canadian officials in 1917, was not incorporated until 1919. Under the provisions of new soldier settlement legislation passed in May 1919, British ex-servicemen and women became entitled to receive full financial, educational and settlement assistance. The 'sentiment in Canada is ... that we need more Anglo-Saxons', cried one senior Soldier Settlement Board official, and British ex-servicemen and women were seen as a vital component in solving the problem.[77]

When the British government first announced its free-passage grants the Canadian government made it abundantly clear that it would retain a firm and independent hand in its selection of overseas immigrants. A precise set of guidelines was formulated governing the type of immigrant Canada wanted to encourage. As ever, agriculturalists remained the top priority. F. C. Blair, Secretary of the Department of Immigration and Colonisation, declared that Canada wanted a class of settler who immediately upon arrival became a producer and not merely a consumer: 'Rapidity of development in Canada at the present time depends almost entirely upon our own ability to develop the natural resources, establish new enterprises with fresh capital and develop further those already in existence.'[78] Canada did not want to attract or assist people who would compete against local labour, or promote the incursion of non-agricultural labour. This was particularly important because of the many Canadian ex-servicemen who were still looking for work.[79]

For ex-imperials wanting to farm under the auspices of the Soldier Settlement Board, Canada was willing to accept only those who were physically fit, morally upstanding, possessed an honourable discharge and could provide a deposit of £200 as a surety before sailing. They also had to have the cash necessary to pay the 20 per cent downpayment required under Soldier Settlement Board regulations for non-Canadian veterans eligible for land, livestock, machinery and building materials obtainable through the board. The selection and medical examination of British soldier settlers would take place in the United Kingdom. The Soldier Settlement Board appointed an overseas representative in February 1919 to disseminate literature, interview and screen prospective applicants and liaise between the Soldier Settlement Board and the OSC. In February 1920 a two-man selection board was established and dispatched to the United Kingdom. The panel travelled throughout the United Kingdom appraising soldier applicants at the various regional emigration offices.[80] Only when the selection board was satisfied that an applicant was suitable did the OSC grant a free passage. However, non-agricultural veterans were eligible under the scheme provided they had assured employment in Canada. Free-passage grants were also available to widows and children of deceased British veterans, women war workers and orphaned children of British ex-servicemen and women.[81]

Despite the establishment of an elaborate administration, preliminary reports indicated that the few British ex-servicemen and women who had already arrived in Canada during 1919 had no intention of pursuing farm work. Some, finding the Soldier Settlement Board's monetary requisite too high, were scared off. Others, not wanting to farm under the Soldier Settlement Board, simply lied about their intentions of embarking upon an agricultural career in order to claim a free passage. Instead, many possessed solid offers of employment through relatives and friends, and were screened and approved as essential but non-agricultural immigrants. A major source of trouble was that many British veterans, provided they met government landing regulations, entered Canada as ordinary immigrants. Problems arose almost immediately as the economic climate in Canada worsened in 1920. To begin with, many of the ordinary ex-service immigrants possessed little or no money on arrival, became impoverished and quickly threw themselves upon the mercy of local charities. Those who arrived under the free-passage scheme also began to find conditions difficult. Destitution quickly blurred the distinction between assisted- and self-financing ex-soldier migrants. In some regions of Canada it was mistakenly assumed that all poverty-stricken British veterans had travelled to Canada under the auspices of the free-passage scheme, thereby bringing the entire scheme into some disrepute.

Confusion persisted as the Soldier Settlement Board and immigration officials tried to clarify the situation. In January 1920 the *Vancouver World* proclaimed that 3,000 ex-imperials were left scattered, stranded and impoverished throughout British Columbia: 'Arriving here in flocks without any properly authorised persons to advise them, these men are unable to take up land as they intended, some are stranded, others fit for charity', while Canadian authorities steadfastly refused to assume responsibility.[82] The Vancouver representative of the newly created Department of Soldiers' Civilian Re-establishment confirmed that the situation was rapidly deteriorating. The majority of the new arrivals were army pensioners with wives and families who had travelled to Canada independently of the free-passage scheme. Many were disabled or mentally unfit and had no previous farm experience or no intention of farming. His view was substantiated by the Commissioner of Immigration in Vancouver, A. L. Jolliffe, who reported that of 150 recently disembarked British ex-servicemen and their families only two claimed farming experience. Approximately one-half were pensioners, many were partially disabled and suffered from a variety of medical problems including shattered limbs, tuberculosis and neurasthenia. Over one-third had applied for immediate financial aid. As the situation became more critical, local repatriation and immigration officials demanded the implementation of preventative steps to halt the entry of disabled imperial veterans, especially pensioners.[83] Officials in Toronto faced a similar dilemma. They reported that an increasing number of ex-imperials were eagerly looking for work, and clearly feared that they would seriously interfere, if not compete, with the re-establishment of Canadian veterans.[84]

The various Canadian veterans' organisations found the problem of the ex-imperial equally trying. The Great War Veterans Association (GWVA), the Army and Navy Veterans (ANV) and the Imperial Veterans in Canada (IVC) came under increasing pressure to provide financial assistance to tide over British veterans until they secured employment. As the number of penniless British veterans grew, the financial strains of supporting their fellow British comrades began to show particularly with the IVC, who bore the brunt of the appeals from impoverished ex-imperials. A spokesman for the Vancouver branch of the IVC implored the Chief of the Imperial General Staff, Field Marshall Sir Henry Wilson, to bring home to British veterans 'the unpreparedness of this country to absorb them into its industrial and agricultural life'.[85]

The federal government accepted the need for more drastic measures to stop the flow of destitute and agriculturally inexperienced ex-imperials into Canada, and in September 1920 displayed a tougher posture. Repeated warnings were dispatched to the OSC that Canadian landing regulations would be strictly enforced. Safeguards, such as a more thorough medical examination at the port of disembarkation, were suggested. Disabled pensioners were singled out, and Ottawa insisted that the physically unfit be stopped at Canadian ports and deported before they become a public charge.[86] The Soldier Settlement Board emphasised continually that only those ex-imperials selected and accepted by its overseas office would be eligible for the benefits under the 1919 Act.[87] If 'other Imperial ex-Service men should happen to arrive without a ticket or without money for meals, it will be entirely their own fault, because they have been warned time and time again not to leave . . . without being thus provided'.[88] In many cases, Canadian officials put the reasons for failure squarely on the shoulders of the ex-imperials themselves. They professed to believe that many had become destitute during the voyage by squandering their savings through gambling. They also assumed – without evidence – that the rigours of military life and routine had impaired the abilities of many British ex-servicemen to adjust to post-war civilian conditions: 'It seems to be a hard thing for ex-soldiers to get rid of the idea that they are no longer in the army and must shift for themselves. Most of them expect that upon arrival at a Canadian port they will be met by an official who will provide them with billets, rations, transportation, or cater to their needs until such time as they can find employment.'[89]

Amery was dismayed by Canada's increasingly hard-nosed attitude towards British ex-servicemen. Canada's eagerness to co-operate, as expressed by Canada's Prime Minister Arthur Meighen in October 1919, had vanished. Rather, it had been replaced by stringent selection guidelines rigidly enforced in London and at Canadian disembarkation ports.[90] In an attempt to clarify federal immigration policy, J. A. Calder, the Canadian Minister of Immigration and Colonisation, met Milner and Amery in London in September 1920. When Calder broached the subject of extending the free-passage scheme for another year Milner made it abundantly clear that the extension would be contingent upon a greater degree of 'corresponding action' on behalf of the dominions, in particular an equal share of the financial responsiblity. Milner stressed that because of the already enormous demands placed upon the British taxpayer an increase in the expenditure on overseas settlement could be defended only if it was shown to be essential in the context of the larger imperial policy of Empire development. He also raised the issue of the self-governing dominions' attitude towards its new British citizens. The dominions showed a tendency to regard the arrivals from the mother country 'too much from the point of view of the immediate utility of their labour and too little from the point of view of their potential value as citizens in the Dominions'.[91] New settlers had to be made welcome and not regarded as 'mere working hands [or] drudges'.[92]

Of the 31.3 per cent or 26,905 British ex-servicemen and their families who arrived in Canada under the auspices of the free-passage scheme, approximately two-thirds were women and children. The total number of ex-imperials who migrated is much higher but impossible to ascertain because the figures do not exist for those who entered Canada as ordinary immigrants. What is clear from the sketchy statistics that have survived is that the free-passage scheme failed to bring large numbers of ex-imperial agricultural immigrants. For example, of the 1,382 applicants approved in the period October–December 1921, only 136 were classed as agricultural. The majority had experience in shipbuilding, railways, engineering, construction, metal working, electricals and commerce. Similarly, of the sixty-five female ex-service applicants in the same period, only eight were classified as agricultural and were categorised as inexperienced farm hands.[93] The number of British farm applicants chosen through the Soldier Settlement Board in London was minimal. In its first annual report, the Soldier Settlement Board reported that 'some hundreds' of ex-imperials had been examined and selected but no specific figure was cited. Four months after the ex-imperial guidelines were announced Commissioner E. J. Ashton reported that 159 ex-soldiers had paid the £200 deposit and had been granted selection certificates. Owing to shipping shortages in the spring of 1920 only fourteen had managed to sail. According to Soldier Settlement Board records 340 ex-imperials were selected in 1920 as suitable for farming in Canada, but only 266 actually reported to the board upon arrival. Of these, 134 withdrew their deposit before or during training and only a paltry sixty-nine were assisted under the OSC free-passage scheme.[94]

Australia received the largest share of British ex-servicemen, their wives and families. Of the final total, Australia received 37,576, or 43.7 per cent,[95] Australia proved the most energetic and yet at the same time the most frustrating dominion with which the British government had to deal. The problems stemmed from two sources. Unlike Canada, Australia did not have a paternalistic and centralised immigration or land settlement administration. Furthermore, it failed to develop a national soldier settlement or economic development strategy. In London, both the Commonwealth and the states possessed their own individual immigration offices and conducted separate propaganda campaigns to attract prospective settlers. Lack of co-operation and co-ordination between the states and the Commonwealth led to fierce competition. Friction increased as wealthier states like New South Wales and Victoria offered larger inducements and enticed more immigrants to the detriment of their weaker, poorer and less-organised rivals. The same was true within Australia itself. The lack of interstate co-operation and the ruinous competition between the state and Commonwealth levels spoilt any chance of formulating a harmonious national land settlement policy.[96]

The second problem was the states' reduced ability to borrow money to finance their public works projects as the result of the war. Many public works projects such as railway extensions, road construction and land settlement had been postponed until the end of hostilities. The Commonwealth government had agreed to assist the states in public works projects which facilitated land settlement, but the Commonwealth itself faced strong pressure to find new sources of capital. States like Queensland, Western Australia and New South Wales, professing eagerness to attract British ex-servicemen, turned to the British government for capital loans or guarantees.[97]

The Colonial Office realised that the speed of land settlement in Australia depended upon the state governments' ability to borrow money to build essential communications. However, they regarded many of the actual programmes as wasteful, extravagant, impractical, unnecessary and over-optimistic.[98] Despite the warnings for caution from several state Governors the Colonial Office believed that the initial teething problems encountered by the Australian repatriation machinery would be solved, allowing for the predicted influx of British ex-servicemen. Throughout 1919 discussions between the OSC and Australia representatives focused on passage rates, fare equalisation and shipping accommodation. Once the free-passage scheme was in full swing in 1920 the scarcity of shipping began to hamper severely Australian operations. Sir Ronald Munro-Ferguson, Governor-General of Australia, called upon the Colonial Office to discuss the problem with the Ministry of Shipping. The Australians were anxious that if the free-passage scheme was to be terminated at the end of 1920 hardly any advantage would have accrued and put tremendous pressure on Amery to extend the scheme.[99] Reluctantly the Treasury agreed to extend the scheme for another year.

But like the Canadians, Australians soon complained about the number of ex-imperials who arrived physically unfit and unable to undertake employment of any kind. Conversely, reports emerged that several state authorities were not looking after the ex-imperials as promised. 'So many of the men you have sent out are wandering the streets here workless and destitute', pleaded a representative of the Imperial Service Men's Association to the Colonial Office, 'that something ought to be done.'[100] Some Australians began to wonder about the wisdom of the free-passage scheme, and as the depression of 1920–22 deepened and unemployment steadily rose popular attitudes towards assisted immigrants became increasingly hostile.[101]

Was the free-passage scheme for ex-servicemen a success or failure? There is no question that it was an administrative landmark which provided the corner-stone for the expansion of assisted migration encompassed in the Empire Settlement Act of 1922, itself a 'major revolution of policy'.[102] Statistically, its architects regarded the free-passage scheme as a tremendous success. Just over 86,000 people were assisted at approximately £28 per head at a total cost of £2,418,263 between April 1919 and March 1923. The scheme accounted for 12 per cent of the total number of British emigrants who settled in the Empire between 1919 and 1922.[103] For the emigrants themselves it provided the chance for a new life overseas; an opportunity that may never have existed had they had to rely upon their own means. This was particularly important for those who embarked for Australia and New Zealand. Under normal circumstances these fares would have been the highest, deterring many who instead might have travelled to Canada. Fare equalisation through government subsidisation allowed for cheaper access to the antipodes, somewhat nullifying Canada's geographical advantage.

Nevertheless, the final tally was a far cry from the initial estimates of early 1919. It is true that the shortage of shipping during the first eighteen months hampered efforts. However, it was the onset of the short, sharp post-war depression of 1920–22 which paradoxically both made and broke the scheme. It was clear that had unemployment not been such a serious problem the British government would not have supported the idea of free passage and its subsequent extension. But at the same time the dominions were suffering from the same economic and social problems created by the post-war depression. The inability of the dominion governments to satiate the demands from their own veterans for jobs and housing led to the growing animosity towards the ex-imperial and the subsequent tightening of immigration regulations.

The underlying problem, however, was the neo-mercantilist rationale behind the free-passage scheme. The emphasis on agricultural settlement in the dominions, the creation of a landed imperial yeomanry which would strengthen imperial defence, enhance primary production and act as a protected market for British manufactured goods, ignored the profound economic and social changes which were transforming the imperial relationship. The Empire 'as an organic system, harmoniously balanced between industrial metropole and agricultural periphery' was quietly dissolving as the dominions began to develop, expand and intensify their own industrial base.[104] The failure of the numerous soldier settlement policies throughout the Empire had more to do with the incorrect presuppositions in the United Kingdom and the dominions about the economic relationship between them than it did with over-optimistic administrators settling inexperienced settlers on marginal land at a time of depressed prices for primary produce.

Notes

1 John A. Schultz, 'Finding homes fit for heroes: the Great War and Empire settlement', *Canadian Journal of History*, 18, 1983, p. 99.
2 National Archives of Canada (hereafter NA), Record Group 76, vol. 5, f. 41, part 3, Cory to W. D. Scott, Superintendent of Immigration, 19 August 1914.
3 *Ibid.*, memorandum by Scott, 8 October 1914; Scott to Cory, 3 September 1914.
4 Public Record Office, London (hereafter PRO), Colonial Office Papers, CO

323/726/52106, T. C. Macnaghten, chairman of the Emigrants' Information Office, to Lord Islington, Under-Secretary of State for India, 31 October 1916.

5 PRO, CO 323/693/52767, Steel-Maitland to Bonar Law, 2 November 1915; minute by Steel-Maitland, 19 November 1915.

6 Trevor Reese, *The History of the Royal Commonwealth Society*, London, 1968, p. 161; Royal Commonwealth Society Archive (hereafter RCSA), 1910 Emigration Conference File, E. T. Scammell and A. R. Pontifex to James R. Boosé, Secretary of the RCI, 7 February 1910; Scammell to Boosé, 1 and 10 March 1910; *Official Report of the Emigration Conference held on May 30–31, 1910. Convened by the Royal Colonial Institute*, London, 1910, p. 26; *The Times*, 14 May 1910.

7 PRO, CO 532/76/48673, Sir Arthur Pearson, newspaper proprietor and member of the Standing Emigration Committee, to F. G. A. Butler, 26 November 1914.

8 H. J. M. Johnston, *British Emigration Policy 1815–1830*, Oxford, 1972; Robert England, 'Discharge and disbanded soldiers in Canada prior to 1914', *Canadian Historical Review*, 27, 1946, pp. 1–18; J. K. Johnson, 'The Chelsea Pensioners in Upper Canada', *Ontario History*, 53, 1961, pp. 273–89; G. K. Raudzens, 'A successful military settlement: Earl Grey's Enrolled Pensioners of 1846 in Canada', *Canadian Historical Review*, 52, 1971, pp. 398–403; W. R. Jourdain, *Land Legislation and Settlement in New Zealand*, Wellington, 1925, pp. 22–3; M. Streak, *Lord Milner's Immigration Policy for the Transvaal 1897–1905*, Johannesburg, 1970.

9 PRO, CO 532/76/48673, minute by Butler, 27 November 1914; Butler to Pearson, 1 December 1914; RCSA, Empire Migration Committee, memorandum by Pearson, 21 December 1914.

10 PRO, CO 532/82/26960, minute by Macnaghten, 12 June 1915; quotation cited in Schultz, 'Finding homes fit for heroes', p. 102; CO 532/76/48673, minute by Macnaghten, 27 November 1914 and minute by Sir John Anderson, Permanent Under-Secretary of State for the Colonies, 30 November 1914.

11 PRO, CO 532/76/48673, minute by Macnaghten, 27 November 1914.

12 PRO, Ministry of Labour Papers (hereafter LAB) 2/1230/LE 27353/2, memorandum by W. Windham, 17 November 1916.

13 Bodleian Library, (Oxford), Round Table Papers, Mss. Eng. Hist. c. 777, paper entitled 'The Colonial Institute', 17 June 1912, no author; Harold Begbie, *Albert, Fourth Earl Grey, A Last Word*, London, 1917, p. 11 and p. 81; Mary E. Hallet, 'The Fourth Earl Grey as Governor-General of Canada', Ph.D. thesis, University of London, 1969, pp. 23–5 and pp. 82–5.

14 Schultz, 'Finding homes fit for heroes', p. 100; Joseph M. Fewster, 'Documentary sources concerning Australia in Durham University', *Durham University Journal*, 50, (n.s.), 1988, p. 65; PRO, CO 532/76/48673, Grey to Islington, 3 December 1914.

15 PRO, CO 532/82/2090, Grey to Islington, 23 December 1914.

16 For these negotiations see Schultz, 'Finding homes fit for heroes', pp. 101–2; PRO, CO 532/83/30739, minute by Anderson, 6 July 1915.

17 A full transcript of the interview appears in the RCI periodical *United Empire*, 6, 1915, pp. 680–90.

18 For details of the mission and the reaction of the official mind see D. S. Higgins, *The Private Diaries of Sir Henry Rider Haggard 1914–1925*, London, 1980, pp. 51–73; H. Rider Haggard, *The After-War Settlement and Employment of Ex-Service Men in the Oversea Dominions*, London, 1916; Peter Pierce, 'Rider Haggard in Australia', *Meanjin*, 37, 1977, pp. 200–8; House of Lords Records Office (hereafter HLRO), J. C. C. Davidson Papers, f. 15, Sir Ronald Munro-Ferguson, Governor-General of Australia, to Bonar Law, 24 May 1916; CO 532/84/27819, minute by Macnaghten, 20 June 1916.

19 RCSA, Proceedings of the Deputation to the Secretary of State for the Colonies and the President of the Board of Agriculture, 10 August 1916, pp. 1–4.

20 PRO, Ministry of Reconstruction Papers (hereafter RECO) 1/685, Nash circular to Boards of Agriculture and Trade, Local Government Board, Colonial Office, Scottish Office, Home Office and War Office, 11 August 1916.

21 PRO, RECO 1/683, War Office to Reconstruction Committee, 31 August 1916; RECO 1/684, Local Government Board to Reconstruction Committee, 6 September 1916;

Board of Agriculture to Reconstruction Committee, 10 October 1916; PRO, Board of Trade Papers (hereafter BT) 13/70/E 30346, Board of Trade memorandum, 30 August 1916.

22 PRO, CO 532/89/26194, minute by Macnaghten, 5 June 1916.

23 PRO, CO 532/89/37065, minute by Macnaghten, 10 August 1916.

24 PRO, CO 532/89/38085, minute by Macnaghten, 15 August 1916.

25 PRO, CO 532/89/47507, Bonar Law to Governors-General of Canada, Australia and South Africa, and Governors of New Zealand and Newfoundland, 21 September 1916.

26 Schultz, 'Finding homes fit for heroes', p. 107.

27 Wiltshire Record Office (hereafter WRO), Walter Long Papers 947/609, Devonshire to Long, 12 January 1917.

28 PRO, CO 532/91/6463, Munro-Ferguson to Long, 3 February 1917; WRO 947/601, Lord Buxton, Governor-General of South Africa, to Long, 20 December 1916. New Zealand did not need prodding as Prime Minister Massey, who had been in the United Kingdom since October, discussed the matter with the Colonial Office direct. PRO, CO 532/85/46077, Lord Liverpool, Governor of New Zealand, to Bonar Law, 26 September 1916.

29 Schultz, 'Finding homes fit for heroes', p. 108.

30 *Report of the Empire Settlement Committee, 1917*, Cd. 8672, X, 1917–18. See PRO, CO 532/89/62468 for the detailed correspondence concerning the selection, constitution and format of the committee.

31 PRO, CO 532/91/4023, Long to Tennyson, 16 January 1917.

32 Dominions Royal Commission, *Final Report*, 1917, Cd. 8462, X, 1917–18, p. 83 and pp. 92–4.

33 *Empire Settlement Committee, 1917*, pp. 21, 24.

34 Ian Drummond, *Imperial Economic Policy 1917–1939*, London, 1974, pp. 50–1; PRO, CAB 23/40, minutes of Imperial War Cabinet, 24 and 26 April 1917.

35 Schultz, 'Finding homes fit for heroes', p. 107; PRO, CO 532/98/28638, minute by Macnaghten, 12 June 1917.

36 Colonel Henry Pilkington, *Land Settlement for Soldiers*, London, 1911; Charles Bathurst, 'The land settlement of ex-service men', *Nineteenth Century and After*, 78, 1915, pp. 1097–1113; F. E. Green, 'Home colonisation by soldiers and sailors', *Nineteenth Century and After*, 79, 1916, pp. 888–905; 'Sailors and soldiers on the land', *Quarterly Review*, 226, 1916, pp. 135–51; A. D. Hall, *Agriculture After the War*, London, 1916; W. H. Warman, *The Soldier Colonists*, London, 1918; C. G. Woodhouse, 'Returning the soldier to civilian life', *South Atlantic Quarterly*, 17, 1918, pp. 265–89.

37 Introduction and Part I of the *Final Report of the Departmental Committee Appointed by the President of the Board of Agriculture and fisheries to Consider the Settlement and Employment on the Land in England and Wales of discharged Sailors and Soldiers, 1916*, Cd. 8182, X11, 1916 Part II of the *Departmental Committee . . . Discharged Sailors and Soldiers, 1916*, Cd. 8277, X11, 1916. Edith H. Whetham, *The Agrarian History of England and Wales*, vol. 8, *1914–1939*, Cambridge, 1978, pp. 109–41.

38 WRO 947/586, Prothero to Long, 7 December 1918; P. B. Johnson, *A Land Fit For Heroes*, Chicago, 1968; L. Orbach, *Homes for Heroes*, London, 1977, p. 42; M. Swenarton, *Homes Fit For Heroes*, London, 1981, pp. 67–87; K. Morgan, *Consensus and Disunity*, Oxford, 1979, pp. 26–45; S. Ward, 'The British veterans' ticket of 1918', *Journal of British Studies*, 8, 1968, pp. 155–69.

39 S. R. Graubard, 'Military demobilisation of Great Britain following the First World War', *Journal of Modern History*, 19, 1947, pp. 297–300; W. Kendall, *The Revolutionary Movement in Britain 1900–21*, London, 1969, p. 188.

40 PRO, CAB 24/69/GT 6270, memorandum by Mond, 12 November 1918.

41 S. Ward, 'Intelligence surveillance of British ex-servicemen, 1918–1920', *Historical Journal*, 16, 1973, pp. 179–80; Christopher Andrew, *Her Majesty's Secret Service*, New York, 1986, pp. 224–9.

42 PRO, CAB 24/96/CP 429, 'Revolutionary Organisations in the United Kingdom', report by the Home Office, 9 January 1920; PRO, Treasury Board Papers (hereafter T)

172/1121, deputation from the National Federation of Discharged and Demobilised Sailors and Soldiers, 6 February 1920. For an examination of British ex-servicemen's organisations as pressure groups see G. Wootton, *The Politics of Influence*, London, 1963.

43 Ward, 'Intelligence surveillance of British ex-servicemen', p. 187; David Englander and James Osborne, 'Jack, Tommy, and Henry Dubb: the armed forces and the working class', *Historical Journal*, 21, 1978, pp. 593–621.

44 Amery Papers, Box E.61, Amery to Lloyd George, 14 November 1918; Box 54, folder B, Milner to Amery, 12 February 1919; original diaries of L. S. Amery, 20 March 1918. I would like to thank Julian Amery, MP for his kind permission to examine his father's private papers and the original diaries. Although the diaries have been published by J. Barnes and D. Nicholson, (eds) *The Leo Amery Diaries*, 2 vols, London, 1980 and 1988, the majority of the overseas settlement material was omitted. Diary material not included in the published version will be cited as Amery diaries while published material will be cited as Barnes and Nicholson. I would also like to thank Mr John Barnes for his invaluable assistance concerning the contents of the Amery papers.

45 Stephen Constantine, *The Making of British Colonial Development Policy 1914–1940*, London, 1984, p. 47.

46 Amery diaries, 14 January 1919.

47 PRO, CAB 24/75/GT 6846, 20 February 1919.

48 PRO, CO 532/146/10143, minutes by E. Harding and H. Lambert, junior Colonial Office officials, 17 and 18 February 1919; minute by G. V. Fiddes, Permanent Under-Secretary, 18 February 1919.

49 Drummond, *Imperial Economic Policy*, p. 56.

50 Amery Papers, Box 54, Folder B, Amery to Milner, 12 February 1919.

51 Barnes and Nicholson, *The Leo Amery Diaries*, I, p. 253 and pp. 256–7; PRO, LAB 2/1229/ED 20058/4, secret memorandum, 3 February 1919; CO 721/3/f. 52, Phillips to Macnaghten, 30 January 1919.

52 HLRO, David Lloyd George Papers, F/39/1/9, Amery to Lloyd George, 1 March 1919; Barnes and Nicholson, *The Leo Amery Diaries*, I, pp. 256–8; Drummond, *Imperial Economic Policy*, p. 60; Amery diaries, 4, 5 and 10 March 1919.

53 PRO, CAB 23/9, minutes of War Cabinet, 31 March 1919; Amery diaries, 31 March 1919.

54 S. Ward (ed.), *The War Generation*, Port Washington, NY, 1975, p. 22.

55 PRO, CO 532/143/20660, Amery to Milner, 7 April 1919.

56 PRO, CO 721/1, Note on the cost of the proposals contained in the memorandum of the Emigration Committee', n.d. In Dane Kennedy's article, 'Empire migration in post-war reconstruction: the role of the Oversea Settlement Committee, 1919–1922', *Albion*, 20, p. 415, the figure is misquoted as 450,000.

57 PRO, CO 532/143/20660, Chamberlain to Amery, 8 April 1919; Amery diaries, 8 April 1919; Hansard, *Parliamentary Debates*, House of Commons, vol. 119, cols 1857–8.

58 PRO, CAB 27/115/C.U. 40, Amery to Worthington-Evans, 1 October 1920; Drummond, *Imperial Economic Policy*, p. 62.

59 Drummond, *Imperial Economic Policy*, pp. 62–4; PRO, T 161/73/S 5691/1, minute by G. C. Upcott, junior Treasury official, 4 October 1920; T 161/30/S 1710, minute by Chamberlain, 8 November 1920.

60 PRO, T 161/86/S 6527/06, copy of an OSC information flyer on the ex-service free-passage scheme.

61 G. F. Plant, *Oversea Settlement*, London, 1951, p. 73.

62 Kennedy, 'Empire migration in post-war reconstruction', p. 406; Amery diaries, 9 April 1919.

63 Central Archives Depot (hereafter CAD), Union Buildings, Pretoria, Department of Lands, LDE 20593, I, Box 1081, minute from the South African Prime Minister's Office, 14 March 1919; PRO, CO 532/134/5280, South African High Commission to Amery, 23 January 1919; CO 721/2/f. 39, minute by Fiddes, January 1919; South African Parliamentary Papers, Select Committee Report, S.C. 4a – 1918, Provision for South African Forces in the Present and Previous Wars.

64 Kent Fedorowich, 'Creating an Imperial Yeomanry in South Africa: British Ex-Servicemen and Imperial Emigration, 1914–1930', paper presented to the Southern Conference on British Studies, Norfolk, Virginia, 10 November 1988; Plant, *Oversea Settlement*, p. 74. The Figure for South Africa is slightly misleading as it includes an unspecified number of ex-servicemen who settled in Rhodesia. The final total also included approximately 2.5 per cent or 2,133, who settled in a variety of miscellaneous imperial destinations. A breakdown between men, women and children does not exist for the final total, but one was given in the OSC's 1922 annual report. Of the 82,196 granted free passage, 37,199 were men, 21,672 were women and 23,325 were dependants; *Report of the Oversea Settlement Committee for 1922*, Cmd. 1804, X11, 1923, p. 29.

65 Jourdain, *Land Legislation and Settlement in New Zealand*, pp. 46–9 and pp. 189–99; J. O. Melling, 'The New Zealand Returned Soldiers Association, 1916–23', M.A. thesis, Victoria University of Wellington, 1952, pp. 78–98; J. M. Powell, 'Soldier settlement in New Zealand, 1915–1923', *Australian Geographical Studies*, 9, 1971, pp. 144–60.

66 W. H. Oliver (ed.), *The Oxford History of New Zealand*, Oxford, 1981, p. 232; Haggard, *After-War Settlement and Employment*, pp. 22–4; Higgins, *Private Diaries of Sir H. Rider Haggard*, pp. 65–6; PRO, CO 532/84/33878, Liverpool to Bonar Law, 9 June 1916.

67 C. Turnor, *Land Settlement for Ex-Service Men in the Oversea Dominions*, London, 1920, pp. 29–30; PRO, CO 721/5/f. 82, New Zealand government to J. Allen, New Zealand High Commissioner, 13 March 1919, tabled at meeting of OSC advisory committee, 14 March 1919; PRO, CO 209/303/24178, Liverpool to Milner, 31 March 1920.

68 PRO, CO 721/25/3825, Cameron to Plant, 30 March 1921.

69 *Quick March*, monthly magazine of the NZRSA, 10 March 1921, p. 36 and 11 July 1921, pp. 55, 57 and 59.

70 *Ibid.*, 10 July 1922, pp. 33–4.

71 Plant, *Oversea Settlement*, p. 74.

72 Desmond Glynn, ' "Exporting outcast London": assisted emigration to Canada, 1886–1914', *Histoire sociale/Social History*, 15, 1982, pp. 209–38.

73 PRO, BT 56/45/CIA/1958, memorandum by Wilfrid Eady, Secretary of the Industrial Transference Board, 8 July 1929.

74 PRO, LAB 2/1235/EDO 220, Clark to Amery, 10 January 1929; Ministry of Labour memorandum, 4 March 1929.

75 PRO, CO 721/5/f. 82, conference between OSC, Agents–General and High Commissioners, 5 March 1919.

76 *Canada Year Book*, 1920, p. 29: *Canadian Annual Review*, 1919, pp. 599–600. For an examination of Canada's soldier settlement policy see Desmond Morton and Glenn Wright, *Winning the Second Battle*, Toronto, 1987, pp. 100–4 and pp. 142–54.

77 *Canadian Annual Review*, 1917, pp. 530–1; *ibid.*, 1920, p. 243; PRO, CO 721/2/f. 17, E. J. Ashton, Canadian Soldier Settlement Board Commissioner, to Macnaghten, 12 January 1919.

78 NA, RG 76, vol. 585, f. 821340, pt 1, Blair to Cory, 30 June 1919.

79 *Ibid.*, pt 2, Blair to Obed Smith, 29 and 30 September 1919; Obed Smith to Plant, 7 October 1919.

80 *Canadian Annual Review*, 1920, p. 243; First Report of the Soldier Settlement Board of Canada, 1921, p. 27; PRO, CO 721/2/f. 17, Lieutenant-Colonel K. C. Bedson to Macnaghten, 12 February 1919; NA, RG 76, vol. 610, f. 901346, pt 8, information bulletins released by C. W. Cavers, Director of Information, Soldier Settlement Board, 10 December 1919, 4 and 9 January 1920.

81 *Canadian Annual Review*, 1920, p. 243.

82 *Vancouver World*, 15 January 1920.

83 NA, RG 76, vol. 585, f. 821340, pt 2, W. Butterworth to R. P. Porter, 9 December 1919; Jolliffe to Blair, 30 and 31 January 1920; pt 4, Joliffe to Blair, 3 and 30 August 1920, and 3 September 1920.

84 *Ibid.*, pt 2, regional reports submitted to the Deputy Minister of Immigration and

Colonisation, January 1920; *ibid.*, pt 4, Harold Buckle, Acting Secretary of the Ontario Soldiers' Aid Commission, to Blair, 15 September 1920.

85 *Ibid.*, Blair to Obed Smith, 29 September 1920; PRO, CO 721/20/2478, W. H. Roberts to Wilson, 25 June 1920.

86 NA, RG 76, vol. 585, f. 821340, pt 2, Blair to Jolliffe, 19 January 1920; Blair to Dr J. A. Amyot, Deputy Minister, Department of Public Health, 31 January 1920.

87 *Ibid.*, vol. 610, f. 901346, pt 8, S. Maber, Secretary of the Soldier Settlement Board, to the Deputy Minister of Immigration and Colonisation, 26 July 1920; *ibid.*, vol. 585, f. 821340, pt 3, memorandum by Maber, 18 March 1920.

88 *Ibid.*, vol. 585, f. 821340, pt 4, Obed Smith to Blair, 31 August 1920.

89 *Ibid.*, W. R. Little, Acting Secretary of Immigration and Colonisation, to F. A. Walpole, Office of Secretary-Treasurer, GWVA, 23 September 1920.

90 Amery Papers, Box F.73, Meighen to W. H. Greenwood, 18 October 1919; Amery to Meighen, 25 November 1919; NA, RG 76, vol. 585, f. 821340, pt 4, Amery to Calder, 15 June 1920.

91 PRO, CO 721/13/2491, Milner to Devonshire, 1 October 1920.

92 PRO, CO 721/17/2491, Colonial Office memorandum dealing with the interviews between the Colonial Office, Calder and Obed Smith at Brown's Hotel, 19 September 1920.

93 NA. RG 76, vol. 585, f. 821340, pt 7, overseas employment register for October–December 1921 compiled by the Ministry of Labour, 1 January 1922.

94 First Report of the Soldier Settlement Board, p. 27; NA, RG 76, vol. 585, f. 821340, pt 3, Ashton to Blair, 23 April 1920; PRO, CO 721/63/3848, Ashton to Plant, 18 June 1923; Plant to Ashton, 13 July 1923.

95 Plant, *Oversea Settlement*, p. 74.

96 PRO, CO 418/158/47624, Munro-Ferguson to Bonar Law, 31 July 1917; CO 721/39/2489, Munro-Ferguson to Churchill, Colonial Secretary, 6 April 1922; J. M. Powell, 'Australia's "failed" soldier settlers, 1914–23: towards a demographic profile', *Australian Geographer*, 16, 1985, pp. 225–9; *ibid.*, The debt of honour: soldier settlement in the dominions, 1915–1940', *Journal of Australian Studies*, 5, 1980, pp. 64–87.

97 PRO, CO 532/79/36749, minute by Harding, 13 August 1915; CO 532/84/42220, Munro-Ferguson to Bonar Law, 19 July 1916; CO 532/85/56089, Government of Western Australia to Bonar Law, 22 November 1916; minute by Macnaghten, 24 November 1916; CO 532/113/60584, John S. Cormack, New South Wales Immigration and Publicity Agent, to W. A. S. Hewins, Under-Secretary of State for the Colonies, 13 December 1918; CO 721/5/f. 82, C. G. Wade, Agent-General for New South Wales, to Amery, 26 February 1919.

98 HLRO, Lewis Harcourt Papers, Box 479, Munro-Ferguson to Harcourt, 10 March 1915; PRO, CO 418/158/47624, Munro-Ferguson to Bonar Law, 31 July 1917; CO 532/125/5864, minute by Lambert, 11 February 1918; Bodleian, Viscount Milner Papers, Mss. Eng. Hist. c. 707, ff. 99–100, ff. 103 and ff. 119–22, W. E. Macartney, Governor of Western Australia, to Milner, 19 February, 25 March and 9 June 1919.

99 PRO, CO 418/186/13070, Munro-Ferguson to Milner, 10 March 1920; minute by Macnaghten, 16 March 1920; T 161/24/S 1237, Harding to F. Skevington, junior Treasury official, 12 August 1920; CO 721/14/2478, meeting of Australian Agents-General, 14 April 1920 and Amery's reply, 4 May 1920.

100 PRO, CO 721/25/2452, Senator E. D. Millen, Australian Minister of Repatriation, to Amery, 4 January 1921; CO 721/36/3819, E. Radford, Secretary of the New South Wales branch of the Imperial Service Men's Association, to Plant, 6 April 1921.

101 Stuart Macintyre, *The Oxford History of Australia*, vol. 4, *1901–1942*, Melbourne, 1986, pp. 207–11; G. Sherington, *Australia's Immigrants 1788–1978*, London, 1980, pp. 104–14.

102 Drummond, *Imperial Economic Policy*, p. 43.

103 Plant, *Oversea Settlement*, pp. 74–5.

104 Kennedy, 'Empire migration in post-war reconstruction', p. 417.

CHAPTER FOUR

'The healthy, wholesome British domestic girl': single female migration and the Empire Settlement Act, 1922–1930

Janice Gothard

Female migration was an immediate priority of the Oversea Settlement Committee (OSC), the British government body dealing with Empire migration from its establishment in 1919. Before the war, the migration of single women to the dominions had been extensively assisted both by private women's migration societies and the dominion governments themselves. With the findings of the Dominions Royal Commission in 1917 underlining the importance of continued female migration, the OSC adopted an aggressive stand on the question. Under the Empire Settlement Act of 1922, Canada, Australia and New Zealand all offered passage assistance to single British domestic servants, an occupational group much in demand in both the United Kingdom and the dominions. As part of persistent efforts to stimulate the supply of female migrants, training institutions were established in the United Kingdom from the mid-1920s at the instigation of the OSC to prepare inexperienced women for domestic service overseas. These institutions functioned to direct the women the United Kingdom most wished to see migrate towards employment in the dominions, to meet the dominion demand for domestics without threatening the United Kingdom's own supply, and as part of the process of selecting the 'right type' of migrant.

The assisted migration of single women to the dominions under the Empire Settlement Act was an exercise in state-controlled labour migration which also sought to meet certain social and population ends. The scheme can be seen as being only partly successful, given the changing and often contradictory motives of the British and dominion governments. Practice stood at odds with stated policy. While the British government's desire to export female labour was equalled by the dominions' demand for working women, even the institution of training sometimes failed to mesh successfully the differing requirements of the United Kingdom and the dominions. By the end of the 1920s economic conditions forced the withdrawal of dominion funding both for training and for assisted passages. The numbers of women who migrated under the Act did not keep pace with demand for domestic labour in the dominions, and in spite of the OSC's efforts, training did little to augment the supply. When the British government renewed its interest in migration towards the end of the 1930s, the emphasis had by then moved to the migration of women within families.

In spite of the perceived importance of female migration to the development of Empire during this period, neither the British nor the dominion perspective has been adequately covered in the existing literature, although the subject has attracted more interest recently. Two older works on British women's migration societies – G. F. Plant's *A Survey of Voluntary Effort in Women's Empire Migration* (London, 1950) and Una Monk's *New Horizons* (London, 1963) – concentrate on the activities of the Society for the Oversea Settlement of British Women (SOSBW) in their discussion of the inter-war period; they remain the standard texts in the absence of more broadly focused work. Recent articles by Brian Blakeley and Dane Kennedy shed a more critical light on the British organisation of inter-war schemes for women's migration.[1] From the dominion point of view, and showing greater concern with the migrant experience itself, Marilyn Barber, Joy Parr and Barbara Roberts have all written on female migration to Canada,[2] but publications on the subject of female inter-war migration are virtually non-existent in the Australian or New Zealand context.[3]

The requirements of the dominion governments influenced the British government's stated pursuit of the goals of Empire migration. While a detailed comparison of the policies pursued by the Canadian, Australian and New Zealand governments is beyond the range of this chapter, it is possible to draw general conclusions about the attitude of the dominions. Despite the rhetoric adopted by these governments in their advertising material, the dominions were more concerned with economic than social considerations. For the British government also, the Empire's need for British mothers and British homes conveniently tallied with the requirements of the home government for markets and her local population for employment. Ultimately, however, the scheme was not a success since the dominion demands for women were not met. Fewer than 100,000 single women were assisted under the Empire Settlement Act.[4] This was due not simply to the failure of the participating governments to practise consistent and compatible migration policies but also to the growing disenchantment of British women with the prospect of paid domestic labour.

Aims and opportunities

In its report for 1923, the OSC stated:

> [T]he true aims of Empire settlement are to ensure that the fresh population required by the Dominions should as far as possible be British in sympathy, in spirit, and in origin, and at the same time to remedy fluctuations of trade by developing this country's markets and increasing the numbers of its customers, thus permanently minimising the risk of unemployment here and overseas.[5]

For the British government, controlling and stimulating the movement of women to the dominions was fundamental to these twin imperial aims of building up the United Kingdom's population overseas and its economic well-being at home. While the OSC advised the government in 1919 that it did not anticipate a need to provide direct state financial aid to migration in general, it recognised 'special grounds for granting State aid to the emigration of women, and for supplementing the existing provision for the emigration of juveniles, more particularly of girls, by direct Government grants'.[6] Nineteenth-century British rhetoric on female migration had stressed the need to redress the imbalance of the sexes between the United Kingdom and its colonies and, in the aftermath of the war, the language of sexual balance was once again invoked by the British government.[7] To this was now added the same purpose which underpinned the programmes of the imperialistic British female migration societies: to populate the dominions with 'new settlers, British by birth and British in sympathies'.[8] British wives and mothers meant British families. The experience of the Boer War had convinced the imperialistic women's migration societies that Dutch mothers and British fathers too often resulted in children with Boer sympathies. This was particularly relevant to Canada, with its mixed population of British and French and its proximity to the United States of America. As the OSC constantly reiterated, 'the thinly populated territories overseas require population to ensure their safety',[9] and women, as the standard bearers of Empire, had a particular defensive role to play against the enemy within as well as without.[10]

In the economic sphere as well, the role of migrant women in dominion family life contributed significantly to British financial security. Women as paid and unpaid domestic labourers supported both the production of raw materials vital to British industry and raised the level of consumption of British manufactured goods, as well as local products, through the creation of more families. In addition, the migration of women to the dominions directly reduced the level of female unemployment in the home economy. Five months after the end of the war, more than 500,000 British women were still receiving out-of-work benefits, although householders were crying out for domestic servants.[11] A number of government inquiries had already focused on the problems created by the war for women workers and women's work.[12] In March 1919, Lady Rhondda, President of the Women's Industrial League, urged the Ministry of Labour to conduct a further inquiry into the conditions of women's unemployment, arguing that women who had served during the war in well-paid and skilled occupations were not prepared to return to a life of drudgery.[13] In the prevailing climate of demand for domestics, the representative of the Ministry of Labour could respond only that 'if there is not enough work to go round, . . . women who have been accustomed to laundry work must go back to it'.[14] Migration, the OSC suggested, was a happier alternative:

> [I]n present circumstances, in view of the lack of employment in this country, there are no doubt many suitable women who would be glad to avail themselves of favourable opportunities of proceeding overseas, where the immediate chances of employment and ultimate prospects of happy married life are better than they are here.[15]

The established women's migration societies supported moves to relocate British women in the dominions, but were reluctant to move too hastily. Ten days after the Armistice, representatives of the Joint Council of Women's Emigration Societies (which as the Society for the Oversea Settlement of British Women later functioned as the women's advisory branch of the Oversea Settlement Department) wrote a warning to the press in response to the froth of publicity which already surrounded the idea of female migration for the women now being discarded by the peacetime economy:

> The Dominions have lost heavily in man-power, and, in the displacement of war, will have many women thrown out of work, who must find employment before any incoming wage-earners will be welcome. Secondly, until the Oversea troops are repatriated it is impossible that there should be much shipping accommodation left over for any women except *fiancées* of Oversea soldiers.[16]

But representatives of the women's service were particularly concerned that the possibility of dominion migration for women be addressed immediately. In March 1919, at a meeting of dominion and British government representatives to discuss migration, the numerical imbalance of the sexes in the dominions and in the United Kingdom was raised, and it was argued that the training which British women had received during the war would now fit so-called surplus women for employment avenues overseas previously closed to them.[17] A suggestion was adopted from Lady Londonderry, Director-General of the Women's Legion, that representatives of the women's war services tour the dominions to ascertain the extent of the openings available and, within four months, women delegates for Canada, Australia and New Zealand were ready.[18] As the delegates were to be funded by the British government, the scope of the inquiry was broadened to include openings for all women.[19] British-government funding of the inquiry reflected both the government's new-found initiative in directing migration to the dominions, particularly of ex-service people, and its special interest in the settlement overseas of all classes of British women; the Treasury specified that it would not fund an investigation into openings for other categories of migrants, such as men.[20]

Faced with the immediate problem of a large number of skilled unemployed women, the British authorities were prepared to be more innovative in their attitude to women's work overseas than they were at home. In a letter to the Canadian delegates, T. C. Macnaghten, Vice-Chairman of the OSC, instructed them that

> the most important part of your duties will be to ascertain to what extent the new kinds of work in which women have engaged in this country, and the experience which they have acquired in the course of this work, are likely to increase their chances of employment and the facilities for their settlement.[21]

The delegates also had a special brief to inquire into opportunities for women from the war services and the Land Army.[22] Each pair of delegates included a woman experienced in agriculture and sought 'to ascertain what openings there might be for the employment and settlement of women upon the land', as well as to investigate industrial and commercial openings.[23] The attitude of dominion representatives was less pioneering. While the British delegates attributed apathy and outright hostility to the notion of opening up new employment to ignorance of the work done by British women during the war,[24] a Canadian government correspondent pointed pragmatically to the existence of considerable unemployment in that country. War opportunities for Canadian women had been much more limited than in the United Kingdom, and Canadian women who had entered non-traditional employment had since returned to their former occupations.[25] An optimistic correspondent to The Times had reported from Sydney in 1916 that new employment fields for women had opened up in Australia during the war and predicted that '[a]fter the war no policy will be tolerated which thrusts [women] out of work'.[26] But the delegates found no evidence to support this hopeful prophecy, in Australia or elsewhere.

For the people of the dominions the imbalance of the sexes was not the concern it was considered to be by the British government. Delegates Pughe Jones and Simm discovered that the numbers of brides brought back by the men of the Australian Imperial Forces raised local doubts as to the community's need to absorb further women,[27] and an estimated 30,000 Canadian servicemen had also married in Europe before repatriation.[28] Many of these women had encountered some hostility when they arrived from local women who felt supplanted.[29] In Australia the delegates found that the national government was involved in repatriation of returned servicemen and considered the investigation of openings for women 'premature'. Encountering marked opposition to any proposal to send out women land workers, the Commissioners were forced to advise the OSC that all intending settlers to Australia be warned of antagonism towards migration to that country.[30] In commercial and industrial fields also, it was evident 'that the Labour organisations throughout Australia are strongly opposed to the wholesale introduction of female labour'.[31]

The delegates' reports effectively strangled at birth the expectation that the dominions would offer employment opportunities commensurate with the proven capabilities of large numbers of British women. What emerged most clearly was the value to all three dominions visited of paid and unpaid domestic labour. As was the case in the United Kingdom, domestic service was desperately depleted of women workers. Demands for domestic workers was very high in the cities of the dominions, but in rural areas it was urgent. In Canada the farming housewife had to contend not simply with caring for her own family, but also with cooking, laundry and mending for all hired hands, who customarily lodged in the farm house. Thus 'the strain borne by the housewife [was] almost intolerable'.[32] In Australia the decline in the birth rate was blamed in part on the lack of domestic assistance available, particularly in the country, for '[w]here men are engaged as primary producers, women must make the homes, and every woman needs help at some period of her life'.[33] The development of rural districts was retarded as lack of domestic assistance forced families into towns.[34] In New Zealand the delegates considered that the lack of domestic assistance approached crisis levels, and was a matter of 'national importance', New Zealand's Minister of Agriculture asserting that one important factor contributing to a decline in New Zealand's wheat production was 'the almost total absence of domestic labour in the homes of the farmers'.[35] Though all the delegates' reports made much of possible openings for trained ex-service women of initiative as outdoor workers on the land, in industrial and in business areas, their conclusions were unequivocal: the real demand was for domestic assistance.

In addition to the immediate pressing demand for paid domestic labour, other short-term economic constraints added to the attractiveness of domestic immigrants for the dominion governments. The prevalence of the institution of live-in service ensured that domestic workers found both employment and home immediately on arrival, thus lessening the government's need to provide hostel accommodation. The Canadian government, through the Canadian Council of Immigration of Women for Household Service, had assumed a far greater responsibility than the Australian and New Zealand governments for the reception and aftercare of women immigrants through the provision of hostels, but private organisations such as the YWCA, the Girls' Friendly Society, Women's Institutes and the Salvation Army were largely left to meet this need elsewhere, with a mixed measure of success.[36] Other employment openings were becoming available for single working women in the dominions, but the need for accommodation was a critical factor for migrants without family support.[37] The OSC delegates to Canada in 1919 expressly warned that the cost of living for women workers obliged to live in hired rooms was quite prohibitive, a finding substantiated by the New Zealand Commissioners.[38] Particularly for unskilled women factory workers, wages offered were considerably below the amount needed to survive independently and, in any case, accommodation in many dominion cities for single workers was at a premium.[39]

The migration of domestic workers also contributed implicitly to dominion government social and population goals. Introducing a supply of single women already equipped with domestic skills helped to satisfy the longer term requirements of the dominions for quality domestic workers as wives and mothers in their own families. Such women fitted very comfortably into the British government's mould for future mothers of the Empire. Thus the population concerns of the dominions agreed with those of the British government and were expressed in the concept of the 'right type of girl' which had constant currency in contemporary discussions of female migration.

'The right type of girl' was the healthy, wholesome British domestic girl at whom much of the government migration publicity of the period was aimed. She was not to be found among factory workers, for many such women had already proved unsuccessful as migrant domestics before the war. The major fault of those women lay in their reputed lack of knowledge of the domestic arts but perhaps more importantly in their apparent inability and reluctance to learn. 'The better type – especially experienced domestics – made good, and secured excellent wages, comfortable homes and generally married satisfactorily within a year or so', according to the pre-war superintendent of female migration to New South Wales.[40] The appeal and the success of the 'right type' lay not simply in her experience but in her willingness to conform to the notion of domesticity. Factory work, located outside the home and with its more independent life-style – the very factors which were increasing its attractiveness over domestic service for British women – was not deemed such a satisfactory preparation for the submission to domestic authority required of a paid servant, nor in inculcating acceptable values in one's own children.

A special correspondent for *The Times* noted in 1921 that the women the dominions ought to encourage, given the limited supply of experienced domestics available for migration, belonged to 'that large body of unclassified women, generally of a more educated type, who, for one reason or another, have never worked regularly for pay, and to whom the freer and more complete life of the Dominions makes a strong appeal'.[41] One British woman who had migrated to Canada before the war observed in 1919 to the OSC Commissioners that 'many persons, she herself included, prefer to work strenuously in Canada rather than in England'.[42] An article on opportunities for women in New Zealand appealed to 'energetic, self-reliant, educated young women who, while skilled in cookery and really fond of household work and management, would not dream of entering domestic service here at home'.[43] Seeking out the right type for migration involved appealing either to a declining supply of women with paid domestic experience, the women the United Kingdom sought to retain and who arguably had little to gain from migration to the dominions, or more particularly to those women who might never before have needed to work outside their own homes, apart perhaps from war service, but who had good domestic skills and an inclination for home-making.

Assistance and publicity

Cheap passages were considered one of the prime factors in stimulating the flow of migration, particularly in the case of single women.[44] For women between positions or out of work, their very lack of funds made them most vulnerable to the pull of migration and its promise of a more secure future. Under the Empire Settlement Act of 1922, Canada, Australia and New Zealand all offered preferential passage rates to single women as household workers, as well as to other specific categories of male labourers and their families. The Canadian government's agreement advanced the ordinary third-class ocean fare of £16 to all preferred migrants, with an additional rebate of £6 offered to single women domestics after a year's residence on a Canadian farm.[45] Australia offered both nominated and selected passages to assisted migrants, who were entitled to a free grant of one-third of the £33 third-class fare, and a loan of the remaining two-thirds of the fare. A further loan of £3 was made in special cases for selected single domestics and single male farm workers.[46] The New Zealand government offered the most attractive passage: selected single domestics travelled out free and were also granted £2 pocket-money, the only group so favoured. Nominated single migrants, male and female, were granted fares of £16 10s, half the ordinary fare.[47]

From April 1925 the cost of passage for domestics to Australia was reduced to £11, with that amount available as a loan in certain cases; and rates to Canada were also reduced, with fares to various destinations ranging from £3 to £9.[48] The following year domestics were offered free passage to Australia.[49] From 1927 an agreement concluded between the British and the Southern Rhodesian governments also entitled approved women proceeding to situations as domestic helps in that country to a free grant of £35 towards the full fare.[50]

The publicity circulated by the dominion governments as part of their programme of assisted migration in the 1920s appealed very directly to the prospect of social and economic security for the migrant. The booklet *Australia Invites the Domestic Girl*, for instance, published early that decade, was directed to

> the healthy, wholesome British domestic girl – the girl who, in some capacity, can help in the home as a first step towards entering into a home of her own. For Australia, above everything, is a land of home-making, and for the rapid multiplication of homes she needs more and more of the right type of girl, and there are not enough of the native-born to go round.[51]

The dominions' own needs were couched in terms of the migrant woman's longer term social role. In a fleeting call to duty, the pamphlet pointed out the extent to which Australia *needed* the domestic worker. Thousands of homes would offer her the best in wages and conditions in competing for her services; by implication, an equal range of offers would come from Australia's surplus men, the 'sturdy hearty Digger[s]'. But the chief thrust of the publication lay in meeting the migrant's own desire for security. 'The point is that the domestic girl in coming to Australia has the certainty not only of a good living while she needs to earn one, but also of greatly improving her chances of satisfactory marriage and ultimate establishment in a home of her own', assumed to be every woman's desire. Domestic service was of particular value in protecting such a destiny for 'it is the girl who knows how to keep a home who generally makes the surest appeal to the thrifty man who aspires to surround himself with domestic ties in a young and developing country'.[52]

The prospective migrant was also offered more concrete inducements, downplaying those features of domestic service life in Britain which women found increasingly unacceptable. A correspondent for *The Times* noted in 1921 the repugnance with which contemporary women regarded domestic service and envisaged only one solution: '[d]omestic work must be made less arduous, more attractive, and freed from that social stigma which so obstinately clings to it'.[53] This writer looked to 'those young countries, less hampered by old and often bad traditions, less hide-bound by circumstances, and to whom this question is absolutely vital, to point us the way' for '[s]urely the women of the dominions will find a means of making a calling of such vital national importance one to which it will be an honour for any woman to belong'.

Thus, publications such as *Australia Invites the Domestic Girl* and the rather similar *Sunny Ontario for British Girls* made much of the ease of housework in dominion homes, with superior design, more advanced technology and labour-saving devices easing the load of the domestic worker. In 1924 a woman who had visited New Zealand advocated the construction in London of a New Zealand-style house, said to be 'so well planned from the woman's point of view for easy working, with all its fitted-in furniture, its easily-mopped polished floors, its few stairs, its electric or gas fires and stoves, its airy rooms and spacious verandahs'.[54] The ease and speed with which housework could be accomplished also suggested that the domestic could expect longer leisure hours, better terms of employment and broader recreational opportunities. Specifically the level of wages was said to be higher.[55]

The other major plank of government propaganda related to the more egalitarian way of life possible in the newer countries.[56] This was directed particularly at the woman who might not previously have worked as a paid domestic. In the dominions, the domestic servant required was the general rather than the United Kingdom's more prevalent specialised servant, who was reminded of the need for flexibility in learning dominion ways.[57] The general's role was marketed as assistant to the mistress and her daughters, all of whom often worked 'a great deal harder and longer than the maid'. If she were 'a nice agreeable girl', the immigrant would live 'very much as one of the family'.[58] The notion that domestic servant and mistress worked shoulder to shoulder tackling the household chores was part of the attempt to raise the status of overseas domestic work in the migrant's perception. It promised both social advancement and maintenance of social status.

Perhaps not surprisingly, the ideological message of dominion publicity was less significant in attracting female migrants than the prospect of improved economic circumstances and easier conditions of employment, which were the causes of greatest disappointments. Most criticism and complaints related to misrepresentations of the strenuous workload.[59] Longer hours of work, limited time off, the higher cost of living and wages which, for the newly arrived immigrant in her first situation, did not match the levels promised, were all specific areas of dissatisfaction. The actual labour was usually as physically demanding as in the United Kingdom, and more so in rural areas. Even where superior technology was available, the smaller number of servants employed increased the burden on the usually sole domestic; and the very existence of labour-saving devices often raised the standard of housework expected.[60]

The ideological content of migration publicity also drew some criticism. One Australian advertising feature depicted the immigrant domestic's progress in the home of a wealthy landowner:

> the girl was shown dusting in a genteel way . . . the next scene showed the squatter's son paying attention to the maid, and of course, they were eventually married. In the last scene the mother-in-law was sitting by the fireside with her knitting, while the new mistress of the house attended to the household affairs.[61]

Such publicity was rightly condemned by disappointed migrants, societies such as the Victoria League which concerned themselves with migrant conditions in the dominions, and in this particular instance, an outraged member of the Australian Parliament.[62]

In 1919, when Commissioner L. E. Simm suggested to Victoria's Immigration Officer that female immigrants could not be expected to take the worst positions the government offered them, he replied, '[t]hey must', adding, 'when we pay, they must go where we send them'. On that basis, Simm had pointed out to Macnaghten that the Victorian Agent-General's advertising material, 'Take a trip to the land of sunshine' and 'Have a six-weeks joy ride to Australia', was at best misleading.[63] Throughout the 1920s the promise held out to women migrants by government advertising and publicity contradicted reality.

Training

Despite the lure of publicity and of cheap passages, the OSC failed to attract the numbers of women the dominions sought. The committee, in fact, doubted whether success was fully possible, for 'having regard to the large excess of women in this country and to the deficiency overseas . . . the supply in the United Kingdom of those who possess the necessary qualifications even for the unspecialised type of domestic work required falls far short of the demand overseas'.[64] Further strategies were called for. Training had been an important feature of the work of the women's migration societies before the war, and their training programmes had earned approval in the Final Report of the Dominions

Royal Commission in 1917.[65] In an effort to convert the numbers of women available in the United Kingdom into the categories required in the dominions, the OSC appealed throughout the 1920s for the dominions themselves to take on the financial responsibility previously assumed by voluntary organisations, in placing more emphasis on training women for domestic service.

In 1912 the British Women's Emigration Association's executive had reported before the Dominions Royal Commission that the women's societies had always faced opposition from British employers of servants to the recruitment of experienced domestics for the dominions and colonies.[66] Thus, their training schemes had been directed at middle-class women – who could pay for the privilege – who would not have entered domestic employment in the United Kingdom. In training women without previous domestic experience, the OSC similarly could draw on a pool of otherwise unemployed women, who in changed economic circumstances now sought paid occupations, and avoid antagonising the home population. In any case, experienced and skilful domestics were highly valued in the United Kingdom and would arguably gain little through migration. Training therefore served to create a supply of workers acceptable to the dominions from a group less in demand in the United Kingdom.

Immediately after the war, the Women's Advisory Committee of the Ministry of Reconstruction had earmarked training as part of a cure for the reluctance of women to enter domestic service, arguing that training schemes and the consequent professionalisation of housework raised the status of the occupation.[67] Dame Katharine Furse, wartime head of the Women's Royal Naval Service, had advocated building on 'the war spirit of service' in establishing a professional reserve of trained ex-service women for domestic work in the United Kingdom,[68] and a comparable corps for migrants had been advocated in late 1918 by Caroline Grosvenor of the Colonial Intelligence League, an organisation which sought openings in the dominions for the educated woman.[69] Military training and discipline had already been perceived as an advantage for migrants in adapting to conditions overseas, and in 1919 both Canadian and New Zealand householders stated a preference for ex-service-women over untrained women,[70] a reflection of the dissatisfaction felt by employers with the standard of skill of some of the female migrants dispatched before the war.[71] Although these quasi-military schemes were never implemented, training was clearly indicated as a factor in raising the status of domestic service, attracting more recruits to the ranks of the type the OSC considered 'vital to the progress and well-being of the communities overseas',[72] and consequently increasing employer and dominion satisfaction.

The OSC initially expressed a preference for training to take place in the dominions,[73] but training women in the United Kingdom, with costs shared between the British government and the dominions, appeared to be more economical and more practical. Some private organisations, such as Barnardo's, successfully implemented training schemes in the dominions, particularly in the area of juvenile migration,[74] but other attempts were less successful. In Australia Mrs Beatrice Macdonald attempted to establish a domestic training hostel in Sydney in 1923, through her Domestic Immigration Society, where up to 150 young single women migrants could be trained in cooking and housework before employment in New South Wales country districts. The SOSBW had approved of this scheme with its basis of co-operation between voluntary societies and government authorities, but ultimately costs precluded success.[75] Further, since training institutions functioned as part of the selection process, screening out undesirable or incompetent women, it was clearly advantageous from the point of view of the dominion governments (and not least for the women themselves) that this took place before departure.

Canada had already practically acknowledged the value of pre-migration training through the Khaki University of Canada, an early training initiative established in the United Kingdom. In addition to its primary function of training men, the wives and fiancées of the Canadian Expeditionary Forces and some single women were instructed in Canadian housewifery in classes funded by the Canadian government through the London County Council; but this exercise ceased in July 1919.[76] The OSC particularly approved of training wives proceeding to the dominions, in line with the committee's perception of the need for women skilled in mothercraft and housewifery as workers in their own homes,[77] but this experiment was not repeated over the next decade of Empire settlement, as the greater concern of the OSC remained to train women for paid domestic labour. Immediately after the war, the United Kingdom's Central Committee for Women's Training and Employment had begun training women without previous domestic experience in an attempt to ease the United Kingdom's own domestic servant crisis, and such programmes could be readily extended to include women migrants.[78] However, the difficulty of using British government funds to train people for the benefit of the dominions[79] and the reluctance of the dominion governments to invest further funds into training schemes for women hampered OSC aims well into the 1920s.

The need for women in the dominions as both paid household workers and as wives and mothers was constantly restated throughout the 1920s,[80] but the very urgency of this demand worked against the OSC's proposals for the establishment of training institutions. With the flow of experienced household workers to the dominions still short of the numbers wanted, untrained women were now accepted for assistance by the dominions and were quite able to obtain domestic positions overseas. The dominion governments had shown no further inclination to finance training schemes for women, and given the ongoing call for domestics within the United Kingdom, the OSC could not contemplate spending public money on such a venture.[81]

None the less training remained a priority for the OSC, within the limits of the British government's expressed interest in meeting imperial needs overseas. From the committee's point of view the rural areas of the dominions seemed to be in most urgent need of domestic workers, and although the idea does not seem to have been taken up, in 1925 the OSC advocated the establishment of short courses designed to prepare women to offer general assistance around the farmhouse or homestead while still filling the servant's role indoors.[82] Such courses were not intended to fit a woman to earn her living outside the home in a rural occupation. The OSC's emphasis on training was not to broaden employment opportunities for British women beyond the domestic sphere, but to provide a better quality of domestic support where the committee considered it most necessary, in particular in supporting the growth of population and rural production.

In 1926 the Australian government established the Australian Development and Migration Commission, heralding a greater interest in the question of the migrant's role in the development of Australian society and in migrant training. Women were included in this process. Prime Minister Bruce, discussing the creation of the commission in London that year, commented on the great part women had played in Australia's pioneering days, and foreshadowed the implementation of training schemes which would facilitate their continuation in those roles.[83] This was a change of direction for the Australian government. While Bruce was attending the Imperial Conference in London, British delegates to the Empire Parliamentary Conference in Perth, Western Australia, drew attention to the comparative lack of interest in that country in the migration of women.[84] The initiative took shape in December 1927 with the official opening of a jointly funded British–Australian domestic training centre at Market Harborough in Leicestershire.[85] About forty women at a time were to be trained in a residential course set up by the Central Committee for Women's Training and Employment.[86] The course, lasting six to ten weeks, included practical instruction in cooking, laundry work, caring for a house and needlework. More than 200 women annually could undergo training, after which they would be eligible for a free passage to Australia where, the OSC reported, they would readily find employment.[87]

Shortly afterwards another training exercise for women migrants was established in conjunction with the Canadian government. Lord Lovat, Chairman of the OSC, had toured Canada in August 1928 and encouraged Canadian authorities to contribute financially to domestic training centres for women in the United Kingdom.[88] Over the next two years, four residential domestic training centres for women opened under the auspices of the Ministry of Labour. One for Catholic women, in Portobello Road, North Kensington, was run by the Dominican sisters. Three others were located in depressed mining and industrial areas: the Newcastle upon Tyne Migration Committee's hostel at Harden, Benton: the Church Army's hostel at Cardiff; and the Centre for the Scottish Women's Committee on Training and Employment at Millersneuk, near Lenzie, Glasgow.[89] The hostels were designed to equip young factory and shopwomen for domestic service, in Canada in particular, through an eight-week training course in housework, with the Canadian government meeting part of the cost of the Canadian equipment used. The provincial governments of Ontario, Manitoba, Saskatchewan and Alberta also contributed $20 towards each trainee's passage, and the cost to the Canadian government was minimal, one factor in inducing it to participate.[90]

Demand for domestic workers was not as responsive to changing economic conditions as the demand for male labour,[91] and in all the dominions it remained high and unsatisfied as economic conditions worsened. Even in 1929, with assisted migration to New Zealand for most classes virtually suspended because of poor economic conditions and severe unemployment and rural depression in Australia, the OSC still recorded unabated demand in all three dominions for domestic help.[92] But in November that year the Australian government indicated its intention to suspend assisted migration almost entirely.[93] At the British government's request the Commonwealth continued to assist the migration of household workers but funding for Market Harborough ceased.[94] From 31 December 1930, Canada and Australia followed New Zealand's lead in withdrawing facilities for free and assisted passages for household workers.[95] By then the other hostels had reverted to the Ministry of Labour for the training of women for domestic employment in the United Kingdom.[96]

Though short lived, the training centres proved themselves in a sense, for as dominion restrictions relating to eligibility for assisted passage tightened in a constrained economic climate, fewer inexperienced women were accepted.[97] The dominion governments had previously been inconsistent in enforcing their requirements that all women be experienced or trained because of the unsatisfactory numbers of women coming forward.[98] The London County Council authorities had conducted tests through the Borough Polytechnic in the 1920s to assess the standard for overseas service of women who had not received formal training but had worked within their own homes, but by 1928 not enough women presented themselves for testing to justify the system's continuation, for as the SOSBW complained, the dominion authorities would accept women without previous experience.[99] The number of inexperienced women who were assisted to migrate as domestics under the Empire Settlement Act is not on record, but only 2.3 per cent had received any special training, under these or other schemes.[100] From Market Harborough, 564 women sailed for Australia; only 507 women were trained for Canada under the Ministry of Labour schemes, and a far smaller number for New Zealand.[101] However, the opportunity to examine the state's role in directing migration through training institutions outweighs the fact that so few women ultimately participated.

Training gave participating governments the best chance to intervene in shaping the ideal migrant. It provided an opportunity both to sieve out the unwelcome and shape others into a particular mould, as well as offering a specific incentive to migrate to a broader field of women. The women trained through Market Harborough, coming on the whole from lower middle-class backgrounds and semi-skilled occupations, fitted closely the model of the 'better type' who scorned both Ministry of Labour training and entering domestic service in England.[102] The Market Harborough experiment seemed to signal a concern on the part of both the British and Australian governments with population and social goals tied up in the idea of the 'better type'. Even so, there is evidence that British authorities quite deliberately neglected to use the training home as a selection or screening process. One Market Harborough trainee interviewed by Paula Hamilton missed out on most of her training because of an injury to her leg sustained in her first cooking lesson, but 'was told not to limp . . . or she would be refused passage'.[103] Government authorities in Australia quickly detected a decline in standards of personal character among the trainees, and in many cases an intention to renege on the requirement of twelve months domestic service.[104]

The British government's establishment of training hostels in depressed areas served a different purpose, that of alleviating unemployment in the United Kingdom in the late 1920s. The Ministry of Labour hostels drew on working-class women from distressed regions and were aimed quite explicitly at redirecting unemployed female factory, mill and mine workers into domestic service in the dominions, with the concurrence of Canadian federal and provincial governments. From the mid-1920s, the Canadian government's recruitment of domestics from Continental Europe to keep up with the demand for domestic assistance had undermined the British government's intention through migration of keeping the Empire's mothers British.[105] On the closure of Market Harborough in 1930, Colonel Manning of the Migration and Settlement Committee remarked that the dominions' choice of inexperienced domestics would now be confined 'practically to the factory worker and although some of this class undoubtedly make good settlers ... limitations of choice will tend to lower the standard'.[106] In Canada, many who received the Ministry of Labour trainees would have endorsed Manning's views, for they were evidently quite unprepared for domestic service and were judged by some to be more trouble than they were worth.[107] Far from being what the British government considered a 'better type', or raising the status of domestic service and of the immigrant domestic, women who received their eight-weeks preparation for Canada at the Ministry of Labour training institutions were ill-prepared for domestic service and unpopular with Canadian employers.

The OSC's shift away from recruiting and training the 'right type' to the Ministry of Labour scheme was a function both of worsening economic conditions at home, with pressing female unemployment, and a recognition that the dominions' own economic and financial constraints prevented the active pursuit of specifically social policies, given the immediate and contradictory labour demands of unemployment and the continuing shortage of female domestics. The Canadian government's apparent unwillingness to take further control of the selection of migrants through the introduction of training schemes earlier in the decade, as well as the recruitment of non-British domestics, also suggested an indifference to stated British imperial concerns. As the OSC had constantly reminded them, domestic training schemes provided the dominion governments with the best opportunity for direct intervention in shaping the female migrant, an option the dominions largely declined to take up. Throughout the 1920s, the population of the dominions had expressed some scepticism at the imperialistic motives of the British government.[108] The OSC's role in redirecting mining and factory women to the dominions through the Ministry of Labour hostel training scheme supports those suspicions. But a study of training also provides evidence of the underlying reluctance of the dominion governments to pursue longer term social goals, the failure to fund more substantial schemes suggesting a greater preoccupation with finance and immediate labour needs.

Experiences

Brian Blakeley has pointed out that one of the problems with the implementation of the Empire Settlement Act lay in the British government's inability to attract the numbers of women required by the dominions.[109] As early as 1923 the OSC reported that '[o]n the whole it seems probable that when every possible endeavour has been made to increase the flow of single women to the Dominions, the majority of women settlers will proceed overseas by the more natural method of family migration'.[110] In assessing the migration policies pursued by the British and dominion governments under the Act, the experiences and motives of those 'unnatural' women who did migrate independently must be given some precedence. Canada, attracting 80 per cent of migrant domestics under the Empire Settlement Act, was clearly the most popular destination, despite its higher fares; New Zealand, with its offer of free passage throughout this period, was least popular. Proximity to the United Kingdom was presumably only a draw given some intention to return or to assist others to follow. Even in the further dominions, authorities expressed surprise at the number of women who did not intend taking up permanent residence in the new country.[111] It would be instructive to assess how many migrants intended returning to the United Kingdom. Chain migration has also been a feature of female migration. Joy Parr's study of non-domestic women migrants to Canada has already shown the significance of female-led chain migration within a particular occupational group.[112] The number of single women who joined relatives in the dominions is often lost where a dual assistance scheme of nomination and selection operates, as was the case under the Empire Settlement Act; similarly, the extent to which pioneering domestics were instrumental in encouraging other family members to follow is obscured. The effect of training in attracting women to the increasingly unpopular ranks of domestic service and its influence on their careers after migration are also important questions, particularly in view of the British government's emphasis on the role of training in broadening the pool of eligible migrants. Exploration of these questions is largely beyond the scope of sources pertinent to a study of policy. Migrant women themselves – and those who chose not to migrate – must provide the answers.

In Canada and Australia historians have begun reconstructing the female migrant experience through the collection of first-hand accounts.[113] In her article 'Sunny Ontario for British girls', Marilyn Barber has analysed the experiences of four British domestics assisted to Ontario in the first decades of the twentieth century, and underlines the perceived attraction of higher wages and better opportunities in Canada as the motive for immigrant women. For immigrants to Australia as well, the chief lure was the prospect of improved material circumstances, rather than the call to imperial duty. Paula Hamilton's interviews with migrants to Australia have reinforced the role played by government publicity in the decision to migrate. The promise of higher pay for lighter work, an attractive climate and a more democratic society were the ultimate draw.[114]

By their own account, marriage was emphatically not the goal but was very often the destiny of migrant women.[115] Despite the promise of increased social autonomy, domestic service in the dominions was as socially restrictive as in the United Kingdom, and for many migrant women was a barrier to social integration.[116] Marriage therefore functioned for some women as a means of escape from the drudgery of paid domestic labour. Others sought to redefine the roles the state intended for them; the control exercised by the British and dominion governments over the migration process still left room for personal initiative. Mary Hutchinson migrated with her sister from their crofter home in the Shetlands to Sydney. She was assisted under the Empire Settlement Act but quickly gave up her position as a domestic to work for a department store, using traditional skills from her home to earn a living by knitting Fair Isle sweaters.[117] Other women sought positions as domestics in commercial establishments or worked in factories to escape from the isolation of their employers' homes. Such occupational shifts were generally possible only after a migrant was sufficiently established socially and financially to be able to turn her back on a live-in situation and, in theory at least, could not take place before the woman had worked twelve months in a domestic position, under the conditions of her assisted passage.

For other women domestic service itself, a traditionally migratory occupation in the United Kingdom, offered the key to mobility. In 1924 an article in the British press entitled 'The touring servant', headlined the opportunities available to the domestic in New Zealand where 'servants are very, very scarce . . . despite high wages, extraordinary privileges, and labour-saving houses'.[118] Much of the article was couched in the familiar and often misleading terms of conditions which seemed 'extraordinary when compared with the duties . . . regarded as customary' in the United Kingdom. But its emphasis on the phenomenon of the touring domestic who worked her way across the dominions from one position to another, which the ready availability of domestic employment made feasible, was an option exercised by a considerable number of migrant women. One was Ada Ford, who migrated to New Zealand in the early 1920s at the age of twenty. The fourth youngest of a family of eleven from the East End, Ford had been between jobs when she was attracted to the tourist posters in New Zealand House in London. Her first application was unsuccessful but at a second interview, she varied her description of her skills a little and was accepted for an assisted passage. She had no money on arrival in Wellington, but after some months in domestic service there and in Auckland, where she wanted to work near friends she had met on the passage out, Ada Ford had saved enough to travel on to Sydney, where once again she found work as a domestic. She eventually married there.[119]

Fewer than 100,000 women altogether were assisted to migrate as domestics under the Empire Settlement Act. Had more single women been attracted to migration, allowing the dominions greater room for selectivity, the dominion governments' perceived social goals might have been pursued more rigorously. The British government's imperial interests also fell victim to the dominions' increasing indifference to these questions, and to worsening unemployment at home. In 1926 Leo Amery, Secretary of State and President of the OSC, protested at a meeting of people interested in female migration that 'migration must not be regarded (in the United Kingdom) as an easy means of getting rid of the poor and unemployed, nor in the Dominions as a means of securing cheap and handy labour for the employer'.[120] Despite the underlying social possibilities within government policies of assisted female migration, examination of the practice suggests that, by the end of the 1920s, Amery's denial appears to have had little substance.

Notes

I would like to express my thanks to Dr Paula Hamilton, University of Technology, Sydney, for permission to use her two unpublished papers on British women migrants to Australia in the 1920s.

1 Brian L. Blakeley, 'The Society for the Oversea Settlement of British Women and the problems of empire settlement, 1917–1936', *Albion*, 20, 1988, pp. 421–42; Dane Kennedy, 'Empire migration in post-war reconstruction: the role of the Oversea Settlement Committee, 1919–1921', *Albion*, 20, 1988, pp. 403–19.

2 Marilyn Barber, 'The women Ontario welcomed: immigrant domestics for Ontario homes, 1870–1930', in Alison Prentice and Susan Mann Trofimenkoff (eds), *The Neglected Majority: Essays in Canadian Women's History*, vol. 2, Toronto, 1985, pp. 102–21; Marilyn Barber, 'Sunny Ontario for British girls, 1900–1930', in Jean Burnet (ed.), *Looking into My Sister's Eyes: an Exploration in Women's History*, Toronto, 1986, pp. 55–73; Marilyn Barber, 'The gentlewomen of Queen Mary's Coronation Hostel', in Barbara K. Latham and Roberta J. Pazdro (eds), *Not Just Pin Money: Selected Essays on the History of Women's Work in British Columbia*, Victoria, B.C., 1984, pp. 141–58; Joy Parr, 'The skilled emigrant and her kin: gender, culture, and labour recruitment', *Canadian Historical Review*, 17, 1987, pp. 529–51; Barbara Roberts, ' "A Work of Empire": Canadian reformers and British female immigration', in Linda Kealey (ed.), *A Not Unreasonable Claim: Women and Reform in Canada, 1880s–1920s*, Toronto, 1979, pp. 185–201.

3 Brian L. Blakeley, 'Women and Imperialism: the Colonial Office and female

migration to South Africa, 1901–1910', *Albion*, 13, 1981, pp. 131–49, and Jean Jacques van Helten and Keith Williams, ' "The Crying Need of South Africa": the emigration of single British women to the Transvaal, 1901–1910', *Journal of Southern African Studies*, 10, 1983, pp. 17–38, both deal with female migration to South Africa before the war; A. James Hammerton, *Emigrant Gentlewomen*, London, 1979, is a study of female migration to all the dominions in the nineteenth and early twentieth centuries; Paul Hamilton's forthcoming book, '*Working for the Family': Domestic Servants in the Australian Home, 1880–1940*, will include a discussion of migrant domestics to Australia in the inter-war period.

4 Barber, 'Sunny Ontario for British girls', p. 56, estimates that 80,000 British women went to Canada in the 1920s as domestics. Paula Hamilton, ' "Everywoman's Calling"?: British Domestic Workers to Australia in the 1920s', unpublished paper presented to the Australian Historical Association Conference, Adelaide, 1986, p. 5, suggests that approximately 6,000 women were selected to migrate to Australia as domestics between 1925 and 1930; other statistics are not available but probably no more than a further 5,000 women migrated in the earlier years of the Empire Settlement Act. Approximately 4,500 domestic were assisted by the New Zealand government in the 1920s, *Appendices to the Journals of the House of Representatives*, D–9, Department of Immigration, Annual Reports, 1921–1933.

5 British Parliamentary Papers, *Report of the Oversea Settlement Committee for 1923*, Cmd. 2107, X1, 1924, p. 17.

6 *Report of the Oversea Settlement Committee for 1919*, Cmd. 573, XXII, 1920, pp. 5–6.

7 *Ibid.*, p. 3.

8 *Ibid.*

9 *Report of the Oversea Settlement Committee for 1922*, Cmd. 1804 XII, 2, 1923, p. 8

10 See Roberts, ' "A Work of Empire" ', pp. 199–201, for a discussion of this theme in the 1920s Canadian context.

11 *The Times*, 19 March 1919.

12 In the later war years and immediately after the war the British government conducted inquiries into the domestic service problem, Cmd. 67, XXIX, 1919; increased employment of women during the war in the United Kingdom, Cd. 9164, XIV, 1918; women's employment after the war, Cd. 9239, XIV, 1919; and women in industry, Cmd. 135, XXXI, 1919, Cmd. 167, XXXI, 1919; and reported on women in agriculture in England and Wales, Non-Parliamentary Report of the Board of Agriculture, 1920, and in Scotland, Non-Parliamentary Report of the Board of Agriculture for Scotland, 1920.

13 *The Times*, 10 March 1919.

14 *Ibid.*

15 *OSC Report for 1922*, p. 14.

16 *The Times*, 21 November 1918.

17 Oversea Settlement Meetings: Representatives of the Dominions and of the British South Africa Co. Meeting, 5 March 1919, Public Record Office (PRO), London, CO 721/5.

18 *Ibid.*, 9 April 1919, 21 July 1919.

19 Macnaghten memorandum, 18 March 1919, PRO, CO 721/6.

20 Treasury to Under-Secretary of State, 26 March 1919, PRO, CO 721/6.

21 Macnaghten to Girdler and Peers, 31 March 1919, PRO, CO 721/6.

22 *OSC Report for 1919*, p. 7; *Report . . . of the Delegates Appointed to Enquire as to Openings in Australia for Women from the United Kingdom*, Cmd. 745, XXII, 1920, p. 3.

23 *Openings in Australia*, p. 3.

24 *Ibid.*

25 Enclosure in Governor-General's Dispatch, 14 February 1919: letter from Department of External Affairs, 12 February 1919, PRO, CO 721/6.

26 *The Times*, 27 December 1916.

27 *Openings in Australia*, p. 4.

28 Enclosure in Governor-General's Dispatch, 14 February 1919: letter from Department of External Affairs, 12 February 1919, PRO, CO 721/6.
29 Letter from Mrs Rosemary Sheens to Janice Gothard, July 1985.
30 *Openings in Australia*, pp. 3, 4, 14, 24.
31 *Ibid.*, p. 8.
32 *Report . . . of the Delegates Appointed to Enquire as to Openings in Canada for Women from the United Kingdom*, Cmd. 403, XXXI, 1919, p. 4.
33 *Openings in Australia*, pp. 4–5.
34 *Ibid.*, p. 5.
35 *Report . . . of the Delegates Appointed to Enquire as to Openings in New Zealand for Women from the United Kingdom*, Cmd. 933, XXII, 1920, p. 4.
36 The SOSBW played a role in providing reception in the dominions through voluntary organisations and also attempted to persuade dominion governments to improve hostel and aftercare arrangements, but were not always successful.
37 Joy Parr's 'The skilled emigrant and her kin', is a fascinating account of British women who migrated to Paris, Ontario, as hosiery workers. This is an unusual case where the large numbers of migrant women and the factory and town itself stood in place of family support. Parr also stresses the importance of kin networks in chain migration.
38 *Openings in Canada*, p. 7; *Openings in New Zealand*, p. 8.
39 *Openings in New Zealand*, p. 13.
40 *Openings in Australia*, p. 23.
41 *The Times*, 5 September 1921.
42 *Openings in Canada*, p. 34.
43 *Daily Chronicle*, 10 July 1924.
44 *Report of the Oversea Settlement Committee for 1925*, Cmd. 2640, XV, 1926, p. 5.
45 *OSC Report for 1923*, p. 26.
46 *Ibid.*, p. 27.
47 *Ibid.*
48 *OSC Report for 1925*, p. 6.
49 *Report of the Oversea Settlement Committee for 1926*, Cmd. 2847, XI, 1927, p. 30.
50 *Report of the Oversea Settlement Committee for 1927*, Cmd. 3088, XI, 1928, p. 44.
51 *Australia Invites the Domestic Girl*, Melbourne, 1921, p. 1.
52 *Ibid.*, p. 8.
53 *The Times*, 5 September 1921.
54 *Daily Chronicle*, 10 July 1924.
55 *Ibid.*; Barber, 'Sunny Ontario for British girls', p. 66.
56 *Australia Invites the Domestic Girl*, p. 8.
57 Barber, 'Sunny Ontario for British girls', pp. 63–5.
58 *Australia Invites the Domestic Girl*, p. 12.
59 Hamilton, ' "Everywoman's Calling" ', pp. 17, 22; Barber, 'Sunny Ontario for British girls', pp. 65–6.
60 Barber, *ibid.*
61 Speech of Mr Green, House of Representatives, Australian Parliamentary Debates, vol. 130, R. 3425, 3 July 1931, quoted in Hamilton, ' "Everywoman's Calling" ', pp. 16–17.
62 Hamilton, *ibid.*, p. 22.
63 L. E. Simm to Macnaghten, 5 April 1920, PRO, CO 721/22.
64 *Report of the Oversea Settlement Committee for 1921*, Cmd. 1580, X, 1922, p. 12.
65 Dominions Royal Commission, *Final Report*, March 1917, Cd. 8462, X, 1917–18, pp. 98–9.
66 Dominions Royal Commission, *Minutes of Evidence*, Cd. 6516, XVI, 1912, p. 45.
67 *The Times*, 19 March 1919.
68 *Ibid.*
69 Colonial Intelligence League Executive Minutes, October 1913–June 1919, Memorandum on Emigration after the War, November 1918, Box No. 38, Fawcett Library, City of London Polytechnic.

70 *Openings in Canada*, p. 5; *Openings in New Zealand*, p. 20.
71 *Openings in Australia*, pp. 23, 24.
72 *OSC Report for 1922*, p. 14.
73 *OSC Report for 1921*, p. 12.
74 Gladys Pott, 'Report on New South Wales', 23 June 1923, PRO, CO 721/74; Paula Hamilton, ' "A Better Type of Girl": the Training of British Migrant Women for Australia in the 1920s', unpublished paper, p. 8.
75 Memorandum on domestic servants, 31 January 1923, PRO, CO 721/74; Hamilton, ' "A Better Type of Girl" ', p. 9.
76 *OSC Report for 1919*, pp. 9–10.
77 *Ibid.*, p. 10.
78 *OSC Report for 1921*, p. 12.
79 *OSC Report for 1919*, p. 10.
80 *OSC Report for 1923*, p. 17.
71 *Ibid.*, p. 12.
82 *Ibid.*, p. 17; *OSC Report for 1925*, pp. 15–16.
83 *The Times*, 13 November 1926.
84 *Ibid.*, 19 November 1926.
85 *OSC Report for 1927*, p. 21.
86 *OSC Report for 1926*, p. 7.
87 *OSC Report for 1927*, p. 21.
88 *Report of the Oversea Settlement Committee for 1928*, Cmd. 3308, VIII, 1928–9, pp. 19–20.
89 *Ibid.*, p. 28; *Report of the Oversea Settlement Committee for 1929*, Cmd. 3589, XVI, 1929–30, pp. 22–3.
90 Barber, 'The women Ontario welcomed', pp. 116–17.
91 *OSC Report for 1928*, p. 27.
92 *OSC Report for 1929*, pp. 14, 18, 20.
93 *Ibid.*, p. 14.
94 *Ibid.*, p. 15.
95 *Report of the Oversea Settlement Committee for 1930*, Cmd. 3887, XVI, 1930–1, pp. 18–19.
96 *Ibid.*, p. 21.
97 *Ibid.*, p. 19.
98 Barber, 'The women Ontario welcomed', p. 116; Hamilton ' "Everywoman's Calling" ', pp. 8–9.
99 G. F. Plant, *A Survey of Voluntary Effort in Women's Empire Migration*, London, 1950, p. 106; SOSBW Ninth annual report, for 1928, cited in Hamilton, ' "A Better Type of Girl" ', p. 10.
100 Plant, *A Survey of Voluntary Effort*, p. 107.
101 Hamilton, ' "A Better Type of Girl" '. p. 2; Barber, 'The women Ontario welcomed', p. 116. No statistics appear to be available for New Zealand trainees but the number of women trained does not seem to have been significant.
102 Hamilton, ' "A Better Type of Girl" ', p. 16.
103 *Ibid.*, p. 15.
104 *Ibid.*
105 Barber, 'The women Ontario welcomed', pp. 117–18.
106 Memorandum from Colonel Manning, Migration and Settlement Committee, to Secretary, Development and Migration Commission, received 17 February 1930, Australian Archives CRS A1, quoted in Hamilton, ' "A Better Type of Girl" ', p. 22.
107 Barber, 'The women Ontario welcomed', pp. 116–17.
108 *Report of the Oversea Settlement Committee for 1924*, Cmd. 2383, XV, 1924–5, p. 14.
109 Blakeley, 'The Society for the Oversea Settlement of British Women', pp. 435–40.
110 *OSC Report for 1923*, p. 12.
111 Hamilton, ' "A Better Type of Girl" ', p. 19.
112 Parr, 'The skilled emigrant and her kin', p. 543. In this reference Parr suggests that

female-led chain migration is atypical. Hasia Diner, *Erin's Daughters in America: Irish Immigrant Women in the Nineteenth Century*, Baltimore and London, 1983, suggests that, amongst nineteenth-century Irish female migrants at least, female-led chain migration was not uncommon.

113 Barber, 'Sunny Ontario for British girls'; Hamilton, ' "Everywoman's Calling" ', and ' "A Better Type of Girl" ', as well as her forthcoming publication on domestic service in Australia.

114 Hamilton, ' "Everywoman's Calling" ', p. 18.

115 *Ibid.*

116 *Ibid.*; Barber, 'Sunny Ontario for British girls', p. 71.

117 Hamilton, ' "Everywoman's Calling" ', p. 19.

118 Daily Chronicle, 10 July 1924.

119 Letter from Margaret Churchill to Janice Gothard, 23 July 1985.

120 *The Times*, 13 November 1926.

CHAPTER FIVE

'We can die just as easy out here': Australia and British migration, 1916–1939

Michael Roe

The field of play in 1923, and its master: W. M. Hughes

Over the past generation many analysts have questioned the moral validity of mainstream European experience in Australia.[1] These critics dwell most emphatically on the terrible effect of European settlement/ invasion upon Aboriginal peoples. More generally, European Australia has been presented as a bourgeois-philistine society, where crudity and greed have repeatedly triumphed. Australia's settlers are seen never to have developed affinity with the new land. While wringing it for wealth, they looked with hate and fear at any outsider who might threaten their grasp. One consequence was for Anglo-based racism to flourish, as Mother Britain alone promised to defend its offspring colony. This dependence variously stunted proud and creative nationalism.[2]

The following pages will offer sizeable evidence in support of such a critique, but British Australia had its happier side. There was much popular pride in the transition from the convict camp of 1788 to the federal Commonwealth in 1901 and beyond. Patriots saw Australia as uniquely upholding social welfare and justice. Notions of 'development' were salient, because they promised not only profit but also life and hope. 'Britishness' likewise inspired pride, linking the antipodeans with world history and power.

While such patriotic values spread wide, conflict had its role throughout Australian experience, and migration issues were sometimes its dynamic. Most famously was this the case around 1850 when various groups – liberal moralists and free working men to the fore – gathered in effective opposition to the continued transportation of convicts. In the same decade feelings quickened against Chinese immigrants, harbingers of long-persisting hostility to any variations from the Anglo-Celtic norm. Legislation to confirm a 'white Australia' (by barring 'coloured' immigration) was the initial task of the Commonwealth Parliament. Most workers believed that employers would use such labour to cut wage rates; often enough organised labour looked askance at all schemes of assisted immigration, seeing them as using public resources for master-class benefit.

The establishment of the Commonwealth in 1901 signified both national unity and structured regional conflict within Australia. The new polity was a complex federation, with the six states retaining pride and powers. While the constant trend since 1901 has been for centralising (i.e. Commonwealth) influence to grow, this happened only through persistent and often disputed pressure. Immigration reflected the complexities of Australian federalism. While broad policy was always a Commonwealth concern, /the schemes of assisted migration which had become general by 1914 were essentially state-controlled, but successive Commonwealth Ministers had sought their integration, and in London the Commonwealth's Australia House was the major source of pertinent propaganda and information.[3]

The First World War split Australian society and set the background for the present story. As its agony deepened, opposition to the war strengthened, notably among radicals and (overlapping) Irish-descended Catholics. Ultra-enthusiasts for the war were often respectable, British-loyal, Protestant and bourgeois; but most support was not restricted to these and was often based on a national pride in the country's soldiers.

War-questioners became dominant in the Australian Labor Party (ALP), which in 1916 consequently expelled from its ranks the British-born Commonwealth Prime Minister, W. M. Hughes. Hughes was a millitant social Darwinist, an enthusiast for conflict. He retained office ultimately by forming a Nationalist Party with his erstwhile opponents. Hughes cherished the imperial link because he saw it as Australia's necessary strength and support. He won high place among the Allies during the war and in subsequent diplomacy.

The war shaped Australia's subsequent immigration debate. It gave new (but not all-conquering) force to the ideal of an organic Empire. Thereby, went the argument, Australia might become ever richer through supplying primary produce to the United Kingdom, and that richness might enable many British migrants to find a happy antipodean life. Voiced in the United Kingdom above all by L. S. Amery, such ideas were welcomed by Hughes and many others.

Visions of an organic Empire entailed some dilemmas. Notions of intense rural settlement had been potent in Australian thought since 1788 and grew into a popular mystique-ideal. Economic facts suggested otherwise. Prizes from Australian soil went to mining magnates and sheep kings. Many a small farm suffered toil and poverty: agriculture and dairying became part of the Australian whole, but at a great price. Yet the yeoman ideal remained, and Australia's major effort towards giving its soldier-heroes a fit home was to establish many as small farmers – and the record of suffering began its replay.[4]

The difficulties of small farming help to explain the central fact of Australia's socio-economic reality (in contrast to agrarian myth): the disposition of average citizens, recent migrants most of all, to live in cities. From its earliest days, European Australia was extraordinarily urbanised. To many this seemed unnatural, almost monstrous; Amery (and Hughes) continued that lament. But urbanism remained and intensified. Associated with it was a drive to foster manufacturing industry, notably through tariff protection. That campaign secured new tariff schedules in 1921. Between the wars various British and Australian commentators came to believe that only an industrialised Australia could sustain a much-increased population and events have proved them right.[5] Yet the terms of the migration debate remained in the Amery mould.

In upholding their migration policies, people like Hughes and Amery continued the struggles of 1914–18. Hughes, the social Darwinist, still believed that an enemy (probably Japan) would someday strike at Australia, and that only a densely peopled nation could resist: migration was integral to his *realpolitik*. Likewise, migrants could be seen as likely to quash domestic dissent, increasingly potent after 1916. In early 1921 T. C. Macnaghten, the key man at the Oversea Settlement Department, wrote thus on Australia:

> the extreme attitude of labour, and the revolutionary propaganda which are active in parts of the country, appear to be largely due to the fact that His Majesty's Government has never in recent years concerned itself with the selection of settlers for that country. Meanwhile other powerful influences have been at work. . . . The result is that a large part of the population is of low Irish origin, disloyal, Sinn Fein, and even Bolshevist.[6]

Hughes and Amery would have concurred.

True to such analysis, Australian society of the 1920s divided over migration much as it had over the war. Those who took pride in the latter, usually respectable Protestant-Empire groups, generally sympathised with the former. Within the Labor Party some esteemed 'development' so high as to dally with Hughes-like ideas, but majority opinion went otherwise. Intensifying traditional hostilities to job-competitors was a scepticism towards Empire naturally strong among Irish-descended Catholics, who in turn were central in inter-war Labor politics. Doctrinaire radicalism, as Macnaghten suggested, had its play. More widespread ran a distaste for the wider world and its stench of war: resistance to migration expressed an Australian variant of the pervasive isolationism of those times.

Middle-ground opposition to the war had grown in 1917–18, and similar sentiment continued to gather against migration. One determinant was the economy's precarious balance: a common situation, but contemporary sensitivities were uncommonly acute. There prevailed both hope for general prosperity – and that thereby the sacrifice of war would find justification – and fear that the war had been only the start of a terrible era. Hence there developed a sort of schizophrenia. Populist suspicion of migrants as purloining Australian wealth found its loudest voice in the media, also the most vociferous in proclaiming the vastness of national potential. The electorate kept pro-migration nationalists in Commonwealth government, but Labor often ruled the states. To find logic in this is infinitely problematic.

One patch of communal near-agreement lay in the hostility felt towards migrants from Southern Europe. Most came from Italy, and in 1923 the Italian government proposed a scheme comparable to the Empire Settlement Act.[7] By then the Prime Minister was S. M. Bruce, and he was much less contemptuous of Southern Europeans than Hughes had been. Nevertheless, Bruce's government dismissed the Italian offer, and populist opinion forced it to diminish the very limited aid given to any migrants not of British blood and to impose quotas against Southern Europeans (including Maltese). The net peak of Italian immigration was 6,516 in 1927, enough to prompt demagogic attacks by Hughes against Bruce.

Even so, Hughes was being consistent, and his ideals had been decisive years before in securing passage of the Empire Settlement Act. In 1916–17 he had encouraged Rider Haggard's proposals for the settlement of British ex-servicemen in the dominions.[8] Hughes urged the states to develop plans under which the British could benefit equally with Australians in their schemes for making soldiers into farmers – schemes which, he hoped, the British government would therefore fund. The state premiers eschewed this equal treatment, and the plan died.

Perhaps Hughes took comfort from London, where, during 1917, the Dominions Royal Commission and the Tennyson Committee reported in terms generally supportive of Empire-building. But those inquiries and further opinion in the United Kingdom also remarked that the homeland might need all its available manpower to offset the war's slaughter.[9] At imperial councils in mid-1916 Hughes contested such notions: the United Kingdom must develop emigration plans at once, he insisted, not await a post-war crisis. In October he cabled his Australian deputy, urging that the states and Commonwealth join in complementary action: 'If we are to hold Australia and develop its tremendous resources we must have numerous population. . . . Demobilization of British Army will offer unique opportunity of securing right type of migrant.'[10] ('Right type of migrant' – how often was that phrase to resound?)

In the meantime the British and State governments did more than that of Hughes. The United Kingdom established its Oversea Settlement bureaucracy and determined to pay the fares of all ex-service personnel and their families who sought imperial emigration, while the National Relief Fund and the King's Fund aided others affected by war and desirous of emigrating. By the end of 1922 some 35,000 migrants to Australia had received such aid. Meanwhile the Oversea Settlement Department dispatched to Australia a commission of inquiry to explore opportunities for female migration: it reported bravely, but its members had learnt of trade union antipathy to migration, of widespread jealousy against British women who had married Australian soldiers, and of assumptions that female migrants should work only as domestics and preferably in jobs which locals avoided.[11] State governments had meanwhile resumed migration work, their approval being required for all British-funded migrants; this did not prevent the departure of some who soon proved to be not of 'the right type'. A few states also renewed their own assistance schemes in 1919, despite shipping shortages and other problems. Two of the states' Agents-General in London, C. G. Wade (New South Wales) and J. D. Connolly (Western Australia) urged grand imperial planning.[12]

Hughes re-asserted himself in 1920. In May and July he persuaded the premiers to accept a plan for assisted immigration whereby the Commonwealth would direct policy and the selection and shipping of recruits; the states, however, would continue to determine their particular intakes and attend to migrants on arrival. Hughes spoke of 200,000 as a feasible annual target. He urged premiers to design migrant farm projects which might win imperial backing, while he affirmed that the Commonwealth would *not* now subsidise British immigrants in soldier settlement schemes.[13]

Hughes thereby showed the limits to his imperialism. Likewise, his idea of co-operation with the states was that they should follow the Commonwealth. He had long fought for that shift of the federal balance. The immigration agreement of 1920 signified one victory in his crusade and promised more: as some states'-righters alleged, Hughes may well have hoped that by linking immigration with farm settlement he could gain control over land policy, hitherto altogether a states' matter.[14] Whatever his ultimate plans, immediately Hughes set up bureaucratic agencies both in Australia and at Australia House in London to handle migration, H. S. Gullett and Percy Hunter taking charge, respectively.[15]

Hunter was one of Hughes's few intimates, while another was E. D. Millen, Commonwealth Minister for repatriation. In London in

1920–21, Millen proved crucial in supporting Amery and his co-believers, who had gained standing when the British economy slumped towards crisis such as forecast by Hughes in 1918.[16] It was not that Treasury officials and other sceptics ever approved of imperial dreams: 'Capitalists are afraid of Australian finance', remarked the Chancellor of the Exchequer, Austen Chamberlain, showing conservative dislike of lavish government spending there.[17] (A legitimate charge, but British investment in Australia continued to be heavy, for want of better alternatives.) At an imperial mini-conference in January–February 1921, Millen urged the United Kingdom to underwrite a £20 million loan for the benefit of Australian farming. Chamberlain blocked this, but Millen and Hunter themselves preferred Amery's alternative (acceptable to Chamberlain) of the United Kingdom subsidising individual migrant settlers. They urged Hughes to clinch the offer at the Imperial Conference to be held in mid-1921.[18]

Hughes spoke there with his usual bravura, but prompted no decisive action. Back in Australia, he imposed on the premiers his ideas of linking migration and land settlement, with the United Kingdom helping to provide capital and the Commonwealth master-minding it all. Then, in late November, he put pressure on the British government to make good its half-promises. Amery happily responded, but even within the Oversea Settlement Committee enthusiasm was restrained. An influential member, shipping magnate Oscar Thompson, ridiculed the idea that British taxpayers should maintain the Australian 'fool's paradise', in which loan money merely delayed the reckoning which must result from high wages and high tariffs.[19] Yet Amery had his way, and early in 1922 the Empire Settlement Act was passed. Never were 'Australia' and 'Empire' so nearly synonymous.

Australia quickly concluded agreements under the Act as to both passenger assistance and land settlement. The latter had more immediate importance. Western Australia, New South Wales and Victoria were involved, with 6,000 farms initially targeted for each of the first two and 2,000 for Victoria. All three schemes had a long history, New South Wales's deriving from one for 'a million farms', first advanced in 1917. The British government was to share interest payments on loans to meet the farms' projected establishment cost. Western Australia's plan was especially great, for that state (and Queensland) apparently offered the best scope for growth; moreover, 'group settlement' already prevailed there whereby newcomers learnt under expert supervision.[20]

All these hopes were to founder. The dominance of the Labor Party in the politics of New South Wales and the difficulties in implementing land settlement schemes elsewhere explain that state's limited attempt to activate its own programme. Premiers James Mitchell of Western Australia and Victoria's H. S. W. Lawson must also bear heavy guilt. They ignored the lessons currently being re-taught by the failure of soldier settlers; they appear not to have understood or not to have felt bound by the agreements. Yet they belonged to the respectable-conservative school of Australian politicians, upholders of Britishness, and they were free from the gross corruptions of lucre, drink and sloth which were frequent among other Australian politicians of that day. Such being the Empire's friends, cynics had only to wait.

During 1922 Hughes found no joy in migration. He fought with the premiers as to Commonwealth and state responsibilities, and with Whitehall for its dealings with individual states. The land schemes under the Empire Settlement Act included the Commonwealth, but if Hughes truly had hoped for a centralist coup in such matters, he had failed. Perhaps this rebuff added its venom to Hughes's criticism of the British government in October–November when the Chanak crisis brought the Empire close to war, without consulting dominion leaders. Meanwhile Hughes's domestic problems grew as a Country (i.e. farmers') Party strengthened, partly through attacking the Prime Minister as being a spendthrift and dangerous. In February 1923 Hughes was forced from office.

Public aspects of Australian migration, 1921–29

At Australia House in London, Percy Hunter had established himself as Director of Migration and Settlement since March 1921. Building on earlier state practices and on the Commonwealth–state agreement of 1920, his office oversaw such matters as the approval of migrants subsidised from British sources, and the granting of assistance (normally one-third fare) to others deemed suitable. Consequent on the Empire Settlement Act, a Passenger Agreement rearranged matters, with the United Kingdom and Australia sharing costs. Aid became steadily more generous up to 1927, when each government granted approved adults £11 of the £33 fare, with further concessions for young women (promising to work as domestics) and children; the governments also could agree to share personal loans to meet any shortfall. Should migrants wish to return within two years they had to repay both grants and loans, thereafter merely the loans.

Most assisted migrants were 'nominated' by associates already in Australia who guaranteed help with accommodation and job-seeking. The nominator first sought approval through the relevant state government; little evidence remains of procedures followed in assessing applications, but predictably Labor governments appear to have been tougher, especially as the economy tightened. Overwhelmingly this was a process of family chain migration, most nominators themselves being fairly recent arrivals, and most nominees youngish adults, often with children. The dutiful nominator assumed a heavy burden.

Various church and philanthropic groups had the right of group nomination. The Salvation Army was characteristically paramount in such endeavours (which otherwise were meagre). Barnardo children came in modest numbers, most famously to the farm of Pinjarra (Western Australia) established in 1913 by Kingsley Fairbridge, supreme upholder of a neo-Rhodesian mythology of heroic Empire.[21] Other users of group migration were large-scale employers, various Australian industries thus adding to their skilled workforce.

The second category of assisted migrants were 'selected'. State governments could specify the numbers of such workers they wanted, to be recruited by Australia House. Again, Labor ministries were consistently unenthusiastic in this cause, and all governments more so as the decade progressed. With minor exceptions no government asked for other than prospective domestics among females and land workers among males. The latter category included recruits for the three state farm schemes noted elsewhere, and also (more substantially) plain farm labourers, who in turn divided (about evenly) between adults and boys. These boys worked under a variety of schemes which strove to control their employment, wages and behaviour – altogether constituting a supreme instance of bourgeois-bureaucratic paternalism.[22] In return some effort was made to prevent exploitation. Other selectees were bonded to their specified role for a year. The figures shown in Table 1 make better sense of the statistics.

As Australia's total population in 1921 was 5.4 million and in 1940 7.1 million, its migrant intake was perceptible, more so than in most comparable societies at the time. But for enthusiasts the record seemed dismal, especially by contrast with immediate pre-1914 years (in 1912 net immigration had topped 90,000). The following account reflects such perceptions, perhaps unduly. Likewise it refers almost exclusively to assisted migrants – yet at least one-quarter of all British migrants to Australia proceeded independently. Bureaucrats and commentators paid these self-payers remarkably little attention, leaving the historian bereft of data. Many must have been relatively affluent and skilled, thereby the more desirable by most Australians' criteria. A minority, by contrast, were of another extreme – recipients of private or public philanthropy, unqualified for Empire Settlement Act assistance perhaps through age or disability. Although the matter was hushed to avoid arousing Australians, the British government advised local agencies to suggest migration to their charges on relief. The agencies could and did

Table 1   *Australian migration, 1920–39*

Period	(a)	(b)	(c)	(d)	(e)
1920–4	171,071	139,888	99,680	33,302	11,582
1925–29	177,318	144,793	121,547	25,854	9,067
1930–34	−18,001	−15,626	3,364	na	na
1935–39	35,485	439	3,788	na	na

Notes

1 The columns represent the following information:
   (a) = total net immigration
   (b) = British component within (a)
   (c) = total assisted migration
   (d) = male selectees within (c)
   (e = female selectees within (c)
2 No series establishes out-migration (and gross immigration). The number was always perceptible.
3 In (b) above 'British' is equivalent to 'British Empire', probably around 5 per cent deriving from other than the United Kingdom.
4 All figures are aggregated for the respective five-year period; they are not annual averages.
5 Nearly all assisted migrants came from the United Kingdom. British Parliamentary Papers, *Report of the Oversea Settlement Committee for 1936–36*, Cmd. 5200, XIV, 1935–6 gives figures for emigrants under the Empire Settlement Act which come to about 95 per cent of the numbers in (c) for the appropriate years. Australia did give some aid to people outside the Act, but the discrepancy remains surprisingly wide.
6 The precise breakdown between male and female selected migrants for 1922 is unknown, forcing extrapolation.

Sources: the Commonwealth's Bureau of Census and Statistics issued annually a *Demography Bulletin* and a *Labour Report*. These series differ even within themselves.

subsidise that outcome, although rarely *in toto*.[23]

The sector of assisted migration which received most attention was the (increasingly) less significant portion, namely selectees. This had its logic, however, for the number seemed capable of great expansion, should Australia's state governments so will. This is what migrationists thought; in fact Australia House spent much effort trying to fill the prevailing quotas. Associated in the task were the United Kingdom's Employment Exchanges, which Australia (and Australia alone) used nationwide as migration agencies. Although Employment Exchange officials were instructed not to demand that unemployed persons offer themselves to Australia, the effect was to taint emigration thither as a mode of state coercion. Overall enough adult males could usually be mustered, but boys fell short by some 30 per cent and girls by nearly 50 per cent.

The taint of the Employment Exchange was only one reason for this scarcity. Farm labourers and domestics were in sizeable demand in the United Kingdom itself; boys and girls – mobile, relatively scarce, exploitable – likewise could find their niches at home. This made them more valuable to their own family's economy. Money and sentiment combined to cause many a parent, mothers especially, to abhor Australian attempts to seduce their offspring.

Broader forces militated against migration.[24] Radicals in the United Kingdom insisted that governments had a duty to provide a decent livelihood for all in their own homeland. At grass roots this attitude became evident in widespread reluctance to go overseas; for good and ill, Everyman's spirit of optimistic adventure had been exhausted by war (not whetted, as ardent migrationists appear honestly to have expected). Just as many post-war Australians felt increasingly separate from the British, so did the latter see Australia as more alien. British opinion was remarkably sensitive to stories of migrant hardship and exploitation suffered in Australia, and many such accounts (most dramatically concerning suicides among boy workers in South Australia) had substance.[25] The British economy was not all that much more grim than Australia's: many ordinary homes had more equipment and comfort. Above all, British social services increasingly outstripped Australia's and numbed the expulsive power of want. To many British people, assisted migration seemed akin to the fate suffered by nineteenth-century convicts. The comparison prevailed in Australia, too; the strongest common trait between the masses in the two countries was suspicion of Empire migration.

Even Australian governments and officials formally supportive of migration were conscious enough of political feeling and economic pressures to impose considerable restraints. This was most obvious in restricting assistance to people 'nominated' or 'selected'. Despite all the counter forces, many British enquired about migration, only to be rebuffed. Even when eligible, applicants found themselves enmeshed in forms, demands and queries: above all they faced a stiff medical test, repugnant at best and damaging to their reputations among friends and neighbours when failed. (Meanwhile Australian critics complained endlessly about degenerates and imbeciles being admitted.)[26]

While state governments were openly restrictive about selection and even nomination, Commonwealth authorities often took a similar (if more discreet) line. They were less enthusiastic than their British counterparts in liberalising fare subsidies and in granting loans to the destitute; in striving thus and otherwise to minimise the ratio of poverty among migrants, they re-made the point that Australia and the United Kingdom alike wanted 'the right type' as their citizens, and alike spurned life's failures and victims. Again, Australia shunned proposals that governments should channel their funding into massive grants to shipping lines, which would then reduce fares, so (hopefully) enabling mass self-paid migration, free from Australia's regulations. British officials were angered by Australia requiring pertinent experience even for domestics and land workers, thus minimising 'selection' of those unemployed industrials (especially miners) whom His Majesty's Government yearned to emigrate. Australia disparaged schemes for training camps which might remedy such lack of experience; ultimately it did contribute to an establishment for domestics, but counterparts for land workers had to be funded entirely by the British Ministry of Labour (which persisted in its migration hopes longer than did the Oversea Settlement Department).

There were complementary tensions about the treatment of migrants in Australia. The British argued that governments there should provide substantial 'after-care';[27] most Australians (politicians, bureaucrats, common people) denied that the migrant had any particular claim against society. The paucity of Australian state welfare was matched by a relatively thin provision of private philanthropy. Only a few Australians helped newcomers. H. S. Gullet established a New Settlers' League devoted to this end, and church and community groups added such work to their agenda. Thus in Sydney a women's Anzac Fellowship, originally formed to provide welfare for soldiers, continued to benefit boy farmworkers in peace time. Ladies of Melbourne's high bourgeoisie, gathered in the imperialist Victoria League, likewise addressed domestics. But the Sydneysiders fought with others in the migration field, and the Melbournites found that many girls resented threats of hegemonic control.[28]

The migrants' social profile was much as might have been expected. The point becomes graphic in a map sampling places of last residence: northern England and southern Scotland show heaviest, south-east England moderate, Midlands and Wales perceptible, the rest minimal (Northern Ireland's inclusion here being the one surprise).[29] Most migrants were poor, selectees often destitute, as, surprisingly, were many nominees although a sprinkling had resources. As suggested above, full-fare payers probably spanned wider extremes. Repeated efforts to recruit the higher bourgeoisie, public school men being the ideal, were failures.

Migrants of this period continued to cluster in cities, where they provided a service and factory work force. Their average skill fell a little below pre-1914 levels, but was important nevertheless, notably (and predictably) in metals and textiles.[30] Despite reluctance to 'select' miners, many came (largely through nomination), and continued their occupation. A large proportion of Australia's domestics in the 1920s must have been migrants – mainly recent ones, for after (sometimes before) serving their bond many girls either married or changed to another occupation. Probably the migrants who contributed most to Australia's economy were the farm workers, and particularly boys, who could be more effectively pressured to stay on the land at modest wages. Although Australian nationalist mythology has as its hero the outback bush worker, in fact few Australians have ever cared for that role, creating a need for such labour. As radicals in both hemispheres (and wider public opinion especially in the United Kingdom) proclaimed, the young land worker faced the exploitation which migrants are ever likely to suffer.

Variations of Australian policy, 1923–39

Hughes's ministry was succeeded by a coalition of Nationalists and the Country Party. It sustained Australia's commitment to 'development' and the concept that the nation's destiny was to produce primary commodities. Country opinion looked askance at industry-sustaining tariffs, but urban interests dependent thereon seemed too strong for any government to flout. Instead the Country Party caused rural expenditure to grow and some rural products (fruit and butter notably) also to receive fiscal aid. Unorthodox and potentially dangerous aspects of the Australian economy therefore intensified. But such remained the Australian way. All could get by, so long as wool and wheat found fair prices, and investment kept coming.

The coalition held office until October 1929, the Prime Minister throughout being S. M. Bruce.[31] Born in 1883 to a wealthy Melbourne family, Bruce took a degree from Cambridge, and gained a rowing blue. In pre-war London he proved a shrewd businessman; thereafter a brave soldier. Returning to Australia this man of splendid talents entered the Commonwealth Parliament and soon the Cabinet. The Country Party found him more amenable than Hughes, and so he rose further. Bruce's style was high-bourgeois, and many a commentator has presented him as an imperial lackey. In fact, he enhanced Hughesian policies of using Empire to strengthen Australia. Bruce, too, saw migration as a pawn in attracting capital and as a necessary play of *realpolitik*, although (having witnessed its evil) he abhorred war as Hughes never did. Likewise Bruce was ready to use migration in asserting Commonwealth ascendancy over the states.

Bruce's most remarkable impact came early, at the Imperial Conference on October–November 1923.[32] Echoing Hughes over Chanak, he warned that henceforth Australians might refuse such sacrifice to Empire as that of 1914–18. His message was that the United Kingdom must reinforce (or buy?) sentiment with policies, based on 'men, money, and markets'. That is, Australia would take migrants if the United Kingdom invested in Australia and gave preference to Australian farm produce. Such notions had a long history but never before such cogent form. Stanley Baldwin gave some undertaking as to preference, and his calling of an election in late 1923 opened the way thither. But the British electorate showed that imperial sentiment had as narrow an appeal there as anywhere. Trade preference fell from the political agenda. Bruce continued his battle, within a restricted field.

With him at the 1923 conference and staying on in the United Kingdom was Senator R. V. Wilson, who assisted the Prime Minister in marketing and migration affairs. Both Bruce and Wilson disappointed British officials by showing little interest in British plans for quickening migration. In early 1924 more energy came from Percy Hunter, who put forward schemes on the Hughes–Millen model, and the premier of Queensland, E. G. Theodore.[33] Comparable to Bruce in his abilities, Theodore was Labor but ardent for 'development': he had earlier attacked Hughes for thwarting a migrant-based land scheme in Queensland. Now Theodore's plans found a responsive ear in Ramsay MacDonald's Labour government, which (contrary to grass-roots labour opinion) approved of emigration.

There ensued fiendishly complex negotiations. Treasury officials at the time and I. M. Drummond since have railed against the Australians' intransigent greed. The outcome was 'The £34 Million Loan Agreement' under the Empire Settlement Act. His Majesty's Government agreed to join the Commonwealth in subsidising loans to the states (via prospective separate pacts); for the first ten years of a loan's run, the United Kingdom would pay 2.137 per cent per annum, the Commonwealth 1.57 per cent and the state 1.293 per cent, in ratio to interest of 5 per cent. The agreement would incorporate the three existing state land-settlement schemes, for which the potential loans were £14 million, while a further £20 million was now allowed. At maximum, the United Kingdom's cost would be £7,083,000, not the £34 million commonly supposed.[34]

Acceptable schemes might establish farms, roads, railways, bridges, irrigation or hydro-electric works, sugar mills, afforestation and other primary-orientated projects. Whereas a state generally could claim £75 loan money for each assisted migrant, for each new farm they would receive £1,000 (soon increased to £1,500) and in return have to take only one family per farm; not every such farm – indeed only half – need be migrant settled. This orientation to primary industry accorded with the traditions of 'development'; it also dimmed Labor's fears of migration as intensifying competition for urban jobs. Pressure from Labor premiers had caused Bruce to agitate for the land settlement clauses, despite his awareness of the problems of pioneering. It seems that he tried, with some deviousness, to frame the agreement so that *no* farms need go to migrants – but British opinion jibbed at such gross Australian selfishness. Further clauses of the agreement sought to ease the migrant's lot, especially through training and aftercare. A British government representative would go to Australia to oversee matters. All this indicated Whitehall's suspicions. Had granting self-government to Australians been a mistake?

With the main agreement signed in April 1925 there began the agony of winning the states' accord. This was compounded in May by New South Wales becoming the fifth Labor controlled state. The new premier, J. T. Lang, abhorred both migrants and Commonwealth centralism; only after Lang's defeat in October 1927 did the senior state sign. The others had done so by mid-1926, although everywhere without parliamentary debate. Most premiers dared neither to shun cheap money nor to espouse immigration.

Bruce now established the Development and Migration Commission (DMC). Most governments push recalcitrant problems sideways, and commissions of independent experts had particular favour in that generation. They wore a halo of efficiency and promised freedom from the venal interference of politicians, Australia's richness in whom sharpened the point. Bruce created many a board, committee and commission. The DMC ranked top in his esteem; in association especially with the concurrently re-vamped Council for Scientific and Industrial Research, it was to enrich Australia through foresight, reason and technology. While specifically charged with vetting state proposals for loans from that £34 million and with supervising assisted migration, the commission was to ponder national growth at large. 'Development' preceded 'migration' in the commission's title and in Bruce's priorities.

Debate on the DMC Enabling Bill had interest. Few of Bruce's colleagues gave effective support. Hughes (outside Cabinet) backed migration with honesty both rare and rank:

> We speak of peaceful penetration, but how did we get possession of Australia? Where are now the legitimate owners of this country? Most of them have disappeared from the face of the earth. We are here by the grace of God and the arm of strength.

Critics attacked clauses which seemingly put the commission beyond ministerial control. Bruce wavered and agreed to amendments, leaving posterity to suspect that here was another sly move that failed.[35]

Chairman of the Commission, receiving a fabulous £5,000 annual salary, was H. W. Gepp.[36] A technocrat-engineer, Gepp's mightiest work had been to create (in Tasmania) a world-ranking zinc refinery, itself a product of imperial wartime needs and subsidised by the British taxpayer. Gepp had made his zincworks a model of benevolent capitalism, blending idealism with achievement. He had guided Australia's part at the British Empire Exhibition and advised Bruce on restructuring the Council for Scientific and Industrial Research. The commission's other original members were C. S. Nathan, a Perth businessman; E. P. Fleming, a career bureaucrat from Sydney; and John Gunn, who thereby forsook the Labor premiership of South Australia. Bruce had endeavoured to transcend factionalism of party and place. The DMC promised to complement his other efforts to co-ordinate (and control) the states' loan raising and expenditure. Thus the battles of federalism continued.

Gepp's first role as Commissioner was to accompany Bruce to the 1926 Imperial Conference. He did well, gaining an extension of the Agreement and strengthening British hopes that at last Australia would give migration due priority. A new dawn promised. But what soon broke were all hopes for a happier world. Migration shrank, and the DMC was doomed.

The state land schemes offered the ultimate example of the commission's intractable problems.[37] That of New South Wales, rooted in plans for a million farms, in fact established thirty-two, and so scarcely counted. However, Victoria had scored about 500 (roughly shared between the 1922 scheme and post-agreement ones), and Western Australia 2,100. In both states there abounded epics of human misery and governmental crassness. Victoria, for example, never fulfilled its promise of providing wages through a two-year initiation period, governments succumbing to popular and political outrage at such largesse to migrants. The first British government representative (W. Bankes Amery) clashed resoundingly with Victorian officials. His efforts contributed to the Commonwealth pressuring Victoria to accept inquiries, ultimately a Royal Commission, and to grant compensation. In Western Australia the situation was less vicious, but bigger and more difficult. There tangled thickest the impossibilities of defining governments' intents and obligations under their pacts. The schemes finally cost taxpayers of this rather poor state very dear. They felt angered, while most migrants had experienced little but hardship, in awful contrast to the utopian hopes for group settlement.

The states, always suspicious of the DMC as a Commonwealth agency, lagged in proposing new schemes. Before the DMC closed, only £9 million had been committed, almost £4 million of this on the land schemes. One complicating factor had been the British Treasury's interference, multiplying bureaucratic maelstroms. But the ultimate problem lay otherwise. Doing its duty, the DMC scrutinised what proposals there were and found several wanting (further land schemes in the West and Queensland, a railway in Victoria). Nor could the DMC itself discover scope for economic growth. Its commentaries were sensible, but usually called for prudence and rationalisation especially of manpower, thus implying a case against migration (a case increasingly endorsed by academic economists).[38] The commission became a scapegoat. Its message told that capitalism, however benevolent and enlightened, had nowhere to go.

Even those schemes that did proceed under the agreement flouted its spirit. The British intended that the states would employ many migrants on the pertinent works and/or otherwise increase their 'selected' quotas. Instead the states sought about as much cheap money as their numbers of (largely nominated) assistees justified, and did no more. This upheld those British Tories and bureaucrats who had long seen Australians as spendthrift buccaneers. They remarked that the agreement, far from controlling the states' extravagance, had intensified it.

Closer British surveillance of Australia further resulted from the agreement. Bankes Amery and his successor (from 1929), E. T. Crutchley, faced impossible difficulties, but sent much intelligence homewards.[39] L. S. Amery went on tour (in 1927), as did various officials. These latter generally deplored Australian ways, above all those of politicians. In 1928 arrived the British Economic Mission, a businessman-junta first proposed by Bruce and Gepp in London in 1926. Presumably Bruce had thought to persuade the mission to boost British confidence in Australia. That was harder by 1928, and the mission's report stressed Australia's problems, in the traditional economist way.[40]

The conditions of Bruce's hegemony were crumbling. Such ideas as his and Amery's for an Empire-strong economy made better sense than Tory-Treasuryism but achieved little. As the international economy choked, Bruce himself accepted that Australian tariffs, wages and public spending were disastrously high – in effect, that the national experiment (and gamble), centred on 'development', had failed. In mid-1929 Bruce invited a political crisis, and it came. He lost his own seat in a mighty swing at the October elections. Labor secured office, with J. H. Scullin its leader. Simultaneously the Great Depression sharpened.

Scullin incarnated Irish-Catholic isolationism. He attacked immigration with a firmness elsewhere apparent through twenty-six fearful months of office only when he forced George V to accept as Governor-General one Isaac Isaacs, Australian-born and anti-migrant.[41] The DMC was dissolved immediately. In February 1930 Scullin, true to Commonwealth centralism, told the premiers to minimise assisted migration; a characteristic protest came from New South Wales, now non-Labor. It availed little, and worsening economic conditions made such dissent otiose. Crutchley kept the passage arrangement on the books, and hoped for effective co-operation with Australia from Whitehall, but all proved sterile. A few schemes staggered along, for example, the Wyangala Dam in New South Wales until 1936, but by then the agreement had folded.

In the 1920s, anger over migration came mainly from Australians, but now migrants stoked the fires. Some protested that Australia's ending of nomination broke prospects of family reunion guaranteed when they negotiated their original move. More stressed the growing disappointment of hope for a decent Australian life. Although leftist thought abhorred migration, a fair number of radicals had come to Australia, and doubtless experience made more. Cecil Sharpley, Australia's major ex-communist confessor in Cold War years, migrated in 1928 under the philanthropic patronage of an Anglican cleric whose son, W. K. Hancock, was currently beginning his fame as the supreme analyst of inter-war Empire.[42]

Migrant protestors found ready listeners at home. In these years of 'bodyline' cricket many a general grievance against Australia probably found sympathy. Radicals in the United Kingdom used the migrants' plight to harass surviving Ministers from 1920s governments, Conservative and Labour, who had endorsed Empire settlement. (One migrant whose life was shattered in Australia was Jennie Lee-Bevan's brother.) A petition to the House of Commons from Australian migrants told that

> suicides are frequent. Some have lost their reason. Young women have sold their virtue, and many of our young men are herded together in camps of unemployed in conditions barely better than the conditions of convicts in British prisons.

Especially vocal were sufferers from Victoria's land schemes. They even persuaded the British government to help pay their return fares. When some state governments sought to mollify their migrant problems by paying return fares, Crutchley called for a veto by the Commonwealth. Many other British migrants scrounged their homeward way; such mobility is usual in migrant life, but now it was made obvious set against the paucity of incomers. Australia experienced a net emigration of 21,500 between 1930 and 1932.[43]

As the world clawed its way from economic abyss towards renewed war, the migration debate revived. Pressure for resumption came from Whitehall. Its spokesmen stressed *realpolitik*, and so advised Australian authorities to consider non-British peoples. This was an interesting prelude to Australia's great demographic shift after 1945, and immediately caused some enquiry in the Netherlands. Through the later 1930s migration from Southern Europe resumed, and against the scarcity of British migrants this re-activated Australia's Anglo-Celtic xenophobia. Under such varied pressures the non-Labor Commonwealth government of J. A. Lyons dabbled with migration, and its brightest young member. R. G. Menzies, showed enthusiasm. Labor and the leftist intelligentsia remained obdurate: H. C. Coombs, later to become a mastermind of Labor's Keynesian-expansionist governments of the 1940s, argued for heavier out-migration.[44] Lyons kept pushing and the state governments shuffled into half-line. Under the 1937 Empire Settlement Act, assistance to migrants renewed much as before, and a trickle of migrants arrived in Australia.

Glimpses into migrant lives

Some migrants found joy and success in Australia; others suffered tragedy; most battled through the ups and downs of life. Earlier pages have pointed towards such conclusions, and those following offer illustrative evidence. The sceptic may remark that such a pattern applies to virtually all experience, and that only in deviating from such generalisation would our subjects have achieved remarkability. That conclusion is excessively negative. These migrants, indeed, were ordinary, but in such degree as thereby to become remarkable, confirming that the supreme effect of migration is to intensify norms of life and consciousness. The venturers pursued one of the worldwide attempts to build a good life in the aftermath of 1914–18. Desperate hope is a common human condition, rarely more so than at this time, and among the migrants it was pervasive.

Docmentation is so full and varied as to allow diametrically opposite interpretations of this story. What follows is one historian's view, possibly telling more of himself than of the objective truth. Likewise the materials demand intense source-criticism. Some derive from pro-migration agencies. More resulted from bureaucratic exchange with somewhat atypical migrants, mainly land-working boys and those who posed problems, often through being laggard in repaying loans granted to assist their passage. As usual, the majority remained silent.

In September 1926 a South Australian farmboy wrote:

> I am very please I have come to South Australia. I have found out what it is to work hard since I have be out. I have a very good and homely boss, he has done a lot for me he has shouted and bully me but that's for my own good, I am just like one of their own. I am well known in Brinkworth now I find them a very nice lot of people, I have played the Australian football I like it better than soccer, my mother wants me to go home this Xmas but I don't

like going and leave Australia.[45]

A counterpart from a girl in New South Wales looked on Australian ways with artless insight:

> I was married in Sydney to my Aussie Boy and we are very happy. My luck in Australia has been the best thanks to the Oversea Settlement Committee. The life here is so free and easy. There is no mistress and maid (in the English meaning). Jack is as good as his master but when home people come out they must lose all their pride (as there is nothing that is a honest living that is looked down on in this country). The best way is to be humble and start at the bottom of the tree. Just start life over again and kid you don't know anything not like the Americans they want to tell us there is nothing they don't know. But Aussie is a young country and we must all be beginners with it. It is really marvellous how quick the English do get to the top although I mustn't give them too much praise before my Aussie husband no matter what I think.[46]

'The glorious sense of space and freedom in the bush districts of Western Australia can only be truly realized by those who have lived and worked in large cities and disliked them, all clatter and smoke', wrote another young woman who had 'married into the real bush life and wherever we pitch our tents there is home.'[47] From distant Queensland a widow told likewise: 'I am very happy here, and thank you for helping me through. My little girl is very happy. This is a beautiful country, all sunshine'.[48] A farm boy in the same state wrote to the New Settlers' League of his employers that 'it is absolutely fine how they treat me, and I also thank you for giving me a job with a Staffordshire man the same as myself. . . . The best part about Australia is there is no picture houses or places to spend your money and you have to save it and when you get a start on saving you do not want to spend it';[49] he hoped to persuade all his mates from home to follow out. Another in the same situation boasted 'I have a good reputation and am noted as being the fastest sheep killer in the district my time for a sheep being three minutes. I am also known as one of the best riders in the district, I can ride buck jumping horses and have seldom been thrown'.[50] From different social and climatic latitudes, an ex-army officer in Tasmania rejoiced to 'have found a happy home in a land of sunshine. Last year I was enabled to retire from active work and to devote my energies to civic and local affairs'.[51]

Of the many stories which contrast with happy sunshine, two concerning South Australian farm boys were particularly poignant. One boy had worked on the land for years, saving £32 to send his mother. He sought aid under an Act which offered to establish farm boys as independent farmers, only to learn that he just missed being eligible. In

1928 he lost his job and in September 1929 suffered a ten years' jail sentence for armed burglary. The case aroused much sympathetic attention, contrasting with the sneers and snarls of much of the reporting of migrant crime. 'His plea was that through unemployment he had many times been starving, and on that account had not viewed things normally', wrote the local bureaucrat in charge of migrant affairs, a man whose office strove hard to do something for its charges, despite massive workload and scant funding.[52] The second case involved a boy who had earlier clashed with his employers: one 'used to call me a Pommie B. time out of number, he callmed me a F B L A P B'; the next 'never realizes that we lads are thirteen thousand miles away from home and friends, it is as much for his sake as for our own that we came out here, we are cheap labour, and some of the farmers take a great advantage over us'. A few months' later the boy had (consenting) sex with a fourteen-year-old girl, and faced assault charges. 'Do me the kind favour of not letting my parents know, as it will break my mother's heart . . . I woud rather do ten years . . . I came out here to do good'. In the accused's support there gathered his local community, led by a remarkable woman ('God saw fit to take my youngest son from me and I felt in these lads I could fulfil a mother's loving part'). The boy was released on personal bond, and well-wishers arranged for him to work a passage homeward.[53]

In other cases disaster had even less relief. A fruitgrower in Queensland wrote anguished letters over many years explaining his inability to repay government. —

> I am full of worries . . . there is poverty here as well as at home [1925]; what a life farming is it is heart breaking [1937]; I am unable to carry on, I think it is terrible after 50 years of hard toil and work (and 30 years of this in the Coal mine) I have now got to depend on my children to find me a home among them, it makes me wish sometimes that I have never come out here, but we never know what is before us, the only outlook and hope for me in life is that God is Good. And he watched over all our ways, hoping you will see me between the lines for it is worse than I can describe [1939].[54]

Various South Australian cases had similar intensity. 'Out here . . . we have met with nothing but reverses, insults, and looked upon with scorn by the average Australian because we have the misfortune to be Pommies', wrote a woman in 1925. 'We have never had a chance since we came here . . . but for my husbands small pension, we should be on the "rations", but I am hoping against hope we shall not be that degraded, two of my boys are working for their keep rather than that, after a long period doing nothing', she continued in 1931. Three years later the debt was written off, when official investigation told of one son and his father suffering much illness, another son and two sons-in-law unemployed.[55] 'Would you kindly let me know when my Wife and children leave for Australia as soon as you can. An I should like my wife to get the news as soon as pospel to let her know that I am Senden for her', went one of several letters from a loving husband-father in 1924; by later 1928 he was asking 'if you are giving assisted passages or taking immigrants to South Africa. We arrived four years ago and find things entirely different as gazetted . . . a hopeless future lies before our children whose ages range from 19. 8. 5. 2 years.'[56]

A domestic was happy enough in reporting her first baby's birth – 'He weighed 7 lbs' in July 1924, but as three others quickly followed 'money matters worry me awfully; I want my Husband to go to England there would be no water carting etc. or cattle & Horses to Water but of course it all takes money.'[57] Another desperate to return ultimately was repatriated after suffering widowhood, trauma and illness. An activist in denouncing migrant wrongs presented her case in rhetorical emotion: 'Remember a *human life* is at stake, but this is great *humour* to many, who brands us with the name of "Pommy" like the Italian is *Branded Dago*.' The woman's parting message had a different but complementary tone: 'I Mrs Wesley does wish to thank you all for what you have all done to help me since I have been out hear as I am very sorry that I have been such a lot of trouble to youse so Please take this little note as I mean what I am writing about.'[58]

Some responded with an anger so pitifully absent in Annie Wesley: 'I am in receipt of your letter dated July 5th in which I learn of your intention to take proceedings against me for not paying my debt to you', wrote one of the workless of 1932, 'also you do not want to embarrass me which by the way your department as done nothing else since I arrived in Australia . . . go ahead if that is your intention then the only thing left me to do will be to further embarrass the Government by drawing rations'.[59] Such a plight was common:

> I am drawing relief and am forced to beg for a living which seems the proper thing to do in Australia.[60] I came to this country in 1927 and like a good many others was thrown to the scrap heap when after the first four months of my arrival in this country I was told to go to the bush and carry my swag and look after myself.[61] Give me a chance to get myself a position to keep my wife and child and myself that is better than living in charity and also help me to regain my manhood.[62]

Between the poles of joy and despair lay stoic survival. This theme sustains perhaps the two most mannered passages in the literature. Angela Thirkell, kin of Stanley Baldwin and Rudyard Kipling, suffered no physical want but worked hard as a Melbourne housemother and fledgling author.

> When I think what I did in Australia between 1920 and 1930 . . . I often wonder why I am alive. I might have been aliver had not all this happened, but anyway it did. . . . One gets through it with courage and goodwill – but one leaves some of one's fleece in the hedge.[63]

In May 1931 one G. E. Clarke, an erstwhile farm boy in New South Wales currently beachcombing in Fiji, lamented the fate of most among his peers:

> The fault is the combined scheme of English and Australian Governments who transported lads, all under age, to a country that was not prepared to assimilate them. They are not to be blamed for coming in their thousands. The promise that could not be fulfilled for three-quarters of them was a magnet which no healthy lad could resist. Take a gold rush, diamond find, a – yes, even a war – Hundreds of thousands of people rush to them with no thought of failure or Death. To them it is adventure, a chance to do something – be something. The aftermath – but these lads, poor devils, they know the track, want, starvation, all honour to them that they have remained law-abiding, with the exception of a small minority. I have heard them singing in the Club room, have sung with them. It has been raining outside and when the sing-song was over, out to a paper bed in the 'Dom' quite a few of our British lads went laughing and joking. Swearing too, telling the lowest of stories, this is fun to them, they have plumbed the uttermost depths, but the spirit of Old England, a tradition handed down for countless ages is theirs.[64]

The stoic note often sounded in simpler terms: 'Life here is not much, its no home.'[65] 'I have a baby but not with my consent however all that is past now.'[66] 'Maybe some fairy will wave her wand & our ambition of having a farm on which we can settle & have an honest living will be realised.'[67] The last contemporary word comes best from W. T. Balls, South Australian farm boy who (like a fair number) encouraged his parents to chain migrate, and paid most of their costs. 'Mum and Dad are settled down now and are quite content', he wrote in August 1926, 'Mum wants to go back to England to die. I reckon we can die just as easy out here.'[68]

The selectivity of time gives a happier cast to those who have long defied such fatalism. The city whence this chapter derives numbers less than 200,000 residents, yet the author has links with various migrants of the 1920s: a student's father, who came (with his two brothers) as a farm boy, and prospered in small business; a friend's aunt, resident here since 1925, rich in positive memories and in mid-1989 making her fourth trip 'home'; a retired upper public servant who writes regular newspaper letters full of shrewd and independent thought; above all, that beloved neighbour who has been our family's support through thirty years.[69] The migrationists wrought no little evil, but their good also has lived after them.

Notes

1 This chapter is based on research for a substantial monograph on the same general subject. The author is conscious that he might seem, especially in the second section, to be offering over-broad generalisations, but affirms in defence that he has researched widely in both hemispheres, most relevantly in series CO 721 and DO 57 at the United Kingdom's Public Record Office (PRO) and via microfilm held at the National Library of Australia (NLA), Canberra. One earlier historian to attempt surveys similar to this is G. Sherington, *Australia's Immigrants 1788–1978*, Sydney, 1980, pp. 104–14; and in J. Jupp (ed.), *The Australian People*, North Ryde, NSW, 1988, pp. 92–6 and 417–9. Nationwide themes are pursued in the context of one state in R. Broome, *The Victorians: Arriving*, McMahons Point, NSW, 1984, pp. 140–50; a documentary overview is J. Lack and J. Templeton, *Sources of Australian Immigration History 1901–1945*, Melbourne, 1988. A recent general history of particular value is S. Macintyre, *The Oxford History of Australia . . . 1901–1942: the Succeeding Age*, Melbourne, 1986.

2 S. Alomes, *A Nation at Last?*, North Ryde, NSW, 1988.

3 D. Pope, 'Assisted immigration and federal-state relations: 1901–30', *Australian Journal of Politics and History*, 28, 1982, pp. 21–31.

4 J. M. Powell, *An Historical Geography of Modern Australia*, Cambridge, 1988, pp. 90–120; M. Lake, *The Limits of Hope: Soldier Settlement in Victoria 1915–38*, Melbourne, 1987.

5 Among Australians to argue thus was the Minister who carried the new schedules, W. Massey-Greene, for whom see C. J. Lloyd, *Australian Dictionary of Biography*, 10, 1986, pp.435–8; among the British, especially striking were the arguments of C. W. G. Eady, for whom see R. Armstrong, *Dictionary of National Biography 1961–1970*, Oxford, 1981, pp. 319–20.

6 PRO, file 2441, CO 721/30.

7 P. Dryden, 'Australian Immigration from World War I to the Depression', Master of Economics thesis, University of Sydney, 1978, p. 127. While primarily a study in economic demography, this thesis has wider value.

8 P. Pierce, 'Rider Haggard in Australia', *Meanjin*, 36, 1977, pp. 200–8.

9 M. Roe, 'Britain's debate on migration to Australia, 1917–39', *Journal of the Royal Australian Historical Society*, 75, 1989, pp. 13–32. This article complements the present chapter (especially the second section) at many points.

10 L. F. Fitzhardinge, *The Little Digger 1914–1952*, Sydney, 1979, p. 353.

11 British Parliamentary Papers, *Report . . . as to Openings in Australia for Women*, Cmd. 745, XXII, 1920; more interesting is the correspondence from a delegation member, L. E. Simm, throughout CO 721/22.

12 For Wade, see especially his *Australia*, Oxford, 1919; the J. S. Battye Library of West Australian History holds a rich series of reports from the state's Agents-General.

13 New South Wales Parliamentary Papers, *Report of the Resolutions, Proceedings, and Debates of the Premiers' Conference . . . May 1920*, and *Conference of Commonwealth and State Prime Ministers . . . July, 1920*, joint vol. I, 1920–1.

14 This feeling became most overt in New South Wales Parliamentary Papers, *Conference of Commonwealth and State Ministers . . . October–November, 1921*, joint vol. I, 1922.

15 For Gullet see A. J. Hill, *Australian Dictionary of Biography*, 9, 1983, pp. 137–9; for Hunter see H. J. Gibbney and A. G. Smith, *A Biographical Register*, Canberra, 1987, I. p. 353.

16 I. M. Drummond, *Imperial Economic Policy 1917–1939*, London, 1974, pp. 63 ff. My debt to Drummond is great.

17 PRO, File 2441, CO 721/30. This file holds much documentation of the 1921 proceedings.

18 Bundle 23, CP 103/12, Australian Archives, Canberra (henceforth AA).

19 PRO, File 2489, CO 721/24.

20 Among the mountainous documentation of these schemes I cite especially enclosures in E. T. Crutchley, letter of 14 August 1930, PRO, DO 57/141, and memorandum of G. Whiskard, 11 October 1935, DO 57/182. For the NSW scheme see further, G. Lewis, ' "Million farms" campaign, NSW 1919–25', *Labour History*, 47, 1984, pp. 55–72; for WA, G. C. Bolton, *A Fine Country to Starve In*, Nedlands, WA, 1972; for Victoria, S. R. McDonald, 'Victoria's immigration scandal of the thirties', *Victorian Historical Journal*, 49, 1978, pp. 228–37.

21 K. O. Fairbridge, *The Autobiography*, London, 1927.

22 The definitive study is G. Sherington, *The Dreadnought Boys*, n.d. (privately published).

23 See, for example, documentation of October 1922, PRO, CO 721/49, and of mid-1924 (especially letter of G. F. Plant, 4 June 1924) CO 721/96.

24 An excellent contemporary discussion is in a memorandum from the Ministry of Labour, January 1925, PRO, CO 721/107.

25 File on T. P. Fogarty, PRO, CO 721/91; more generally, South Australian Parliamentary Paper, *Report . . . on the Boy Migrant Scheme*, 1924.

26 Commonwealth of Australia Parliamentary Papers, *Migrants – Medical Examination in England*, 2, 1923–24.

27 An early expression of such concerns may be discerned in Commonwealth of Australia Parliamentary Papers, *British Oversea Settlement Delegation to Australia: Report, May 1924*, 2, 1923–24; and British Parliamentary Papers, Cmd. 2132, XI, 1924.

28 J. I. Roe, 'Mary Booth', *Australian dictionary of Biography*, 7, 1979, pp. 345–6; for the Victoria League see its correspondence with the SOSBW, Fawcett Library, City of London Polytechnic.

29 Jupp (ed.), *The Australian People*, p. 93.

30 C. Forster, *Industrial Development in Australia 1920–1930*, Canberra, 1964, pp. 171–7; G. Withers, *The Immigration Contribution to Human Capital Formation*, Canberra, 1987, p. 10a.

21 C. Edward, *Bruce of Melbourne*, London, 1965; W. H. Richmond, 'S. M. Bruce and Australian economic policy 1923–29', *Australian Economic History Review*, 23, 1983, pp. 238–57.

32 Vol. 3, CP 103/3, AA, adds crucially to the various printed reports, especially in recording Bruce's interpretation of Australian world-views; W. K. Hancock, *Survey of British Commonwealth Affairs . . . Problems of Economic Policy*, London, 1940, I, pp. 141–8; K. Middlemas and J. Barnes, *Baldwin*, London, 1969, pp. 215–49.

33 PRO, CO 721/96 and 104, generally; memorandum of T. C. Macnaghten, 21 July 1927, T 161/692; I. Young, *Theodore*, Sydney, 1971, especially pp. 41–2.

34 Detail as to the Agreement and work thereunder is in Commonwealth of Australia Parliamentary Papers, *Development and Migration Commission . . . Reports*, 5, 1926–28; 2, 1929; 2, 1929–31.

35 *Commonwealth of Australia Parliamentary Debates*, 29 and 30 June, 1 and 6 July 1926.

36 M. Roe, 'H. W. Gepp', *Tasmanian Historical Research Association, Papers and Proceedings*, 32, 1985, pp. 95–110.

37 See note 20 above, the archival references in which further present a general overview of the Agreement, including statistics quoted below.

38 N. Cain, 'The economists and Australian population strategy in the twenties', *Australian Journal of Politics and History*, 20, 1974, pp. 346–59.

39 Richly complementing the DO files are Crutchley's personal papers, available on microfilm, National Library of Australia.

40 Commonwealth of Australia Parliamentary Papers, *British Economic Mission . . .*

E

Report, 2, 1929.

41 J. R. Robertson, *J. H. Scullin*, Nedlands, 1974.

42 C. H. Sharpley, *The Great Delusion*, Melbourne, 1952; W. K. Hancock, *Australia*, London, 1930, touched upon many issues pertinent to this paper. For an instance of earlier migrant radicalism see M. Roe, 'Strikebound in Cape Town', *Labour History*, 53, 1987, pp. 73–84.

43 See note 9 above.

44 W. D. Forsyth, *The Myth of Open Spaces*, Melbourne, 1942; W. G. K. Duncan and C. V Janes (eds), *The Future of Immigration into Australia and New Zealand*, Sydney, 1937, especially pp. 71, 119 (Menzies), 43–4 (Coombs). Interesting documentation is at file 764/2/2, A 601, and file 46/5/18, A 436, AA.

45 C. O. Jopson, file 999, SRG 7/6, Public Record Office of South Australia (hereafter PROSA).

46 Society for the Oversea Settlement of British Women, *Annual Report* . . . 1925 (London).

47 *Ibid.*, 1923.

48 Catherine King, letter of 8 April 1925, IMM 55, Queensland State Archives (hereafter QSA).

49 Samuel Micklewright, letter of September 1925, IMM 300, QSA.

50 A. H. Hanson, letter of July 1930, IMM/N 120, QSA.

51 *Oversea Settler*, April 1931.

52 G. C. P. Allen, file 975, GRG 7/6, PROSA. The bureaucrat was Victor Ryan; his subordinate who oversaw women migrants' welfare, Jean Anderson, was still more impressive in her goodness.

53 G. N. McCay, file 1516, GRG 7/7, PROSA. The remarkable woman was Louise E. Martin.

54 Arthur Knibb, IMM 55, QSA.

55 Emma Ferguson, file 16, GRG 7/10, PROSA.

56 Robert Prew, file 971, GRG 7/10, PROSA.

57 Nayemi Arzeian, file 134, GRG 7/8, PROSA.

58 File 128, GRG 7/8, PROSA.

59 E. J. Whitton, file 1437, GRG 7/9, PROSA.

60 William Croft, letter of 14 June 1931, file 974, GRG 79, PROSA.

61 Maurice Corner, letter of December 1934, file 1561, GRG 7/9, PROSA.

62 G. Apostolides, letter of 20 April 1931, file 1471, GRG 7/9, PROSA. He was repatriated.

63 M. Strickland, *Angela Thirkell*, London, 1977, p. 160.

64 Letter of 12 May 1931, DO 57/145. The recipient, Miss M. Grant Cooper, worked voluntarily for the group which attended to NSW farmboys' welfare; the pertinent file testifies to her saint-like devotion. When Clarke wrote of 'the track' he meant tramping through the back country; to have 'a paper bed in the "Dom" ', was to wrap oneself in newspapers and lie in Sydney's Domain park, a common resort of the destitute.

65 C. R. Arnall, file 4, GRG 7/6, PROSA.

66 Kathleen Ashby, letter of 2 October 1928, file 208, GRG 7/8, PROSA.

67 W. Fleming, letter of 12 June 1923, T 161/216.

68 File 7, GRG 7/6, PROSA.

69 Respectively the late Mr E. T. Warn, Mrs Florence Priest, Mr W. E. Kallend, and Mrs J. G. Brackenbury.

CHAPTER SIX

Immigration and the making of New Zealand, 1918–1939

Stephen Constantine

The introduction of the ex-servicemen's assisted-passage scheme in 1919 and the Empire Settlement Act of 1922 signalled the Imperial government's conversion to a faith in Empire migration as a solution to several apparent domestic and international difficulties. But it was acknowledged that effective policies depended on the active co-operation of the dominion governments, to increase their quotas for immigration, to accelerate land settlement programmes, to participate in the selection of suitable British migrants, to arrange for their transport and reception, and to share expenses. Attempts were therefore made to persuade the government of even the smallest dominion to co-operate fully with the imperial migration strategy. British wishes were officially relayed to the New Zealand government through the High Commissioner,[1] by dispatches to the Governor-General[2] and by personal lobbying especially when New Zealand Ministers attended Imperial Conferences in London.[3] Amery, as Secretary of State for the Dominions, raised migration matters during his remarkable tour of the Empire in 1927–28, and he was followed by a more circumspect Malcolm MacDonald in 1934.[4] Representatives of the Oversea Settlement Committee also arrived on several occasions to inspect, to listen and to encourage,[5] and their efforts were supported by numerous unofficial operations, for example, by the Royal Colonial Institute, the Empire Development Parliamentary Committee and the Salvation Army.[6] Nor should we overlook the pressure exerted by would-be migrants themselves who besieged the High Commission in London with their enquiries.[7]

There were grounds for thinking that New Zealand might be a willing partner. New Zealand authorities since 1840 had actively if not continuously busied themselves recruiting immigrants, almost exclusively from the United Kingdom. As a result, the non-Maori population was overwhelmingly of British stock, 98 per cent in 1911.[8] Moreover, there seemed to British eyes strong evidence of a natural harmony between the economic and demographic needs of 'mother' and 'daughter' societies. New Zealand was seen, not unreasonably, as essentially a producer of such primary goods as meat, wool and dairy products. These contributed virtually all of the country's exports, and the appetite of the United Kingdom was sufficient to consume 79 per cent of them in 1913. In return, New Zealand's imports were largely of British manufactured goods, and its economy was greatly fuelled by British supplies of capital.[9] It also appeared that this economic exchange could not have reached saturation point. New Zealand in 1918 appeared a recently settled, still immature society, needing further labour supplies from the United Kingdom's over-stocked population to stimulate greater economic production and to absorb yet more British output. Commentators were fond of comparing the population density of England, 650 people per square mile, with that of New Zealand, a mere 11.7.[10] Moreover, in 1911 in the crucial age group 20–39 there were only 879 females for every 1,000 males, whereas in England and Wales there were, 1,099; great opportunities for demographic manipulation appeared to exist, bringing mutual benefits.[11] Furthermore, New Zealand had acquired a reputation in the United Kingdom as the most loyal of settler societies, the most dutiful dominion. It was the 'Britain of the South', its imperial allegiance demonstrated by deed in wartime and frequently by word. Loyalty to the United Kingdom and sympathy for its problems were regularly expressed in much of the New Zealand press and often noted by Governors-General reporting home.[12] It was encouraging to hear Massey, the Prime Minister, agreeing in 1919 that 'One of the most important factors in the building-up and development of the Empire . . . will be the keeping of British citizens within their own Imperial gates.'[13]

There were, of course, economic forces at work which substantially explain the volume and kind of immigration into New Zealand which actually took place between the wars. It was generally recognised in the dominion that the direction and quantity of new investment drawn from domestic and especially overseas sources were of critical importance in the creation of employment and the generation of demand for labour and skills in excess of those locally available. The New Zealand reporter in *The Round Table* noted that 'the question of capital lies at the root of the problem, experience showing that migration has always been largely influenced by the flow of capital to the country to which the immigrant is making his way'.[14] Rates of domestic capital formation and capital imports into the country fluctuated between the wars with consequent effects upon the demand for labour. In turn, investment depended substantially on contemporary New Zealand, Australian and British assessments of the buoyancy or otherwise of markets for New

Zealand products, at home and especially overseas and particularly in the United Kingdom. New Zealand's prosperity was affected by a downturn in trade and prices in 1921–22, by recovery through the mid-1920s, by a further fall from 1927, by international collapse in 1929–31 and by the poor recovery experienced by primary-producing countries in the 1930s.[15] Such oscillations inevitably affected immigration policy-making in New Zealand and government responses to British pressures.

But there was, in addition, a distinctive political aspect to this. Perceptions of economic need and responses to economic events were mediated through the political process in New Zealand. The immigration of labour raised political issues, and the controversy generated also affected the volume and type of immigration encouraged between the wars. The growth in the size of New Zealand's population and labour force had never been allowed to be entirely dependent on either natural increase or on uncontrolled free-market immigration. On the contrary, the New Zealand state in the nineteenth century had performed a significant role in controlling the inflow of migrants. New Zealand's distance from its principal preferred source of immigrants meant that the costs of travel were high compared with passages especially to the United States of America or Canada. Distance had one perceived advantage: it prevented the country from being flooded by masses of unassisted immigrants. On the other hand, when supplies of labour were wanted, the authorities had to bid high to attract them by providing assisted passages and sometimes the opportunity to obtain cheap land for those selected. The New Zealand Company, the provincial governments and from 1871 the central government were thereby granted considerable opportunities through selection, assistance and controls to influence substantially the volume and type of immigration.[16] By extension, they exerted influence not only over the size of New Zealand's population but also partly over the character of New Zealand society. Its composition and development might be significantly determined by immigration. It followed that immigration policies were potentially state-controlled methods of social engineering.

One authority on migration has written: 'The control of population movement has been a natural adjunct of the development of the nation state.'[17] Such a claim raises a critical supplementary question: whose nation state? To many New Zealanders after the First World War, New Zealand seemed still a plastic society, still warm, still capable of being moulded to alternative shapes. Its future depended considerably on which social class controlled, or was at least able to influence by political means, the direction in which the nation state would be allowed to develop. Rival socio-economic groups inevitably conceived of rival destinies, and in a society still substantially drawing upon imported factors of production, the volume and type of imported labour to be attracted or permitted by the state became contentious matters. Assisted immigration, it seemed, had the potential for a radical making, or remaking, of New Zealand, for good or for ill.[18]

The labour movement

Conspicuous among the groups with a determined point of view about the merits of immigration was the labour movement. Trade unionists and trades councils, prominent in New Zeland from the 1870s, were organised nationally into the Alliance of Labour in 1919, succeeded by the Federation of Labour in 1937. Parliamentary representation rapidly rose after the creation of the New Zealand Labour Party in 1916 leading to the formation of a majority Labour government in 1935. The voice of labour was also vigorously expressed through its own newspaper, initially *Maoriland Worker*, and to a certain extent through the Returned Soldiers' Association (RSA), particularly in the immediate post-war years.[19] And from pioneering days, especially in the aftermath of the Vogel immigration programme of the 1870s, labour was in general hostile to state-encouraged immigration.[20] It is true that between the wars representatives could acknowledge that New Zealand was under-populated and that the immigration particularly of skilled labour might accelerate development.[21] But on the whole they claimed that conditions were never quite right for the introduction of further labour supplies. Moreover, once appropriate conditions were established, it was claimed, people of the right quality would flock to New Zealand anyway without the need for tax-financed state assistance.[22] Opposition was inflamed after the war partly by social and economic circumstances in New Zealand and partly by the twin imperial initiatives which the Reform government seemed to be too ready to embrace.

Specific charges were laid against the immigration authorities. Especially in the immediate post-war years the labour movement complained that the introduction of more families would worsen an already desperate housing shortage. 'Mr. Massey', reckoned *Maoriland Worker*, 'desires to flood Maoriland with immigrants at a time when the housing problem has become a national scandal.'[23] Sympathy was expressed for the deceived 'homey': 'Those who come to "God's Own Country" full of hope and enthusiasm quickly find their first disillusionment when trying to obtain a home.'[24] But concern for the plight of the immigrant was at least equalled by anger at the impact of their arrival on those already homeless. The Labour Party conference in 1920 condemned the encouragement of immigration 'seeing that it is impossible for all the people already here to get houses in which to live, and any influx of immigrants will only intensify the present housing diffi-culty'.[25] This was not an issue which ever entirely subsided: a housing shortage was again raised as an objection to renewed immigration in a debate in the Legislative Council in 1939.[26]

However, it was a controversy which was overriden by the apparently more catastrophic effects of immigration on employment. The tradi-tional and persistent labour fear that assisted immigration generated unemployment was inevitably heightened by cyclical downturns between the wars. The Alliance of Labour denounced such programmes at a special conference on unemployment and immigration in 1921, and the Labour Party annual conference in 1922 'emphatically protest[s] against the Government's policy of using the public funds to bring workers here from Great Britain to face unemployment, hardship and distress'.[27] Even after economic conditions improved the issue did not disappear. In 1925 the Auckland Trade Unions' Secretaries Association was still claiming that employment was scarce and assisted immig-ration a scandal.[28] Louder protests were raised when economic down-turn was again widely felt in 1927. The Labour Party annual conference and the Alliance of Labour at another special meeting denounced immi-gration; the New Zealand Workers' Union similarly claimed it was 'the main cause of the excess of unemployment'.[29] Labour in New Zealand had been here before. E. J. Howard complained in Parliament that 'we have travelled the same road as was travelled in Sir Julius Vogel's time. And we have reached the same stage now as was reached then. We have unemployed. We have soup kitchens. We have hungry women and children.'[30]

Some sympathy was expressed for immigrants as the dupes of govern-ment, condemned to unemployment on arrival. The leader of the New Zealand Workers' Union regretted in 1920 that 'already immigrants allured to the country by Government advertisement are learning that all is not gold that glitters', and the RSA lamented that many of the new arrivals 'will have difficulty earning a crust during the approaching winter'.[31] But commiseration was soon edged with hostility. It was claimed that 'the Massey Government deliberately brought immigrants from the Old Country knowing that THEY COULD ONLY BE EMPLOYED BY DISPLACING OTHER NEW ZEALANDERS'.[32] There was talk of 'petted new-comers', and some immigrants met with violence.[33]

Organised labour did not regard the consequences of immigration on employment as merely unfortunate. Militant labour activists inter-preted government policy in the 1920s as part of a class conspiracy launched by the capitalist state on behalf of employers to damage the bargaining position of labour and to reverse labour gains. 'Immigration at the present time', it was said in 1920, 'will benefit no one but the employer, profiteer and landlord. Still, they voted for Mr Massey, and the devil is said to look after his own.'[34] The intention, it was believed, was the creation of a permanent army of unemployed, making the workers 'more amendable to their masters' whip'.[35] One expected consequence of a flooding of the labour market was an attack on wage levels, in spite of arbitration awards. Canterbury Trades and Labour Council, for example, was convinced that 'unemployment has been deliberately created by the Employers, supported by the Government, for the purpose of reducing wages and lowering the standard of living of the working people'.[36] Implicit, too, was an attack upon trade unionism, for immigrants were 'expected to act as scabs when the bosses force the Unions to strike rather than lose what little they have'.[37]

In response, repeated attempts were made to stem the flow of labour to New Zealand by condemning deceitful official propaganda and by putting the real facts before British workers. A Labour conference in 1920 decided that 'the Labor organisation, the Labor press, and the leading daily newspapers of Great Britain be communicated with and that the serious housing situation be placed plainly before them with the object of warning all intended emigrants to New Zealand'.[38] Similarly, a cable was sent in 1921 by the Alliance of Labour to the British Labour MP J. R. Clynes, claiming that 'the Government here are dismissing men and replacing them by immigrants. Unemployment is general, and threatens to become acute'.[39] Further alerts, emphasising unemployment, wage cuts and housing problems, were dispatched to the British Labour Party and the Trades Union Congress on several later occasions between the wars,[40] and individual unions warned their opposite numbers in the United Kingdom.[41] Meanwhile, a delegation from the OSC, investigating prospects for migrants in New Zealand in 1923, was firmly told of ruinous competition for jobs and housing shortages.[42] In addition, labour deputations repeatedly lobbied New Zealand Ministers, there were public demonstrations, and the issue inevitably surfaced in Parliament and as an election issue.[43] Labour remained predictably sensitive in the depressed years of the 1930s and beyond.[44]

What made accelerated immigration so intolerable was the sense among New Zealand labour leaders that they had heretofore succeeded in achieving substantial gains for workers in more prosperous times, perhaps by exploiting labour shortages. This was 'Godzone', a society where working people had advantages denied them in the overcrowded United Kingdom. The Alliance of Labour, meeting the OSC delegation, condemned living standards in the United Kingdom: 'the labour movement in New Zealand were determined that these conditions should not be introduced into New Zealand'.[45] *Maoriland Worker* likewise declared that the 'Labor Party Will Use Every Means to Prevent Old World Conditions Becoming General in New Zealand. Colonial Standard of Living Too High for the London Financiers.'[46] This headline reveals another suspicion among radicals; that 'the immigration policy of our Government was designed more to serve Great Britain than New Zealand'.[47] It followed that labour leaders were suspicious of the imperial authorities, for example of Amery on his tour of New Zeland,[48] and were attracted towards plans which might make the country more self-sufficient economically, more insulated, more independent. Some perceived a prerequisite to be the expansion of domestic secondary industries to reduce dependence on imported manufactured goods and on the export of primary products to pay for them. The RSA, for example, spoke of 'the practical patriotism of building up local manufactures. We cannot always remain dependent on our primary products alone.'[49] Such instincts became more common with the onset of severe depression in the 1930s when the expansion of home industries seemed essential to provide more secure employment.[50] One implication which some non-labour observers drew was that the home market needed to be expanded, by immigration. That deduction was rarely accepted by labour leaders.[51] For them, immigration remained a threat to past gains and present status. They were therefore determined to resist imperial migration pretensions and to impose their wishes upon New Zealand governments. Immigration policies should indeed be a means of social engineering, but designed for labour's benefit. They should be restrictive, to limit the volume of labour locally, to raise its value and its security, and to tip the balance of economic and political power within a more independent nation state towards the organised working class.

Employers

This scenario was, of course, unacceptable to employers, who had traditionally looked to immigration to enhance their labour supplies. Repeatedly they demanded government programmes of assisted immigration, especially in the earlier 1920s and in the later 1930s. For example, the Association of New Zealand Chambers of Commerce forwarded to the Ministry of Immigration in May 1920 their conference resolution that 'as the present labour power of the country is not sufficient to supply the economic needs of the Dominion, the Government be urged to adopt a strong immigration policy'.[52] Similar motions were passed at their conferences in 1922, 1923, 1924 and 1925, and again in 1937 and 1938.[53] In Wellington, thanks in particular to the energies of A. Leigh Hunt, the Chamber of Commerce frequently endorsed calls for accelerated immigration; it sponsored in 1925 the formation of the

Dominion Settlement Association to put the case before the public and the government.[54] Hunt's exaggerated claims that the country could absorb 50,000 immigrants a year probably blunted his credibility, but the general aspiration was echoed elsewhere. The Vice-President of the Auckland Provincial Employers' Association claimed in 1918 that New Zealand could support 'a population of *ten million* in comfort and plenty'; the official organ of the Auckland Chamber of Commerce believed in 1921 that the country 'could easily support twenty times its present population'; and its council was urging a resumption of assisted immigration in 1937.[55] The need to import labour was particularly endorsed by employers in South Island where concern was fuelled by the additional anxiety that the economy and population of the North were growing more rapidly than in the Southern communities, formerly the country's economic heartlands. The Otago Expansion League, the Canterbury Progress League and the Nelson Progress League added their propaganda to the arguments of local Chambers of Commerce and employers' associations.[56]

Frequently employers acknowledged and welcomed the benefits which they believed increased immigration would bring to the Empire in general and to the United Kingdom in particular: reducing the burden of unemployment and dole payments which pressed upon the mother country.[57] But they were primarily concerned with the advantages which they expected would accrue to the New Zealand economy. The scarcity of labour at 'reasonable' rates of pay was a common complaint.[58] Moreover, many employers regarded New Zealand as a still under-developed country, endowed with barely tapped mineral resources, under-settled lands and commercial opportunities, which certainly needed capital and markets for their realisation but also labour.[59] Immigration also seemed necessary because the longer term prospects for the domestic labour supply did not seem good. The natural rate of increase of the population appeared to be slowing down as an alarming consequence of a decline in the birth rate: it had already fallen for the non-Maori population to 21.06 per 1,000 by 1926 and was to plunge to 16.17 per 1,000 by 1935.[60] Contemporaries extrapolated from the trend and predicted the stagnation and perhaps even absolute decline of New Zealand's population with potentially disastrous consequences for national defence, for the domestic market and, not least, for employers' labour supplies.[61]

Such deterioration would further intensify a problem from which employers believed the economy already suffered in the 1920s. It was frequently asserted that New Zealand's rapid development, much financed by government borrowing, had inescapably generated massive state expenditure on debt-servicing, consequently crippling taxpayers, damaging markets and discouraging savings and investments. An increased population, however, inflated by immigration, would reduce the per capita burden.[62] Moreover, much of the development expenditure of government and private enterprise in the past had been incurred laying down the social and economic infrastructure of the country. New Zealand's geographical shape, mountainous terrain, hazardous harbours and poor natural lines of communication had been severe handicaps to overcome, and the services developed were consequently expensive. Here, then, was another argument for increasing the population, to achieve economies of scale and reduce per capita costs to the advantage of New Zealand producers.[63]

There was one other burden from which most employers believed they suffered: 'The absence of domestic assistance in the homes of New Zealand is a matter of national importance.'[64] Employers in towns and on farms had traditionally relied upon the immigration of women from the United Kingdom for their supply of domestic servants, and demand seemed insatiable, not least because of the high propensity for domestics newly arrived in a society with an inbalance between the sexes to be rapidly married and carted off to establish their own independent households. Moreover, as rural employers often complained, there was an annoying tendency for many immigrant domestic servants from interwar urban Britain to stay in the towns or to move there rapidly once they had tasted the delights of rural life in the backblocks. The distinction between the household domestic servant and the female farm labourer was in practice a fine one, and conditions in rural areas could be physically and socially hard. And yet their services appeared essential for economic enterprise, for domestic comfort and for civilised existence.[65] The Women's Branch of the Farmers' Union complained that the lack of servants was throwing an intolerable burden on farmers' wives, while the Victoria League concluded that 'the acute shortage of women in this country for service in the homes is adversely affecting the women and encouraging a declining birth rate'.[66] An effective immigration policy would here seem to have a pretty important social engineering function.

Employers found ample means to express their anxieties and to make their demands on government Ministers through their Chambers of Commerce, the employers' associations, the newspaper press and via their influence within the Reform, Liberal and United parties. They therefore welcomed in general the opportunities presented by the Imperial government's migration initiatives. However, not all employers shared the same vision of New Zealand's future, nor as a result did they agree on the precise purpose and preferred type of immigration.

Manufacturers

A substantial manufacturing sector had developed in New Zealand's economy, adding considerably to the processes of urbanisation. By 1926 almost one-quarter of the occupied population was classified by the census as industrial, not much less than the number engaged in primary production. By then over 58 per cent of the total population was already living in towns, admittedly defined as communities of a mere 1,000 inhabitants or more but including significant cities in Auckland, Wellington, Christchurch and Dunedin.[67] It is true that farming between the wars usually contributed most to GDP, but the output of factories was rising relatively in value, even to exceed the value of farm products for a while in the mid-1920s and early 1930s.[68] Many industries were, of course, intimately connected with rural society, processing farm products and supplying agricultural equipment, but manufacturers even in such activities were aware of their often distinct interests since it was to their advantage and not necessarily to those of rural producers to ensure that the processing of farm produce was carried out in New Zealand and not overseas. In addition, they argued that New Zealand should become not merely a consumer of imports but a manufacturer or at least an assembler of industrial products wanted by New Zealand farmers and other customers. The interests of industrialists could and did collide with those of farmers and their allies, particularly importers. Industrialists therefore became organised to assert their claims, by the formation of manufacturers' associations, by the establishment of the Industrial Corporation of New Zealand (from 1926 the New Zealand Manufacturers' Federation) and by seeking a voice within national and provincial employers' associations and Chambers of Commerce. Moreover, their views were expressed through the press, including their own journals, and by lobbying political parties and government departments.

What they requested inevitably included further tariff protection to guard nascent secondary industries from overseas competition. But they were also keen to increase their supplies of appropriate labour. The drift of population from countryside to town eased general urban labour needs but did not necessarily supply enough workers with adequate skills. This explains their considerable interest in apprenticeships and education. It also explains why, until the onset of depression in 1927 and again with economic recovery from the later 1930s, many industrial employers were keen to encourage selected assisted immigration. For example, in 1919 the New Zealand Employers' Federation, based in Wellington, resolved 'that a deputation, representative of all branches of industry, wait upon Cabinet and urge the necessity of an immediate policy of immigration'.[69] The Industrial Corporation likewise urged the government in 1923 'to give special attention in their immigration scheme to skilled workers in all industries, many of which are handicapped by a shortage of labour'.[70] The Chairman of the Kaiapoi Woollen Company claimed in 1923 that 'it was more profitable for New Zealand to employ her own people in her industries than to send her raw material Home at its lowest value and bring it back as finished goods at the highest value. For those reasons . . . a vigorous and practical immigration scheme should be taken in hand without delay.'[71] Later in the 1930s there were still complaints that 'we do not at the present moment possess sufficient skilled workers in New Zealand to enable those secondary industries to be developed at the pace which we all desire'.[72] The Secretary of the Department of Industries and Commerce reported that 'it is frequently brought under the notice of this Department by manufacturing industries that shortages of labour in their factories are hampering production'.[73]

Manufacturers looked to immigration, however, to satisfy more than their need for labour. They were also conscious that New Zealand's limited population size restricted their domestic market and left them vulnerable to overseas suppliers with large home populations who enjoyed economies of scale. New Zealand manufacturers were therefore keen to see their potential customers increased by immigration and population growth.[74] Such arguments became more frequent after the economic downturn. In 1935 the President of the Manufacturers' Federation revived the campaign for immigration by claiming that there was 'no other solution to the problem of consumption of our increasing farm and factory products than a larger consuming market in our own country'.[75] The argument could also be reversed, to assume that an increased population by immigration was a self-evidently desirable objective for fiscal, defence, social or national status reasons, and then to claim that only an expansion of secondary industries was capable of generating the increased employment such a population growth would require.[76]

Such arguments were enhanced by the further claim that the more balanced economic structure which would be established would allow New Zealand to assert its status as a sovereign nation and escape the ties of economic dependence and cultural subservience which bound her to Imperial Britain. 'Our manufacturing . . . industries', declared the *National Review*, are 'necessary to our progress towards ideal nationhood – an independent and self-supporting community'.[77] Such aspirations were often coupled with critical remarks on the national preoccupation with farming and rural life: 'We do not believe that we are doomed to be a nation of milkers, shearers and slaughtermen for all eternity.'[78] The Auckland Manufacturers' Association, celebrating its golden jubilee in 1936, saw New Zealand evolving 'from the extraction of crude products and raw materials towards a higher economic and social development'.[79] A country locked predominantly into farming would also remain culturally stunted; on the other hand, manufacturing would encourage 'the development of various businesses which comprise a town and are catering for the needs of the luxuries of modern civilisation'.[80] 'Populations that can sustain large cities have the advantages of greater education and cultural opportunities.'[81] In brief, manufacturers and their urban allies perceived New Zealand as becoming a more urbanised, more industrialised and, in their eyes, more civilised nation state. They were asserting not only their economic interests but also their status within society. And they addressed immigration as one tool for the economic and social engineering of New Zealand to advance their class interests, against organised labour and against the resistance of traditional rural society.

Farmers

The thrust and tenor of these claims were unacceptable to representatives of rural New Zealand and their allies in the importing and service sectors. Their protests, amplified by the Farmers' Union through its journal, much of the press and the Chambers of Commerce, which they usually dominated, penetrated political parties and ministerial corridors.[82] Rural society viewed with alarm accelerating urbanisation, emergent secondary industries, tariff protection and assertive trade unions. Farmers were not, however, hostile to immigration. Landowners had traditionally favoured assisted passages, and after the First World War they regarded immigration once again as a necessary tool. However, it should be designed to engineer the satisfaction and protection specifically of rural interests.

Some speculators still believed that the country's rural resources were under-developed. Proposals were floated by investment companies and by enthusiasts like Leigh Hunt for further land settlement either on untouched 'wastes' especially in Otago and North of Auckland or by sub-division and more intensive cultivation: immigration policies should attract new settlers (and their capital) for these tasks.[83] But most rural producers were not keen to increase competition at a time of uncertain markets.[84] Most were anxious only to increase labour supplies for rural jobs. It is true that this period witnessed a further expansion especially of dairying in North Island where labour needs did not individually greatly exceed those naturally available in farm families. Moreover, the labour intensiveness of farming declined with mechanisation. Nevertheless, rural society still required hired labour for sheepruns, arable harvests, dairying and in places for the exploitation of such rural mineral resources as coal and gold. Problems of recruitment, however, were exacerbated by the noted fall in the birth rate and the alarming drift of native-born labour from country to town.[85]

The feared consequence was a labour shortage, or at least a shortage of labour at tolerable prices. The response was a repeated demand for a government programme of assisted immigration to satisfy rural needs. *The Country* lamented in 1923 'that notwithstanding that 94 per cent of the value of our exports are from the land, there is a steady drift of the population from the country to towns. An influx of suitable agricultural immigrant[s] is imperative to combat this unnatural flow'.[86] *Farming First* in 1926 was adamant that 'We need immigration – for the land.'[87] The 1927 manifesto of the New Zealand Country Party demanded that 'when economic conditions warrant, a vigorous policy be instituted to induce well-selected immigrants from Great Britain to settle on the land . . . , and that full advantage be taken of the Imperial Immigration scheme'.[88] Later, in 1936, the Farmers' Union debated a motion 'that the Government investigate the position re the supply of agricultural labour available in New Zealand and if . . . there is not sufficient labour to supply the needs of the country that they immediately adopt an Immigration Policy for supplementing the requirements for agricultural labour'.[89]

Farmers' representatives were particularly interested in encouraging juvenile immigration. The Immigration Department in 1920 asked local Farmers' Unions if they would welcome a proposal to bring in British lads aged seventeen to twenty as farm labourers. The response was enthusiastic. 'This class of labour', began the report from Auckland, 'is in more demand than any other in this Province on dairy farms.' Hawke's Bay was similarly 'heartily in accord with the scheme', and Southern Hawke's Bay 'could absorb an almost unlimited supply'. Poverty Bay 'unanimously approved' and Taranaki was 'entirely in sympathy'. The attraction of young immigrants was that they were expected to be more docile, more adaptable and, once trained up to life in the countryside, more likely to stay on farms than older immigrants. They were also cheaper. Pelorus Sound Farmers' Union complained about 'these days of high wages and bonuses', and proposed that farm lads should receive less than current rates of pay.[90] This interest was sustained right through the period, the Farmers' Union resolving in 1937 'that the Government take into serious consideration the system of training young boys and girls or the possibility of obtaining them from abroad and training them to go on farms'.[91]

There was more to this than an attempt to obtain cheap labour. What appeared also at stake was the status of farmers in New Zealand society. These were anxious decades when rural New Zealand faced the shock of a greater intrusion of urban-industrial interests and alien values. Farmers were prone to claim that other sectors were parasites feeding off and dangerously weakening the agricultural foundations of the country. 'We live on grass', yet the burdens on the farmer felt crippling.[92] A cartoon in *Farming First* portrayed one farmer in 1901 supporting three 'Townies' but staggering under five 'Townies', smug and fat, by 1925.[93] In self-defence farmers deployed the realistic claim that the secondary industries of New Zealand depended greatly upon rural society for much of their raw materials and many of their customers; indeed, given the volume of imports which domestic manufacturers could not yet and probably never could replace and New Zealand's reliance on external sources of capital, the entire economy appeared to farmers to depend on their export success. Obstacles in their way would trip up all.[94]

Common, too, was the claim that rural society was the home of particular virtues, qualities which made New Zealand distinct as a nation and uniquely valuable, qualities lacking in the grim urban and industrial 'home country' from which New Zealand farmers believed their ancestors had fled to preserve the good life in their version of 'God's own country'. The masthead of *Farming First* contained the declaration 'National Health is in exact ratio to the proportion of people having direct interest in the soil.'[95] The concept of health could be physical, in the belief that health in the cities was sadly but predictably below that enjoyed in the countryside: 'there is no life so healthy as that of the Farm worker'.[96] But there was a moral health to be considered, too. *The Farmers' Weekly* praised the self-denial and self-discipline of country dwellers and delicately dismissed towns as 'mere excrescences (callosities, perhaps, but more likely to contain noxious pus)'.[97] Towns were often depicted as colonies of over-crowded slums where the poor competed for survival at the expense of morality and where Bolsheviks picked about among the wreckage. The New Zealand reporter for *The Round Table* commented that

> We are not at present a great manufacturing country, and it is doubtful if we ever could become one, or whether, from a humanitarian point of view, it would be worth our while to try to become one. There is nothing intrinsically attractive in industrialism and much that is repulsive. It means factory, slums and social problems.[98]

One attraction of settling young immigrants as farm labourers was that they would 'become true New Zealanders'.[99]

To many farmers and sympathetic observers, rural New Zealand seemed under threat, economically, socially and culturally. The views expressed echo those of rural representatives in other settler societies facing urbanisation, industrialisation and the growing power of city finance. In response, New Zealand farmers looked to government and not least to immigration policy for protection. Immigration attracted farmers, too, as an instrument of social engineering, but its purpose in their case was conservative, to build a dyke against decay.

Government policies

New Zealand governments between the wars were therefore subjected to very considerable pressures in the formulation and execution of immigration policy. Their decisions could not be merely automatic and dispassionate responses to economic fluctuations, influential though they were. Unassisted immigration, it is true, provoked little domestic controversy: 'There is nothing to prevent people coming out here at their own expense', chirped *The Dominion*,[100] cheerfully ignoring the Undesirable Immigrants Exclusion Act of 1919 and the Immigration Restriction Acts of 1908 and 1920. The former was designed to exclude ex-enemy nationals and the politically unacceptable, especially socialists. The latter, reflecting an overwhelming consensus, barred entry to convicted criminals, the insane, the deaf, dumb and blind, those suffering from contagious diseases and, notoriously, peoples of non-European stock.[101] While social engineering was the purpose of such restrictive legislation, it was the positive proposals for assisted immigration which provoked most political agitation, for or against the practice in general and over specific categories of immigrants in particular. In such circumstances it was impossible for New Zealand Ministers to listen merely to the voices of British imperialists when devising immigration policy.

Given the composition and principal political supporters of the post-war Reform government, it is not surprising that Massey sympathised with employers in their wish to recruit British labour to ease their perceived shortages. Moreover, the Liberals endorsed the need and merely chivvied the government to do more, faster and better. The first post-war immigration policy decision was therefore to revive the pre-war New Zealand programme of subsidising the passages of selected British immigrants.[102] Arrangements were made to inform New Zealand residents and to advertise the attractions of New Zealand to the British public by posters and publications.[103] Not surprisingly in this context, the Imperial government's scheme for the migration of ex-servicemen and women was welcomed, since the cost was to be borne entirely by British taxpayers while the New Zealand authorities retained control over selection.[104] For similar reasons, when that scheme was broadened by the Empire Settlement Act the principle of sharing costs was much appreciated. Indeed, the New Zealand government's Audit Officer was astonished. Henceforth, the country would be receiving the immigrants it wanted substantially at British expense: 'it is difficult to see what present advantages the Imperial Government receives by participation in the scheme'.[105] The first assisted-passage agreement was signed on 28 August 1922. Subsidies from both governments reduced the cheapest third-class fare for the standard approved adult migrant from £36 to £18. Passage agreements were thereafter renewed regularly until 1941. Falls in shipping company costs allowed rates to be cut to a mere £11 by 1926, 'the cheapest fares that have ever existed in the history of the Dominion'.[106]

Before the war New Zealand residents could nominate near relatives in the United Kingdom for assisted passages; in addition domestic servants and farm labourers could be nominated by New Zealand employers or could apply themselves for assisted passages to the High Commissioner.[107] After the war, even under the agreements with the Imperial government, the New Zealand authorities scrupulously retained control over the selection of suitable immigrants and retained the right to increase their subsidies to encourage the immigration of particularly desirable immigrants. Thus, and indicative of the government's desire to satisfy the employing classes, extraordinary efforts were made to attract female domestic servants. An early decision replaced the pre-war cheap reates for domestics with free passages and allowed the lucky recruits £2 each to cover expenses. This generous provision was then made available under the scheme for ex-service personnel and under the Empire Settlement Act.[108]

More potentially awkward was the recruiting of other workers. Pre-war governments had explicitly refused to help industrial employers recruit workers under the assisted passage scheme.[109] However, no administration after the war could ignore the economic importance of the expanding urban and industrial sectors. Moreover, the shift of population made it imperative for politicians to cultivate the urban as well as the rural vote. The Governor-General astutely observed that the farming community was no longer all-powerful even within the Reform Party, that businessmen and manufacturers were also a component part, and that 'the Prime Minister found it necessary to conciliate both'.[110] Massey acknowledged in 1919 that secondary industries were of growing national importance, that they had specific labour requirements and that new immigrants 'would not all be farm labourers'.[111] Indeed, he initiated an official inquiry which reported a factory labour shortage of 12,937 in 1920.[112] One response was to authorise the High Commissioner as the need arose to provide assisted passages without nomination for certain urban workers in particular demand, sometimes mechanics but mainly artisans and building workers. More consequential was the initiation in 1920 of a system of open nomination by which all New Zealand residents could nominate any person in the United Kingdom irrespective of relationship or occupation. The practice allowed employers in all economic sectors (and also certain approved societies) to nominate either specific individuals in the United Kingdom or to request the High Commissioner to recruit on their behalf suitable migrants for particular jobs. In all cases nominators were supposed to guarantee employment and accommodation. The beauty of the system was that government authorities could apparently avoid thereby taking sides in the disputes between rural and urban producers.[113]

Nevertheless, the priorities of Reform administrations in the 1920s can still be discerned. It was, of course, reasonable for those in government to pay particular heed to the rural sector which was still responsible for so much of New Zealand's prosperity. Moreover, the electoral system with its country quota remained weighted towards rural constituencies which it would be foolish to antagonise; even Labour needed to woo rural support. It is also not surprising that 'Farmer Bill' Massey did not forget his roots. But perceptions of the preferred future of New Zealand as a largely rural society imbued with particular values were still evidently deeply entrenched in departments of state. Even in the Immigration Department the Under-Secretary could declare in 1927 that 'the Dominion, by . . . placing [immigrant] youths on the land, . . . gains citizens of the true New Zealand spirit'.[114]

Evidence of this officially sanctioned bias is apparent in various special immigration operations which were launched in addition to the basic nomination system, largely in response to rural expectations. There was, it is true, no attempt to initiate land settlement schemes, beloved of the Imperial authorities, either under the ex-servicemen's programme or under the Empire Settlement Act: the New Zealand government was finding its attempts to establish its own ex-soldiers on the land an expensive and politically troublesome operation. Officials accepted that the quantity of land still available for fresh settlement was limited and its quality generally poor, beyond the skills of immigrant tyro farmers.[115] Instead, the government set out to attract farm labourers. The High Commissioner was authorised in November 1918 to advertise the resumption of assisted passages especially for agricultural workers. This class was also specifically targeted for recruiting under the ex-servicemen's scheme: in October 1921 instructions were sent to obtain one hundred unmarried ploughmen, dairy workers and experienced general farm labourers. Under the Empire Settlement Act the cost of assisted passages for farm workers was further reduced, to £10 for adults when the standard rate was £18.[116] Official sponsorship and government subsidies also encouraged special programmes to bring in juveniles as farm workers. These embraced the introduction of a dozen boys dispatched to the Ruakura Farm Training College with British Empire Exhibition scholarships, a remarkable operation initiated by Taranaki Chamber of Commerce which deposited (sometimes bewildered) English public schoolboys on New Zealand farms, projects for the immigration and training of young farm workers by the Church of England and by the Salvation Army, and the scheme sponsored by the New Zealand Sheepowners Acknowledgement of Debt to British Seamen Fund which brought out orphaned sons and daughters of British seamen and trained them for farm work.[117] One other category singled out for a while for special treatment were miners needed for the expansion of largely rural-based New Zealand coal and gold industries.[118] The Minister of Immigration in 1927 readily revealed his preferences: 'that [immigrants] are being absorbed in the right direction there is no doubt as not more than 35 per cent stay in the cities'.[119]

This commitment to employers' needs and particularly to those of rural New Zealand did not mean, however, that Massey and his successors were indifferent to the objections of organised labour. It would have been foolish politically in the volatile inter-war years to ignore entirely the protestations of labour leaders; their constituency appeal was growing. Moreover, some of their complaints were legitimate and were identified, too, by other observers. There was, indeed, a housing shortage after the war, and unemployment did rise with demobilisation and a trade slump in 1921–22. The head of the Immigration Department urged a suspension of operations in August 1920 because of the housing problem and further restraint in March 1921 because of depression.[120] In July 1922 Massey conceded that 'it may be desirable to go slow with immigration activities while the present depression lasts'.[121] As a rough guide, governments thereafter aimed to introduce no more than 10,000 assisted immigrants a year, increased to 13,500 for 1926, the maximum which it was thought the economy could safely digest; the ambitious schemes for a massive increase in the labour force or the domestic market were disregarded. The totals were still more than labour leaders believed tolerable, but their root objections were effective only from 1927 when once again other observers, including employers, conceded that economic downturn, rising unemployment and potential public disorder warranted initially cuts and eventually in 1931 virtually the abandonment of all forms of assisted immigration.[122] Already by 1928 the Governor-General was reporting 'that any Government which attempted to resume a policy of assisted immigration while unemployment remained ... would have a difficult task and would certainly become unpopular'.[123] The Coalition government formed in the crisis of 1931 was disinclined to resume assisted immigration even as late as September 1935.[124] Thereafter, the Labour government which came to power in November, reflecting at last the fundamental objections of organised labour, remained resolutely opposed to all forms of assisted immigration in spite of very considerable lobbying and in spite of the administration's commitment to the development of secondary industries, for which some imported skilled labour might have been useful.[125] 'We are not going to pay anyone's fare to come to New Zealand ... until we have solved our economic problems', declared Michael Savage.[126]

Some of the consequences of the New Zealand governments' responses to economic circumstances, imperial pressure, domestic

Table 1   *Immigrants intending permanent residence, 1918–39*

Year	Total assisted (year beginning 1 April)	Total UK departures (year beginning 1 April)	Total NZ immigrants (year ending 31 December)
1918	906	na	na
1919	3,811	na	na
1920	10,107	na	na
1921	7,005	11,560	11,135 (9 months)
1922	6,737	11,341	13,845
1923	6,752	11,488	11,762
1924	8,924	12,451	14,314
1925	7,685	10,965	15,704
1926	11,239	14,943	17,868
1927	3,822	6,197	11,327
1928	1,968	3,814	6,339
1929	1,790	3,369	6,343
1930	1,233	2,610	6,917
1931	290	2,258	3,236
1932	56	626	1,572
1933	4	468	1,792 (15 months)
			(year beginning 1 April)
1934	1	491	1,579
1935	0	653	1,915
1936	11	892	2,807
1937	10	1,513	4,341
1938	13	2,020	6,493
1939	8	na	7,315

na   Not available

Sources: *AJHR*, D-9, Department of Immigration Annual Reports 1919–35; *Annual Statistical Report on Population* 1921; *Annual Statistical Report on External Migration* 1922–32, *Annual Statistical Report on Population and Buildings*, 1933/34–1939/40; NA, LI, 22/1/1, memo by H. E. Moston, 4 December 1935.

lobbying and their own priorities may be seen in Table 1. The number of assisted immigrants topped 10,000 in 1920–21 and peaked at 11,239 in 1926–27 before falling away rapidly. The Department of Immigration itself was closed in 1932–33. The total assisted over twenty-two years was 72,372, but the annual average over the decade 1919–29 was 6,805, a significant increase above the average of 3,481 recorded in the ten years 1905–15. Moreover, as Table 1 also shows, assisted immigrants in the 1920s contributed a high percentage of all those arriving from the United Kingdom in the 1920s and a significant proportion of the total number of New Zealand immigrants. Nevertheless, imperial observers could only be disappointed. New Zealand absorbed 14,967 immigrants assisted by the New Zealand government alone (mainly between 1918 and 1922), only 12,671 immigrants at British expense under the ex-servicemen's scheme between 1920 and 1925 (mainly before 1923) and 44,734 jointly under the Empire Settlement Act.[127] Such a modest response reflected, of course, economic circumstances and territorial and climatic realities in New Zealand, limiting conditions which even British observers were recognising by the 1930s. The figures also reflected the political struggle within New Zealand over which the imperial authorities could exercise no control.

That struggle may also be detected in Table 2. Among assisted immigrants the largest single occupational category was made up of domestic servants, either nominated from New Zealand or recruited by the High Commissioner in the United Kingdom to satisfy the demands of the employing classes.[128] A substantial number were textile workers, building craftsmen, electricians, engineers and mechanics, and many were recorded as clerks, typists and shop assistants; they were responding to the needs of the manufacturing and tertiary sector often through the open nomination system. But a still larger volume was headed towards rural society as miners and especially as farm labourers, both adults and juveniles. This occupational spread was not a reflection of the occupational structure of heavily industrialised and urbanised inter-war Britain, nor even of the sectors most disturbed by restructuring and unemployment (although coalminers were badly affected). Nor did the occupational distribution simply reflect the occupational structure of New Zealand. Rather, patterns of assisted immigration by occupation, as by volume, were the result also of struggles between interest groups in New Zealand and their abilities to affect the social engineering practices of government.

Table 2 Occupations of assisted immigrants, 1922–32

Occupation/Category	Year beginning 1 April										Total
	1922	1923	1924	1925	1926	1927	1928	1929	1930	1931	
Bakers, grocers		46	73	55	88	19	7	13	5	2	308
Blacksmiths	27	13	20	22	42	5	1	2	2		134
Boilermakers	33	25	21	10	19	5					113
Bootmakers	25	31	19	49	26	8	2	3	4	1	167
Bricklayers, masons	11	49	51	31	16	8	4	1	2		172
Butchers	13	9	31	24	35	6	2	6		1	127
Cabinet-makers, carpenters, joiners, turners	96	148	183	106	148	24	14	10	6	1	736
Clerks, typists	91	111	171	182	250	94	59	39	16	6	1,019
Domestics	912	951	970	736	1,011	651	441	347	283	76	6,378
Dressmakers, milliners, tailors	26	58	47	61	81	34	12	15	15	2	351
Electricians	25	28	68	44	63	7		5	1	1	242
Engineers, fitters, mechanics	230	190	258	194	340	61	18	34	11	3	1,339
Farming	514	566	971	880	1,015	218	79	58	64	15	4,380
Gardeners	17	16	19	17	39	10	2	1	3	1	125
Glassworkers								12	2		14
Labourers	127	132	201	152	238	39	20	29	6	3	947
Machinists					15	14	15	14	5	3	66
Miners	377	277	269	295	542	102	34	48	20	8	1,972
Motordrivers	21				28	20	8	10	4	2	93
Moulders, patternmakers	19	9	33	27	37	3	3	3	1		135
Nurses			41	36	52	40	18	6	17	3	213
Painters, plasterers, plumbers	36	45	61	49	86	10	3	3	1	2	296
Printers	17	27	35	23	14	7	4	3	1		131
Railways	32										32
Shop assistants, salesmen		77	126	103	126	85	40	46	24	6	633
Teachers			34	30	41	34	25	15	10	5	194
Textile workers, weavers	30	39	37	22	32	16	5	4	3	1	189
Empire Exhibition Scholars					12						12
Church of England Boys					52	97	149	100	96		494
Salvation Army Boys					186	138	100	88	52		564
Public school boys		8	208	157	235	16	15	6			645
NZ Sheepowners Boys and Girls					97	127	90	108	98	24	544
Miscellaneous	676	563	606	497	965	249	101	115	50	17	3,839
Wives and fiancées	1,278	1,156	1,473	1,231	1,771	521	194	191	123	34	7,972
Total	4,633	4,574	6,026	5,033	7,702	2,666	1,465	1,335	925	217	34,576

Source: AJHR, D-9, Department of Immigration Annual Reports 1923–32. Some categories have been amalgamated and minor discrepancies in the original tables corrected. Occupations recorded only for the years included.

Notes

1 New Zealand National Archives, Wellington (henceforth NA), L1, 1914/1614 pt 2, High Commissioner (HC) to Prime Minister (PM) 5 March 1919; L1, 1921/334, HC to PM 1 February, 21 March, 26 May and 10 August 1921. Many Department of Immigration files were accidentally destroyed by fire in 1952: I am grateful to NA staff, including those in the conservation section, for preparing and allowing me to use damaged material. Material from the National Archives is quoted by permission of the Director of the National Archives of New Zealand.

2 *Ibid.*, Amery to Jellicoe 17 March 1921, Churchill to Jellicoe 22 July 1922, Devonshire to Jellicoe 28 February 1923.

3 NA, PM9/5, Imperial Economic Conference 1923; NA, EA1, 158/7/1 pt 1, Imperial Conference 1926; EA1, 151/1/13, Allen to Coates 31 March, 14 and 22 April 1926.

4 NA, EA1, 59/3/201; Public Record Office, London (henceforth PRO), DO 117/84; L. S. Amery, *The Empire in the New Era*, London, 1928; Malcolm MacDonald Papers, University of Durham, box 8/2–5, 79/3 Diary 5–21 December 1934; PRO, DO 35/374/10630/29, Bledisloe to Thomas 7 January 1935.

5 For example, visits by Lord Lovat, Chairman of the OSC, 1928, NA, EA1, 158/7/1 pt 2A; and by Lord Hartington, Chairman of the Oversea Settlement Board, 1937, PRO, DO 114/89, minutes of OSB 17 February 1937.

6 Sir Henry Rider Haggard Papers on RCI Post-War Settlement Mission 1915–16, Royal Commonwealth Society Archives; C. Turnor, *Land Settlement for Ex-Service Men in the Oversea Dominions: Report to the Royal Colonial Institute*, London, 1920; NA, L1, 1921/334, EDPC to Massey 7 November 1921; L1, 1920/1771, Salvation Army Involvement in Immigration 1920–31, especially correspondence from Lamb, Head of Emigration and Colonisation Office.

7 NA, L1, 1914/1614 pt 1, HC to PM 13 October 1918; pt 2, HC to PM, 16 September 1919.

8 M. F. Lloyd Prichard, *An Economic History of New Zealand*, Auckland, 1970, p. 186.

9 *Ibid.*, pp. 209, 217.

10 J. Saxon Mills, 'Unemployment and the Empire', *Contemporary Review*, March 1922, p. 317.

11 Calculated from G. T. Bloomfield, *New Zealand: a Handbook of Historical Statistics*, Boston, 1984, p. 50 and B. R. Mitchell, *British Historical Statistics*, Cambridge, 1988, pp. 15–16.

12 For example, *North Otago Times*, 15 October 1927; PRO, CO 209/309/Gov41033, Jellicoe to Churchill, 11 July 1921, CO 532/275-Gov60555, Jellicoe to Amery, 19 November 1924.

13 NA, PM9/3, speech to British Empire Producers Organisation, 27 May 1919.

14 *The Round Table*, 16, 1925–26, p. 666.

15 Lloyd Prichard, *Economic History*, pp. 266–398; W. B. Sutch, *Poverty and Progress in New Zealand*, Wellington, 1969, pp. 197–204, 214–40; G. R. Hawke, *The Making of New Zealand: an Economic History*, Cambridge, 1985, pp. 42–102, 122–43; D. J. George, 'The Depression of 1921–22 in New Zealand', M.A. thesis, University of Auckland, 1969.

16 The only substantial extended study remains W. D. Borrie, 'Immigration to New Zealand since 1854', unpublished thesis, University of Otago, 1939; see also 'Immigration', in A. H. McLintock (ed.), *An Encyclopaedia of New Zealand*, vol. 2, Wellington, 1966, pp. 130–9.

17 J. A. Jackson, *Migration*, London, 1986, p. 62.

18 For a good study of class interests behind the management of immigration in the provincial period see L. G. Gordon, 'Immigration into Hawke's Bay 1858–1876', M.A. thesis, Victoria University of Wellington, 1965.

19 J. D. Salmond, *New Zealand Labour's Pioneering Days*, Auckland, 1950; B. Brown, *The Rise of New Zealand Labour*, Wellington, 1962; H. Roth, *Trade Unions in New Zealand: Past and Present*, Wellington, 1973; J. O. Melling, 'The New Zealand Returned Soldiers' Association 1916–1923', M.A. thesis, Victoria University of

Wellington, 1952. For the RSA's early links with labour see B. Gustafson, *Labour's Path to Political Independence*, Auckland, 1980, pp. 102–3.

30 For example, see *Trades and Labour Councils' Federation Conference Reports*, 1906, 1907, 1911, Federation of Labour Offices, Wellington; Otago Trades and Labour Council, *The Immigration Fraud*, Dunedin, 1913.

21 *Maoriland Worker*, 24 August 1921, p. 10; *The Standard*, 29 July 1936, p. 1 and 23 September 1936, p. 1; *1919 Conferences: United Federation of Labor 6th Annual Conference, New Zealand Labor Party 3rd Annual Conference*, Wellington, 1919, p. 14.

22 *The Standard*, 3 December 1936, p. 1.

23 *Maoriland Worker*, 17 March 1920, p. 4; see also 28 January 1920, p. 5, 25 August 1920, p. 7, 19 July 1922, p. 5; Canterbury Trades and Labour Council Minutes, A1(f), 31 January 1920, University of Canterbury Library; *Quick March* (RSA magazine), 10 July 1920, p. 73, 10 December 1920, p. 40.

24 *Maoriland Worker*, 11 February 1920, p. 5.

25 *Ibid.*, 25 August 1920, p. 7.

26 *New Zealand Parliamentary Debates* (henceforth *NZPD*), vol. 255, pp. 634–6, 30 August 1939 and p. 700, 31 August 1939.

27 Jim Roberts Papers, Victoria University of Wellington (henceforth Roberts Papers), D 14/1/4, *Report of Conference . . . 7–8 September 1921*; *Maoriland Worker*, 31 May 1922, p. 7; see also Roberts Papers, D 89/1, New Zealand Workers' Union, *Report of Proceedings of Sixth Annual Conference*.

28 Auckland Trade Unions' Secretaries Association Minute Book, D-14, 21 December 1925, University of Auckland Library; see also Canterbury General and Builders Labourers and Related Workers Union Minutes, 1c, 28 September 1926, University of Canterbury Library.

29 *New Zealand Worker*, 9 February 1927, p. 3, 20 April 1927, p. 1, 12 June 1927, p. 8; Roberts Papers, D 21, *Report of Open Conference*, 11 April 1927; Roberts Papers, D 89/2, New Zealand Workers' Union, *Eleventh Annual Conference*, 15 June 1927, p. 31.

30 *New Zealand Worker*, 6 July 1927, p. 11; see also speech by H. F. Holland, Labour leader of the opposition, *ibid*, 25 May 1927, p. 1.

31 *Maoriland Worker*, 7 April 1920, p. 8; *Quick March*, 11 April 1921, p. 46.

32 *Maoriland Worker*, 6 September 1922, p. 9. For a specific accusation against the publishers Whitcombe, Tombs see Otago Letterpress Machinists Union Minutes, 2 May 1921, Dunedin Public Library. See also *Trades and Labour Councils' Federation Conference Report*, 1924, p. 5; *Maoriland Worker*, 11 May 1921, p. 1; *NZPD*, vol. 191, pp. 165–6, 30 September 1921, vol. 195, p. 842, 1 August 1922; W. Nash, 'Immigration, occupation and the land', *The New Zealand Highway*, 2, 10 August 1927, p. 8.

33 *Maoriland Worker*, 4 May 1921, p. 2; W. E. A. Student, 'Economic waste in immigration', *The New Zealand Highway*, 2, 11 July 1927, p. 13; A. Owen and J. Perkins, *Speaking for Ourselves*, Auckland, 1986, pp. 78–9; George, 'Depression of 1921–22', pp. 183–4. There was some official evidence to suggest by 1929 that unemployment was higher among New Zealand-born than among immigrants: *Appendices to the Journals of the House of Representatives* (henceforth *AJHR*), H-11B, 1929, Unemployment in New Zealand.

34 *Maoriland Worker*, 17 March 1920, p. 4; see also 15 September 1920, pp. 8–9.

35 *Ibid.*, 5 October 1921, p. 2; see also 3 May 1922, p. 2 and *New Zealand Worker*, 9 February 1927, p. 4 and 16 March 1927, p. 4.

36 Canterbury Trades and Labour Council Minutes, A1(f), 8 October 1921; see also *Maoriland Worker*, 7 April 1920, p. 8 and 4 May 1921, p. 2.

37 *Ibid.*, 17 August 1921, p. 2; see also 24 August 1921, p. 10, 24 May 1922, p. 4, 22 November 1922, p. 4; *New Zealand Worker*, 5 January 1927, p. 4. Holland complained in Parliament that this was happening in the coal mines of South Island, *NZPD*, vol. 193, p. 264, 11 January 1922.

38 *Maoriland Worker*, 31 March 1920, p. 7; and see 4 August 1920, p. 4. Contemporary

records were inconsistent, using either the spelling 'Labour' or 'Labor'.

39 *Ibid.*, 11 May 1921, p. 3. The matter was raised in the House of Commons, Hansard, *Parliamentary Debates*, vol. 141, cols 1195–6, 5 May 1921.

40 *New Zealand Worker*, 19 January 1927, p. 5 and 27 April 1927, p. 3; Roberts Papers, D 21, *Report of Open Conference*, 11 April 1927, pp. 10, 24; Labour Party Archives, London, British Commonwealth Labour Conference Correspondence 1923–24, BCLC 24/7, Paper for 17 September 1924 meeting, Nash to Henderson 17 February 1923; Trades Union Congress Archives, London, T 146, file Migration Documents, British Commonwealth Labour Conference, Agenda Item No. 1, Emigration, communications from Nash, 26 May and 23 June 1925 and from Roberts 13 May 1925.

41 Otago Letterpress Machinists Union Minutes, 2 May 1921; Trades Union Congress Archives, London, T 322, file 993.1 New Zealand Correspondence, J. Moulton, Secretary Amalgamated Society of Carpenters and Joiners' Industrial Union of Workers, Wellington, 2 February 1937.

42 NA, Nash Papers, 7/0028-43; *The Press* (Christchurch), 18 September 1923, p. 12; *New Zealand Times* (Wellington), 18 September 1923, p. 5. For the *Report of the British Oversea Settlement Delegates to New Zealand – 1923* see British Parliamentary Papers, Cmd. 2167, XI, 1924.

43 *Maoriland Worker*, 26 May 1920, p. 2, 27 April 1921, p. 2, 6 September 1922, p. 8; *Auckland Star*, 13 July 1921, p. 7; *Quick March*, 11 July 1921, p. 49; Canterbury Trades and Labour Council Minutes, A1(g), 12 June and 16 October 1926; *Trades and Labour Councils' Federation Conference Report*, 15 April 1927; *New Zealand Worker*, 27 April 1927, p. 3; Reform Party, *Reform's Record and Achievements*, Wellington, 1922, pp. 76–80; Reform Party, *Sixteen Years' Progress*, Wellington, 1928, pp. 93–4.

44 Auckland District Branch of the New Zealand Amalgamated Society of Carpenters and Joiners Council Minutes, D-31 Box 1, 16 September 1936, and Auckland Trades and Labour Council minutes, D-30, 22 August 1935, University of Auckland Library; NA, L1, 22/1/3 pt 1, Mrs T. Harris, Women's Auxiliary National Unemployed Workers Movement, to PM 28 February 1937; New Zealand Federation of Labour, *Second Annual Report of National Executive 1939*, p. 4, Federation of Labour Offices, Wellington.

45 NA, Nash Papers, 7/0037, statement by Roberts; similarly 7/0040, statement by secretary of the Boot Operatives Union.

46 *Maoriland Worker*, 16 August 1922, p. 5.

47 *New Zealand Worker*, 8 June 1927, p. 4; see also *The Standard*, 18 November 1936, p. 16.

48 *New Zealand Worker*, 7 December 1927, p. 1.

49 *Quick March*, 10 February 1921, p. 41; see also 10 February 1920, p. 43; *NZPD*, vol. 214, p. 299, 22 September 1927; *New Zealand Worker*, 23 March 1927, p. 12.

50 P. W. G. McAra Papers, A-139, Box 26, Series 10/1, *Labour's Plan*, April 1933, University of Auckland Library; *The Standard*, 22 January 1936, p. 6; New Zealand Labour Party, *1938 General Election Manifesto*, pp. 11–12; New Zealand Labour Party, *Twenty-Third Annual Conference*, 1939, p. 14; New Zealand Federation of Labour, *News Bulletin*, August 1938, p. 2.

51 But see the campaign of the Labour MP W. E. Barnard, founder of the Five Million Club, *Evening News*, 19 March 1937, 2 June 1938, Press cuttings collection, Migration, Press House, Wellington.

52 NA, L1, 1920/1649, Association of New Zealand Chambers of Commerce to Minister of Immigration, 28 May 1920; see also *ibid.*, 20 January 1926.

53 *Association of New Zealand Chambers of Commerce/Associated Chambers of Commerce of New Zealand Annual Conference Reports*, 1922–25, 1937–38.

54 *Wellington Chamber of Commerce Annual Reports/Yearbook/Annual*, 1922–23, 1926, 1936, 1939, 1940; NA, L1, 1920/1649, Wellington Chamber of Commerce to PM 2 June 1923, and DSA to Under-Secretary for Immigration, 1 February 1926 and subsequent papers; DSA, *New Zealand for the Britisher: a Vital Empire Question*, Wellington, 1925.

55 *Auckland Provincial Employers' Association Annual Report*, 12 September 1918, p. 21; *The New Zealand Journal of Commerce*, 15 August 1921, p. 1 and see 15 June 1922, p. 1; *Commerce Journal*, 15 February 1937, p. 13, 15 March 1937, p. 22, 25 August 1938, p. 15, 25 July 1939, p. 15; see also *New Zealand Masters' and Employers' Journal* (Auckland), August 1918, p. 4.

56 Dunedin Chamber of Commerce, *Annual Reports*, 1918, p. 20, 1922, p. 15, 1923, p. 16, 1924, p. 16, 1937, p. 21, Hocken Library; *ibid.*, Minutes of Council OCC/3/4, 15 November 1920, 18 September 1922; OCC/3/5, 14 April 1924; OCC/3/7, 20 October 1936, 17 November 1936; Otago Employers Assocation Minute Books. MS 1041/4, 17 September 1920, 22 March 1921, Hocken Library; *Otago Expansion League Annual Report*, 1924, p. 10, Hocken Library; Otago Expansion League, *To Intending Emigrants*, Dunedin, c. 1919; Canterbury Progress League Records, Canterbury Public Library; Canterbury Progress League, *Canterbury – New Zealand*, Christchurch, c. 1921; Nelson Progress League, *The Book of Sunny Nelson*, Nelson, 1925.

57 For example, DSA, *New Zealand for the Britisher*, p. 6; New Zealand Farmers' Union President's Address, Annual Conference 28 July 1925, pp. 1–3.

58 For example, *Commerce Journal*, 26 April 1937, p. 1.

59 For example, Otago Expansion League, *Central Otago: the Land of Promise*, Dunedin, 1925.

60 Lloyd Prichard, *Economic History*, p. 319; R. J. W. Neville and C. J. O'Neill, *The Population of New Zealand: Interdisciplinary Perspectives*, Auckland, 1979, pp. 5–8.

61 *Associated Chambers of Commerce of New Zealand Annual Conference Report*, 1937, p. 32, 1938, pp. 16–19; *Commerce Journal*, 25 August 1938, p. 15; *NZPD*, vol. 248, pp. 365–6; A. E. Mander, *To Alarm New Zealand*, Wellington, 1936.

62 Kaiapoi Woollen Manufacturing Company Ltd, Minutes of Meetings of Directors, A6, Annual Meeting 27 August 1920, Frostick's address, University of Canterbury Library; *New Zealand Masters' and Employers' Journal*, 12 June 1919, p. 2; *NZPD*, vol. 195, p. 849, 1 August 1922, vol. 255, p. 363, 17 August 1939; *The Country*, 20 January 1923, pp. 8–9.

63 *The Dominion* (Wellington), editorial, 17 October 1923; *NZPD*, vol. 242, p. 245, 11 September 1935, vol. 249, p. 19, 2 November 1937; *Associated Chambers of Commerce of New Zealand Annual Conference Report*, 1937, p. 34, 1938, p. 16.

64 *Report to the President of the Oversea Settlement Committee of the Delegates Appointed to Enquire as to Openings in New Zealand for Women from the United Kingdom*, British Parliamentary Papers, Cmd. 933, XXII, 1920, p. 4.

65 *NZPD*, vol. 189, p. 1022, addendum October–November 1920, vol. 251, p. 337, 8 July 1938; *The Press*, 16 February 1921, p. 6; PRO, CO 209/301/Gov 68550, Liverpool to Milner, 4 October 1919.

66 NA, L1, 22/1/4, Notes of Meeting: deputation to Fraser and Armstrong, 18 February 1938; L1, 22/1/3 pt 1, Notes of Meeting: deputation to Savage, 25 November 1938; see also *NZPD*, vol. 186, pp. 693–4, 27 July 1920 and vol. 255, p. 363, 17 August 1939.

67 Lloyd Prichard, *Economic History*, pp. 270, 322. For urbanisation see C. Gibson, 'Urbanization in New Zealand: a comparative analysis', *Demography*, 10, 1973, pp. 71–84, and for industrialisation see Hawke, *Making of New Zealand*, pp. 42–56 and C. A. Blyth, 'The industrialisation of New Zealand', *New Zealand Economic Papers*, 8, 1974, pp. 1–22.

68 Hawke, *Making of New Zealand*, graph on p. 102.

69 New Zealand Employers' Federation Minute Books, 29 October 1919, NZEF offices Wellington; similarly *New Zealand Capital and Labour Review*, 28 December 1918, p. 4.

70 *New Zealand Times*, 23 February 1923, p. 4; also report of Canterbury Industrial Association in *The Press*, 18 September 1923, p. 12.

71 *Lyttleton Times*, 30 May 1923, cutting in NA, IC1, 20/86. The efforts of the Kaiapoi Woollen Company to recruit labour in the United Kingdom may be traced in the Minutes of Meetings of Directors, University of Canterbury Library.

72 *NZPD*, vol. 255, pp. 595–6, 24 August 1939. Shortages of labour are also recorded in

the records and reports of the Otago Employers' Association and Dunedin Manufacturers' Association, Hocken Library, and of the Auckland Provincial Employers' Association and New Zealand Ironmasters Federation, University of Auckland Library.

73 NA, ICI,20/86, Collins to Under-Secretary Immigration Department, 3 October 1921; see also ICI,31/140, Annual Conference of NZ Manufacturers' Federation, 27 February 1929, remit from Auckland, and ICI,31/140/1, Notes of Deputation from Auckland Manufacturers' Association, 24 March 1939.

74 For example, *Auckland Provincial Employers' Association Annual Report*, 12 September 1918.

75 *New Zealand National Review*, 15 December 1935, pp. 52–3; see also 15 February 1937, p. 13 and *NZPD*, vol. 255, pp. 588–9, 24 August 1939.

76 For example, Kaiapoi Woollen Company Minutes, A8, speech by chairman to shareholders, 31 August 1927; *Auckland Provincial Industrial Association Annual Report*, 26 May 1926, p. 12, Auckland Public Library; *New Zealand National Review*, 15 February 1937, p. 11.

77 *Ibid.*, 15 April 1925, p. 27.

78 *Ibid.*, p. 23.

79 NA, IC1,31/140/1, proofs of *Auckland Manufacturers' Association Golden Jubilee Booklet*.

80 *Auckland Provincial Employers' Association Annual Report*, 12 September 1918, p. 22.

81 Arthur Fraser in *Evening Post*, 3 March 1937, Press cuttings collection; see also A. Fraser, *A Case for Immigration*, Wellington, 1936.

82 R. J. Bremer, 'The New Zealand Farmers' Union as an Interest Group: some Aspects of Farm Politics, 1918–1928', M.A. thesis, Victoria University of Wellington, 1966; T. W. H. Brooking, 'Agrarian Businessmen Organise: a Comparative Study of the Origins and Early Phase of Development of the National Farmers' Union of England and Wales and the New Zealand Farmers' Union, 1900–1929', Ph.D. thesis, University of Otago, 1978.

83 NA, L1,1921/334, deputation about Maraetai and Matarawa lands, 16 August 1923; *The Country* (official organ of Auckland Farmers' Union), 20 January 1923, pp. 8–9, 20 February 1923, p. 13, 20 October 1922, pp. 10–11, 20 August 1924, p. 7; NA, EA1,158/7/1 pt 1; A. Leigh Hunt, 'New Zealand's Latent Wealth – National Development Scheme', January 1923; *Dunedin Chamber of Commerce Annual Report*, 1927, p. 28; *Evening Post*, 13 June 1934, Waikato Land Settlement Society, Press cuttings collection. The opposition Liberal party in the 1920s especially emphasised sub-division and land settlement to encourage immigration: *New Zealand Times*, 11 July 1923, p. 6, 21 September 1923, p. 4.

84 For example, see defeat of land settlement motion at Annual Conference of Associated Chambers of Commerce of New Zealand, *Report*, 1926, and *Farming First* (official organ of Auckland Farmers' Union), 25 June 1937, p. 25.

85 *The Country*, 20 February 1925, p. 14.

86 *Ibid.*, 20 October 1923, p. 10; similarly 20 September 1923, pp. 12–13, 20 March 1924, p. 14, 20 June 1924, p. 8.

87 *Farming First*, 10 August 1926, p. 17.

88 *Ibid.*, 10 August 1927, p. 14. For the Country Party see B. D. Graham, 'The Country Party idea in New Zealand politics, 1901–1935', in R. Chapman and K. Sinclair (eds), *Studies of a Small Democracy*, Auckland, 1963, pp. 175–200.

89 *New Zealand Farmers' Union Annual Dominion Conference Report*, July 1936, pp. 14–15, General Assembly Library, Wellington; see also motions proposed at the Women's Division NZ Farmers' Union, *Conference Report*, 1936, pp. 9, 12; *Farming First*, 15 November 1935, p. 4, 25 April 1936, p. 3, 25 May 1936, p. 4, 25 January 1937, p. 8, 25 May 1937, p. 9; *Point Blank* (official organ of the NZ Farmers' Union), 15 January 1936, p. 30, Federated Farmers of New Zealand Offices, Wellington.

90 NA, L1,1920/2739. In practice, the head of the Child Welfare Department claimed, farmers 'are able to obtain the services of immigrant lads for less than the usual

wages': NA, CW40, 57/-, memo by Strong, 15 September 1928.

91 NA, L1,22/1/3 pt 1, NZ Farmers' Union to Acting PM, 25 May 1937; see also *Point Blank*, 15 June 1937, p. 19, 15 July 1937, p. 63.

92 *Farming First*, 25 April 1938, p. 8.

93 *Ibid.*, 10 December 1927, p. 11.

94 *New Zealand Farmers' Union Annual Conference Report*, President's Address, 28 July 1925, p. 12.

95 The quotation was from J. A. Froude.

96 *The Farmers' Weekly*, 18 April 1925, pp. 6–7.

97 *Ibid.*, p. 7 and 23 May 1925, p. 27; see also 20 September 1924, p. 10, 18 October 1924, p. 37 and *Auckland Weekly News*, 27 September 1923, p. 23.

98 *The Round Table*, 12, 1921–22, p. 917; similarly *The New Zealand Journal of Commerce*, 15 August 1921, p. 1.

99 *The Country*, 20 September 1923, p. 20.

100 NA, EA1,59/3/201, pt 1, *The Dominion*, 29 November 1927.

101 Oversea Settlement Department, *Handbook on the Dominion of New Zealand*, London, 1926, pp. 18–19. Between 1931 and 1936 a further Immigration Restriction Amendment Act limited the right of entry of even British citizens, particularly unemployed Australians. References in support of a 'White New Zealand' policy especially immediately after the First World War are legion in the records of trade unions, *Quick March* and *NZPD*. See also F. A. Ponton, 'Immigration Restriction in New Zealand: a Study of Policy from 1908 to 1939', M.A. thesis, Victoria University of Wellington, 1946; P. S. O'Connor, 'Keeping New Zealand white, 1908–20', *New Zealand Journal of History*, 2, 1968, pp. 41–65; G. R. Warburton, 'The Attitudes and Policies of the New Zealand Labour Movement towards Non-European Immigration, 1878–1928', M.A. thesis, University of Canterbury, 1982.

102 NA, L1,1914/1614 pt 1, HC to PM, 13 October 1918 and reply 22 November 1918. The pre-war programme, launched in 1904 and analysed in J. S. McBean, 'Immigration into New Zealand 1900 to 1915', M.A. thesis, Victoria University of Wellington, 1946, had been virtually suspended during the war, see *AJHR*, D-9, Department of Immigration Annual Reports 1915–19.

103 NA, L1,1914/1614 pt 1, Thomson, Chief Immigration Officer, to Minister of Immigration, 12 March 1919; Thomson memo. 3 February 1919; cable to HC, 17 April 1919.

104 *Ibid.*, HC to PM, 5 March 1919, reply 13 March 1919, HC's cable 11 April 1919, reply 29 April 1919. For the operation of the scheme see L1,1920/533, HC to PM and subsequent correspondence.

105 Negotiations, and the Audit Office memo of 16 January 1923, may be traced in NA, L1,1921/334; also see PRO, CO 532/209/Gov43604 and subsequent files and CO 886/10 Confidential Print Doms No. 89.

106 NA, EA1,158/7/1 pt 1, memo by Thomson with letter of 13 August 1926; L1,22/1/1, Immigration Agreements, memo for Minister of Immigration, 4 December 1935.

107 *AJHR*, D-9, Department of Immigration Annual Report 1914, p. 2; Emigrants' Information Office, *New Zealand Handbook*, London, 1914, pp. 26–7.

108 NA, L1,1914/1614 pt 1, cable to HC, 22 November 1918; *ibid.*, pt 2, Bell to HC, 13 March, 10 April, 5 and 10 May 1919; L1,1920/533, Thomson to Nosworthy, 4 August 1920; L1,1921/334, memo from Audit Office, 16 January 1923. Examples of assisted domestic servants may be found among the few surviving personal records in L1, box 127, Schedules of Nominated Immigrants 1923. See also a useful short study by L. B. Davis, 'An examination of the New Zealand Government's scheme of Assisted Immigration for Domestic Servants in the 1920s', M.A. research essay, University of Auckland, 1973.

109 McBean, 'Immigration', pp. 37, 59, 75.

110 PRO, DO 35/48/Gov5935, Fergusson to Amery, 26 April 1928.

111 *New Zealand Times*, 6 December 1919, p. 5.

112 NA, L9, Accession 1232; *AJHR*, D-9, Department of Immigration Annual Report 1921, p. 1.

113 The system was explained in *AJHR*, D-9, Department of Immigration Annual Report 1921, p. 1; see also NA, ICI,20/86, Thomson to Department of Industries and Commerce, 11 October 1921. For examples of industrialists using the system see NA, L1, box 127, Schedules of Nominated Immigrants 1923 and *The Press*, 16 January 1924, p. 8.

114 *AJHR*, D-9, Department of Immigration Annual Report 1927, p. 2. For Massey's preference see W. J. Gardner, the *Farmer Politician in New Zealand History*, Massey Memorial Lecture, Palmerston North, 1970, p. 10. See also G. Warren Russell, Minister of Internal Affairs, *New Zealand Today*, Christchurch, 1919, pp. 165–7: 'The fiat to Adam was: "Go forth and replenish the earth and subdue it".'

115 NA, L1,1914/1614 pt 2, Thomson to Minister of Immigration, 3 February 1919; L1,1921/334, Allen to PM, 21 March 1921; PRO, CO 532/211/Gov4212, Jellicoe to Devonshire, 14 December 1922 and minutes; William Downie Stewart Papers, Hocken Library, MS 985 series 1, Coates to Amery, 22 May 1926. See also J. M. Powell, 'Soldier Settlement in New Zealand 1915–23', *Australian Geographical Studies*, 9, 1971, pp. 144–60 and A. Maloney, 'A Land Fit for Heroes: the Otago Experience of the National Soldier Settlement Scheme after World War One', B.A. long essay, University of Otago, 1982.

116 NA, L1,1914/1614, pt 1, cable to HC, 22 November 1918; *ibid.*, pt 2, Bell to HC, 13 March 1919; L1,1920/533, cable to HC, 21 October 1921; L1,1921/334, memo from Audit Office, 16 January 1923.

117 *AJHR*, D-9, Department of Immigration Annual Reports from 1924; PRO, DO 35/36/Doms OSD 1149 for British Empire Exhibition Boys; NA, L1, box 128 for Reports on Farm Boys 1926; L1,1920/1771 and AGR40,1962/60C for Salvation Army scheme; AGR40,1937/33B and CW3,2/11 and Nash Papers 1443/0069 for New Zealand Sheepowners' operations.

118 NA, L1,1921/334, memo from Audit Office, 16 January 1923.

119 *New Zealand Worker*, 16 March 1927, p. 1; similarly *Associated Chambers of Commerce of New Zealand Annual Report*, 1925, p. 31, speech by Immigration Department Under-Secretary.

120 NA, L1,1920/533, Thomson memos 4 August 1920 and 15 March 1921. For the effect on one migrant and his family see the papers of Alfred Rose, especially letter from HC, 10 May 1921: I am grateful to Mr Eric Rose of Stokes Valley, Hutt, for his courtesy in allowing me to see this material, copies now in NA.

121 *NZPD*, vol. 195, p. 652, 25 July 1922.

122 Ministerial concern about 'excess' immigration and the Labour Party's exploitation of the issue was first expressed in November 1926, Downie Stewart Papers, Stewart to Coates, 9 November 1926; a reduction except for juveniles, farm labourers and domestics was announced in February 1927, *The Press*, 17 February 1927; further cuts, sparing domestics was announced in September 1927, *NZPD*, vol. 214, pp. 374–5, 23 September 1927; and assistance for domestics was discontinued on 31 March 1931, *NZPD*, vol. 228, p. 206, 3 July 1931, leaving only a handful of separated families to be helped thereafter. Widespread support for the cuts is recorded in the press, see cuttings in NA, EA1,158/7/1 pt 2A, in the *Associated Chambers of Commerce of New Zealand Annual Conference Report*, 1927, by the National Industrial Conference (of employers and trade unionists) in *Report of Proceedings*, Wellington, 1928, p. 359, and by the Governor-General in his dispatches to the Dominions Office, for example, PRO, DO 35/24/GovNZ5948, 28 April 1927.

123 PRO, DO 35/48/GovNZ2266, Fergusson to Amery, 26 January 1928; the message was endorsed in subsequent dispatches in 1928 and 1929.

124 *NZPD*, vol. 243, p. 1, 27 September 1935.

125 Parties of skilled craftsmen needed for the government's house-building programme were encouraged to immigrate but at their own expense, NA, L1,5/3/15 and *Evening News*, 29 June, 28 July, 12 and 24 August 1939, Press cuttings collection.

126 *The Standard*, 3 December 1936, p. 1; see also correspondence and response to deputations 1937–9 in NA, ICI,20/86; L1,22/1/3 pt 1; L1,22/1/4; also PRO, DO 114/89, minutes of meetings of Oversea Settlement Board, Nash, 1 December 1936,

and Savage, 17 June 1937.
127 Mysteriously, figures for ex-servicemen and Empire Settlement migrants taken from New Zealand official reports differ from those published by the Oversea Settlement Committee and cited elsewhere in this book.
128 Including 4,503 selected between 1922 and 1932 under the special scheme for women domestic servants; *AJHR*, D-9, Department of Immigration Annual Reports 1922–32.

CHAPTER SEVEN

'Leaven for the lump':
Canada and Empire settlement, 1918–1939

John A. Schultz

Canada proved at best a reluctant partner in Empire settlement. Few in Ottawa shared Amery's vision of a Greater Empire through emigration. Although the country had historically depended on a steady influx of immigrants to take up land and develop its economy, immigration had always been highly controversial.[1] Desirable as it might be in principle, the practical result frequently prompted dismay and second thoughts. Empire settlement would be no different. 'Nothing new', observed a laconic Commissioner of Immigration when details of the British proposals reached his desk in 1921.[2] His comment would prove prescient. Before it died in the depression of the 1930s, Empire settlement would arouse the hopes of those who saw in it the means to ensure the predominance of British values in Canadian society, and the hostility of those who cavilled at the idea that the dominion should become a dumping ground for the unfit on the pretext of patriotism. At the United Kingdom's prompting, Canada would participate, but never wholeheartedly. In the end, imperial patriotism flagged in the face of growing problems.

Obstacles

From a Canadian point of view, the timing of the new scheme was less than auspicious. For much of the late nineteenth century, the new dominion had struggled to attract enough immigrants to take up its empty western lands. Handicapped by climate and competition from the United States of America, the country turned eventually to Eastern Europe where, under the energetic direction of Clifford Sifton, vast numbers of 'sturdy peasants in sheepskin coats' were recruited. The rush of new faces in the decade before the First World War prompted vocal complaints. The strangers drifted into city slums; took jobs from native Canadians; constituted an undigestible lump of population; polluted the country's racial stock. Government officials, originally hired to encourage immigration gradually came to see it as a 'problem', best dealt with by restricting further entry as much as possible. Their efforts, together with the outbreak of war in 1914, reduced immigration to a trickle; post-war depression and dislocation coupled with the problems of soldier resettlement discouraged any resumption of recruitment.[3]

Conversely, the war had also stimulated feelings of imperial patriotism and aroused a sense of Empire solidarity. Both the war and the post-war 'Red scare' focused attention on the foreign-born. Many were beginning to suspect what census data would subsequently confirm – that the percentage of Canadians of British background had slipped to less than half the population – and agreed with Prime Minister Borden that Canada's 'capacity for assimilating people whose conception of government is often strangely inconsistent with our institutions and traditions' had been reached. Canada's vast empty spaces demanded an active immigration policy, but one which recognised the problems posed by the large number of aliens.[4] By adding a generous leaven of British stock the unassimilated lump of non-Anglo-Saxons could be absorbed and 'Canadianised'. Only in this way could the dominion fulfil its destiny as the future home of a true imperial race.[5]

In short, Canadians were of two minds about the desirability of immigration, something that became apparent as word of the Imperial government's decision to initiate a large-scale policy of state-assisted settlement within the Empire began to spread. Officialdom was unenthusiastic. Assisted settlement and colonisation of one kind or another, sponsored by companies or individuals with government guarantees, had been tried regularly in the years before 1900 when Canada had been attempting to attract immigrants. 'You will recall,' the Commissioner of Immigration reminded the Deputy Minister, 'that these schemes were not a success'; moreover, 'the majority of the groups . . . were made up of people from Great Britain'.[6] The explanation was simple. Intending emigrants who needed a handout were obviously failures, very likely to fail again; assisted schemes by their nature delivered a poor class of low-quality stock. In the officials' view, Empire settlement was wrong in principle: it 'would produce a great many settlers who are not likely to make a success on the land and who would give our country a black eye'.[7]

The only official to consider the proposal on its possible merits appears to have been R. H. Coates of the Dominion Bureau of Statistics. Coates attempted to analyse whether the United Kingdom could, in fact, supply the population, capital and markets Canada needed, in an effort to determine whether, therefore, Empire settlement was worth pursuing either as a practical proposition or as a way of securing the imperial tie. In theory at least, he concluded, it seemed viable: the

United Kingdom had sufficient surplus labour to make good Canada's projected shortfall; adequate capital to meet Canada's expected requirements in employing that labour would be generated by the British economy. Moreover, the increase in the production of foodstuffs and other commodities which the combination of capital and labour would generate could be absorbed by the British market. In sum, the scheme appeared to be statistically sensible, with much to recommend it.[8]

None of this much impressed Coates's colleagues in the permanent civil service, who regarded the British proposals as hopelessly grandiose. 'Immigration on a vast scale', argued one, 'is neither possible nor desirable':

> If we get and absorb . . . 8,000 a year . . . we shall do very well. . . . In the past we have brought into this country immigrants by the hundred thousand only to discover at the next census that they had all vanished. We must build solidly for the future, and disregard paper schemes for the transfer of millions from the United Kingdom.[9]

Paper statistics were in any case beside the point: the fact was that the dominion lands theoretically available were not suitable for settlement by 'people from overseas'; only experienced western pioneers could hope to succeed. Moreover, what would westerners currently having a hard time of it think of a system of financial assistance for these newcomers? And what of Canadians who might like a subsidy to go on the land? In all likelihood, an influx of assisted settlers from the United Kingdom would have the undesirable consequence of driving native Canadians out, probably as emigrants to the United States of America. 'Plus', added one bureaucrat, 'there is the headache of getting all the provinces to agree.' The proposal for child migration held some promise – more, at any rate, than adult immigration – but otherwise the scheme had little to recommend it.[10]

These doubts and suspicions were shared by the bureaucrats' political masters. From the perspective of Parliament Hill, investing in Empire settlement subsidies looked like a way of buying trouble, something the ruling Liberals under Prime Minister Mackenzie King made it a habit to avoid. Never a visionary, King's natural inertia was reinforced in this case by both the attitude of the bureaucrats and the advice of political confidants. P. C. Larkin, King's long-time mentor, wrote from London that personally he had 'grave doubts' that emigrants of the sort proposed would do well in Canada or take to farm life; King should go slow. The British needed the scheme far more than Canada, and were prepared to go to any lengths to promote it.[11] Politically dependent on the western Progressive party for his hold on power, King was inclined to be careful.

Participating in the settlement plan would cost money, at a time when practical politics meant guarding the porkbarrel. 'Please do not forget', cautioned Cabinet colleagues, 'the attitude of our supporters whom we are unable to satisfy when the question of giving large grants for this, that, and the other indefensible purpose is under discussion.'[12] Moreover, within his own caucus many were suspicious if not aggressively hostile towards anything that smacked of old-fashioned imperialism. Empire settlement, in this view, was another plot 'designed to establish plantations of Imperialist settlers in different parts of the dominion who may serve future Imperialist plans . . .' or, alternatively, 'another game to dump upon Canada a number of people who will become a charge on the Canadian public'.[13] Canada had had an earlier experience with 'remittance men', and their 'superior insolence' still rankled:

> British Columbia is suffering from the presence of a large number of Englishmen, who are unemployed, who do not want to work, and who take the superior attitude that this country owes them a living. . . . you will recall that when we were discussing unemployment relief, our colleague from Alberta told us that fully 98% of the inmates of the Unemployment Relief Station at Edmonton during the winter of 1921 and 1922 were Englishmen. It is, therefore, the part of wisdom not to add to the number of these people by furnishing means for men of their class to come to Canada.[14]

Clifford Sifton, the well-known architect of pre-war western settlement, rejoined the fray by denouncing Empire settlement as a 'crime against Canada'. The leading Liberal newspaper, the Toronto *Globe*, echoed these sentiments, condemning the 'dumping' of British workers into Canadian cities where many were already unemployed as 'criminal folly'. According to the editor, the best 'assistance' the Canadian government could give to intending British immigrants would be to ensure they got a square deal in purchasing land:

> This country has been built up largely by the energy and enterprise of immigrants . . . who put their own savings into the adventure. . . . Canadians will continue to welcome . . . workers of the United Kingdom who come to the new land as they themselves or their fathers came in other days. But they assuredly do not favour the granting of assistance from the Dominion Treasury to these new home seekers.[15]

Whitehall was well aware of these reservations. Amery attempted repeatedly to allay Canadian suspicions and to encourage Canada's wholehearted participation. He tried especially to scotch the idea that the United Kingdom was bent on dumping its unwanted population on the dominions. Empire settlement, he argued, was not merely a matter of shifting surplus labour, though certainly a better distribution of population within the Empire promised to solve many problems including trade and defence. Instead, he assured King, assisted emigration was a means of nation-building, of enriching spiritual growth by common endeavour, and developing healthy citizenship.[16] As for the charge that assisted migrants were automatically undesirables, Amery denied it absolutely:

> One of the features which differentiates the migration situation to-day from that before the war is . . . the cost of passages. Before the war the Atlantic passage was a mere trifle . . . and most decent working men could without difficulty afford to pay their passages themselves. In fact the presumption was that men who could not find their cost of transportation to Canada probably belonged to the unemployable sediment which always exists at the bottom of a big industrial population, and your Government took the very natural line of discouraging assisted migration.
>
> To-day the ocean passage alone costs £17 . . . . Further the unemployed of to-day who cannot produce money towards their transportation include . . . something like a million of fit, healthy, vigorous young men, most of them with good war service to their credit, who would make good citizens and good workers on the land if only they got their chance.[17]

If the immigrants were properly selected for character, and adequate housing and training provided, he argued, the problems in the past – especially the drift of workers back to the towns – could be easily avoided. Ironically, he added, the only objection raised to the bill in the British House of Commons was the charge that the United Kingdom was encouraging its best to go to the dominions and leaving itself with only the worst.[18]

King remained unpersuaded. To placate Amery and appease imperial sentiment in Canada, he made reassuring noises about the government's 'genuine desire' to pursue 'an active policy' which would 'aid in the solution of the distribution of population in a manner which would serve the highest ends of British citizenship'.[19] Meanwhile, he cast around for palatable alternatives, preferably ones which did not require government sponsorship. The terms of the Empire Settlement Act left the door open to the participation of private organisations. J. A. Robb, the Minister of Immigration, thought that perhaps men like Sir Joseph Flavelle of Toronto and Charles Gordon of Montreal might be interested in forming a private loan company which would acquire land and issue low-interest loans to British settlers, the scheme to be financed by British government guaranteed bonds issued against the land. The United Kingdom would save on dole payments, and the Liberals would be safely at arm's length. Alternatively, the Ontario Association of Boards of Trade suggested tinkering with the income tax act: suitable adjustments might attract a stream of 'fairly well-off' migrants from the

United Kingdom's moneyed classes who would put their funds into developing Canada. If British immigration was to be encouraged, why opt for the unemployed residue?[20] Or there was the Western Canada Colonization Association, organised by land speculators and railway companies and promoted by long-time Liberal J. S. Willison. King was eventually persuaded to endorse the association on the strict condition that 'the government of Canada accepted no responsibility for its undertakings', but he remained wary. Whatever the political attractions of rewarding one's friends while keeping an official distance, the proposals all stood for 'the kind of patriotism which means profits to private citizens' which in turn meant a potential for scandal. Plus, 'there is always the danger, in immigration matters, of a class of settlers being landed in the country who are not wholly suitable, but who are brought in in order that nominal conditions surrounding Government subsidies and grants may be fulfilled'.[21]

In the end, the King government agreed to participate in Empire settlement, but only reluctantly and only after lengthy negotiations. Under the terms of the draft agreements signed in April 1923, Canada would offer limited assistance to three classes of intending British migrants: household workers; agricultural workers nominated by a Canadian farmer; and children between eight and fourteen years of age sponsored by an established voluntary society.[22] The child migrants would be subsidised by a direct grant of $40, but all other assistance was to take the form of 'passage loans', of which half would be advanced by each government. To qualify, the immigrant or nominator would have to contribute 'substantially' to the costs of fares. Immigrants were expected to begin work within a week of their arrival and to pledge to stay in Canada for at least a year (or until the loan was repaid). The Minister of Finance earmarked $600,000 in the Estimates to cover the advances, and arranged with the chartered banks to handle the repayments.[23] It was an unenthusiastic, niggardly response, far short of Amery's grand vision.

That much was clear early on, when the Canadians refused to consider increasing the passage money for child migrants and balked at Whitehall's attempts to open the door a bit wider by working around the Canadian demand that would-be agriculturalists and domestics put up at least one-quarter of the costs themselves:

> concerning nominated passages it appearing majority cannot provide missing twenty-five percent transportation cost what sum would Canada guarantee towards their settlement supervising if Imperial Government furnished missing twenty-five percent transportation by grant?[24]

Ottawa's reaction, typical of the unenthusiastic attitude of Immigration Branch officials, held out little hope for flexibility:

> the possession of some funds on the part of an immigrant, is to an extent a guarantee of industrial fitness. If he lives on the verge of poverty and has nothing, it may indicate, not that he has been out of employment but that he is industrially unfit. It would not be any blessing to Canada or the British Government to step in in such cases and make a grant . . . . The amount of money proposed for expenditure this year on nominated passages is not very great and we can get some who will be able to contribute a part towards their passage.

As for settlement, the presumption was that 'there will be some friend or relative who will offer a home and employment'; Canadian officials did not propose to invest much time or effort in supervision.[25] London was advised that, owing to 'public opinion', nominated passage would be confined to 'those who themselves or their friends [are] able to contribute substantially twenty five percent cost'. 'So far', lamented the Chairman of the Oversea Settlement Committee, 'Canada has shown small disposition to co-operate, and the schemes concluded with her are very negligible.'[26]

The administration of even these limited arrangements proved equally disappointing. The summer shipping season slid away and with it any chance of recruiting substantial numbers; meanwhile little was done. Of the $600,000 allocated for Empire settlement in 1923, only a little more than one-third had been spent by the year's end, the bulk of it on children and domestics; only a tiny fraction, $38,000, was loaned to assist British men and their families make a new start.[27] The relative handful of Empire settlers compared to the more than 50,000 Europeans arriving the same year prompted T. C. Macnaghten to comment bitterly that for all the talk of imperial ties Canada obviously wanted 'hewers of wood and drawers of water' to do the rough work, not British farmers.[28] Canadian officials offered a variety of excuses, including 'unsettled conditions', the lack of administrative machinery in some provinces, and the potential problems in keeping track of large numbers of young boys and girls. Privately, however, the same officials acknowledged their unwillingness to pursue the programme vigorously in view of what they construed as a lack of unanimous support:

> so far as I can recall there has never been a year when there has been so much discussion of Immigration. . . . The discussions in the House indicate not only that Parliament and the country is taking a great interest in immigration, but also that there is a wide divergence of views as to what should be done. . . . It is evident that there is not whole-hearted support to any scheme of assisted passage.

From this standpoint, the permanent civil servants could be well pleased with their efforts and count the results (or rather, the lack of them) a success: 'it has', noted the Director of Immigration Branch in late August, 'so far been considered the part of wisdom for the first year to exercise the greatest care in the grant of passage assistance'.[29] A year later with a second season almost over, the Minister could explain disingenuously that he intended to visit the United Kingdom to 'consult with the Overseas [sic] Settlement Board in an endeavour to arrive at a mutual and equitable arrangement for the settlement of Britishers in Canada' – the existing agreements notwithstanding.[30]

Rising pressure

Criticism of the government's lacklustre programme quickly emerged. While some members of the Cabinet continued to doubt the wisdom of any co-operation – 'why should we keep men overseas offering loans to induce very *doubtful* farmers but very *certain* Tory advocates to come to Canada?' – critics bemoaned what they saw as a lost opportunity. For every complaint that the Salvation Army was loading the country with worthless girls and waifs, there were a dozen arguing that Canada was throwing away its future:

> Canada must have more people and these must be placed on the land. The British settler does not require assimilation – a very important feature. He, and especially his offspring, will be a leaven of tremendous value to Canada. Each settler successfully established in Canada is an asset. He has a distinct money value to the country. . . . Hence Canada . . . should be prepared to meet a considerable share of the incidental expenses and losses in the movement of British people.[31]

Newspaper articles lamenting the lack of success in attracting Empire settlers appeared regularly throughout the summer and autumn of 1923, often comparing Canada's poor showing with the more aggressive approach of Australia and New Zealand.[32] Fears that Canada was going to lose out to the other dominions in the scramble to get large numbers of 'the right class' of immigrants from the United Kingdom along with a fair share of the Empire Settlement Act assistance money turned up frequently in both the press and private letters.[33] Why was Canada dragging its feet? Why were the prejudices of 'high officials' being allowed to endanger Canada's future development and prosperity? The explanations varied. Some saw in the restrictive administration a plot by Charles Stewart, the Minister of the Interior, against Jews; others suspected that Quebec was holding the Liberal government back from an energetic settlement policy. Whatever the cause, the cure was obvious: a bolder effort to attract the best British stock.[34]

Stung by the criticism, Mackenzie King blamed it on a 'whispering campaign' organised by his political enemies.[35] Canada was eager to secure every British immigrant it could; if the government had appeared a little slow, it was only out of concern 'that we have our house so in order that when we invited the people of [Britain] to come to Canada, conditions as to employment and settlement might be such that they would find it easy to . . . become satisfactorily established'. 'I think', King announced at the Imperial Conference,

> we are now at the point where we can welcome immigration of the right kind to our country. Certainly no stock could be more welcome than British stock of the kind which helped make our country and Empire what it is.[36]

King's soothing reassurances notwithstanding, pressure for an expanded programme continued to mount. The provinces were complaining that their interests were not being looked after and were anxious to see the federal authorities adopt more-extensive measures to encourage settlers; in the interval Ontario went ahead with its own arrangements.[37] The British meanwhile made no secret of their disappointment in the dominion response, and pressed for a bolder policy, including the clearing of land for group settlements, increased facilities for juveniles, and the grant of assisted passages in a less-restrictive fashion. If any large-scale emigration was going to take place, admonished Ramsay MacDonald, the dominions must be prepared to accept representatives of the mass of the United Kingdom's population, rather than continuing to try to select only the best and most skilled.[38]

By the summer of 1924 changed circumstances in Canada added weight to the demands for a more-active immigration policy. The post-war economic downturn had passed. On the prairies the lean years were over, and western interests were becoming aware that improved freight rates and other services depended on an increasing population to bear the costs and give the farming areas greater influences in Ottawa.[39] Business interests agreed. 'The business view', noted one of King's correspondents, is that 'nothing but wide open immigration of Europeans, barring sub-normals, is necessary if we are to have development and prosperity. It is not merely land settlers but throughout all North America labour in every form needs to be further supplied with outside workers.' The promise of prosperity, agreed another, argued for opening the door:

> Our railways and manufacturers are clamouring for population. Our National debt demands more shoulders to carry it. Sentiment largely takes a part in emigration and a belief that good times are coming draws emigration as well as investment.[40]

Canada's need for more immigrants was compounded, in fact, by the prosperity of its southern neighbour. Passage of the American quota system threatened to exacerbate an already worrisome tendency. By restricting entry of the foreign-born but allowing the unregulated admission of native Canadians seeking better paid jobs, the American system threatened to leave Canada with an unassimilated residue. Concern over the impact of the system prompted the Immigration Branch in 1925 to begin to track the movement carefully. The figures revealed what many feared: almost 60,000 'real' Canadians a year were being drained away. British stock was needed now more than ever to leaven the remainder and keep Canada a British country.[41]

Government commitments

All of this prompted the federal government to accept the need for an increased level of immigration, though it continued to be chary of becoming involved directly in the business of assisted passage. To answer the demand that more be done to encourage British immigration it arranged to pay a bonus of $15 to the White Star, Cunard and Canadian Pacific steamship lines for British passengers destined for Canada.[42] But in the autumn of 1925 the government also signed an agreement with the railway companies permitting them to recruit labour in Russia, Estonia, Latvia, Danzig, Poland, Czechoslovakia, Austria, Hungary, Yugoslavia and Rumania. The result was an 'immediate and heavy increase' in immigration from Southern Europe. The bonus for the British, by contrast, accomplished little; British immigration increased only slightly, mainly, noted officials, because '90% of the men who would go and could go have not the means of buying a ticket'.[43]

Conscious of the criticism the heavy influx of 'non-preferred' European immigrants was likely to provoke, officials took a significant initiative in establishing the '3,000 Families Scheme' under the terms of the Empire Settlement Act. Advertised as a 'demonstration of what might be accomplished by private land owners in the way of assisting settlement' (King still preferred private to public programmes), it seemed to demonstrate instead the potential results of a very small effort on the part of the bureaucracy. For its part, the federal government made available lands which had been acquired earlier for soldier settlement and either not used or turned back to the Soldier Settlement Board; the British government in turn advanced settlers funds for stock and equipment. The intention was to settle 3,000 families over three years; despite restrictive terms and a formidable process to gain approval, it proved impossible to process the flood of applications.[44] The families scheme was greeted in Canada with universal approval. The railway agreements, by contrast, provoked only anger and hostility. The general synod of the Anglican Church condemned what they regarded as a plot by French-Canadians to establish Roman Catholicism in Canada, charging that Canada was being flooded with Southern Europeans while British Protestants were being kept out. Western opinion was especially outraged. Bishop Lloyd of Saskatchewan angrily denounced the 'denationalising' of the western provinces for the sake of railway dividends, while the Mayor of Winnipeg contended that 'the process of filling up the Western provinces with people of non-British stock . . . constituted a menace to Canada and should be corrected with a new immigration policy on the part of the government'. The premier of Ontario declared that Empire settlement was essential to maintain the 'strength and vitality' of the British Empire and to preserve Canada's dedication to its ideals. 'Can we expect', warned the Reverend Canon Cody, 'the same loyalty to British ideals from those Galacians, Poles and heaven knows who, who are now populating the West?' The Empire settler was more than the equal of his European counterpart: 'if foreigners could make money and own automobiles in Western Canada, then the British immigrant was equally capable of doing so'.[45]

A change in policy seemed the better part of political valour. Struggling to maintain its majority, the Liberal government could ill afford to offend Canadians' imperial sentiments:

> The two questions that seem to be exercising the minds of the people are the thorough investigation of this Customs matter . . . and the question of immigration from Britain. In the west here people are asking how many of these people from Europe like Ukrainians, Mennonites, Austrians, etc. we can bring in and properly assimilate.[46]

With the Imperial Conference of 1926 approaching, party strategists counselled King to capitalise on the success of the 3,000 Families scheme and to try to expand Canada's participation in Empire settlement:

> You know how strongly many of us feel on the question of immigration and settlement . . . and the importance of the Government immigration policy. . . . It does appear to me that you have a great chance to do a big thing for Canada, and a big thing for yourself and the Liberal Party, by developing this scheme on a much larger scale. . . . It would be a great thing if you could come back with an agreement with the British Government which would involve a much enlarged scheme of settlement on the lands in the different provinces of Canada.[47]

What had once been suspect was now to be sought after. 'I have the impression', noted one of King's Toronto backers, 'that a scheme which was proposed from England a few years ago, and not very favourably regarded here either by the Immigration Department at Ottawa or by other more private co-operation which was sought, was nevertheless brought into effect.' In the interval attitudes had changed:

> You will receive the hearty backing of influential people in Canada for anything you can reasonably do in co-operation with British authorities toward securing a good class of British immigrants for Canada in increasing numbers. I am aware that there are whole classes of Britishers that might not be desirable ... [but] there are other classes ... who are excellent material for Canadian citizens.[48]

Always alert to shifts in the political wind, Mackenzie King arrived in London determined to heed his advisers and embrace Empire settlement. There were no problems, he declared, that optimism, confidence and ambition could not solve:

> the great desire of Canada is to welcome more British settlers. The Dominion can absorb many more of the right type of British working people. Canada looks forward to the day when British-born migrants will pour in again to the nearest Dominion, as they did in the years before the war.[49]

King's words signalled a new willingness to co-operate. The Canadian government had already undertaken a series of initiatives, among them the appointment of Robert Forke, a westerner and former Progressive, as Minister of Immigration, and the negotiation of reduced passage rates for would-be settlers. Forke's appointment was hailed as the opening salvo in a progressive immigration campaign; the 'cautious experiment' of the 3,000 Families Scheme could be expanded by a Minister with courage into a $100 million, 100 per cent effort to revitalise Canada from the Maritimes to British Columbia with tens of thousands of British farmers, fishermen, workers and young people.[50] Meanwhile, the new arrangement between the Canadian government, Whitehall and the shipping companies showed what co-operation could accomplish. The British government would contribute in cash towards the cost of passage of house workers, farmers and farm workers an amount equal to that which the Canadian government agreed to spend on placement and aftercare; the transport companies in turn would reduce rail rates in Canada. The cheap rate could be extended to any province or society that wanted to promote immigration if they agreed to spend at least $25 on aftercare over five years for each person selected. Under the agreement, costs dropped substantially for Empire settlement passengers: an approved settler could now be landed at Toronto for $15 (reduced to $10 in 1927), children free, without a loan to be repaid.[51] In short order the number of assisted immigrants more than doubled, during a period when British immigration otherwise declined (see

Figure 1); 'a splendid step in the right direction,' noted the Imperial Order of the Daughters of the Empire (IODE) with satisfaction.[52]

Others soon followed, among them a Boys Training Scheme and Land Settlement Scheme, the expansion of the 3,000 Families Scheme, a training scheme for domestics, a Cottage Scheme and a much-expanded Harvesters Scheme. The Boys Training Scheme grew out of the efforts of the Dominions Office to persuade the Canadian government to become more directly involved in the settlement of juveniles.[53] Assisting British youths to take up a life in the dominion had proved a popular idea, especially among those who saw in Empire settlement the means of perpetuating the British race in Canada; even those suspicious of assistance on the grounds that it amounted to subsidising failures made an exception in the case of young people, for obvious reasons. But under the 1923 agreement, the arrangements had been placed in the hands of approved voluntary societies. If federal and provincial governments would take official responsibility, following the Australian example, Whitehall believed that recruitment could be greatly expanded.

As a result of this prompting, Canada's new Minister of Immigration announced in January 1927 that the federal government would co-operate with the provinces to bring British lads to Canada and train them for farm work. Ottawa would contribute $80 for each boy to pay his passage and assist in his training; the provinces in turn would establish training farms and see to the eventual placement of the 'graduate' with local farmers. Follow-up supervision by the Soldiers

Figure 1 Arrivals at Canadian ports, in thousands
Source: Empire settlement based on warrants issued, figures compiled from Canada, Department of Immigration and Colonization, *Annual Reports*, 1919–39.

Settlement Board would ensure that the boy was 'kindly treated'. Nearly all of the provinces embraced the idea with enthusiasm; some set up special training farms while others used existing experimental farms of agricultural schools.[54] Immigration Branch for their part, found the new programme a convenient way to terminate what had become a highly embarrassing arrangement under which the Salvation Army carried on juvenile immigration in exchange for a generous subsidy.[55] Boys Land Settlement was a natural outgrowth of the initial commitment: boys who had received training and who managed to save $500 as farm hands could borrow up to $2,500 to begin farming. Whitehall would put up half the money; Ottawa the rest. With $5 million earmarked to be spent over ten years, the training and settlement scheme represented the ambitious hopes of Empire settlement advocates; it also typified the disappointment of those dreams. In its most successful year it managed to attract 2,300 British boys and spent only a little over one-third of its yearly budget.[56]

The other bold initiatives did even less well. The Cottage Scheme – under which provincial governments and private organisations were to build cottages for the use of British families while they were being trained in farming – collapsed when it proved impossible in practice to erect a suitable dwelling for the $1,000 proposed. The provinces had, in any case, shown little interest in participating in a programme which required them to make a sizeable contribution from their own funds.[57] The house-worker programme fared better, but still failed to meet the expectations of its proponents. As was the case with farm workers, the supply of experienced domestics interested in migrating was relatively small. Once again the Oversea Settlement Committee took the initiative by establishing training hostels in the United Kingdom to help girls qualify, and paid 75 per cent of the costs. Canada for its part agreed to the usual aftercare, though in the case of single young women the arrangements were more extensive and included close supervision and temporary accommodation at government-subsidised hostels run by the YWCA, the Catholic Women's League and other organisations. These elaborate efforts did succeed in encouraging a substantial increase in female immigration, but for most the journey proved a dead-end. Of the 18,790 who went to Canada under the 1926 agreement, 1,517 eventually married but a similar number, 1,716, returned to the United Kingdom by choice or were deported. The others were trapped by the onset of the depression and remained on the rolls of the Women's Branch which was responsible for their welfare. The romantic notion that young British women would find a virile Canadian mate and breed a future Empire race must have seemed a bitter farce to most.[58]

Even the highly praised 3,000 Families Scheme was to remain a demonstration only; an intimation of what might be done. Described as 'the most successful effort in colonization undertaken by any Government in modern times', the scheme was universally acclaimed even by those otherwise critical of assisted settlement. But efforts by British authorities to expand it proved futile.[59] Although the two governments had agreed in 1926 that family settlement would be continued as a permanent feature of joint settlement policy if the original programme succeeded, when the Chairman of the Oversea Settlement Committee proposed in 1928 that 20,000 families be settled on Canadian farms, Ottawa balked. The expanded scheme was to be financed by the sale of Canadian bonds guaranteed by the British government; Canada would select the settlers, arrange their transport and provide subsequent supervision. The immigrants selected would, in turn, repay the cost of land and equipment by instalments. Ottawa's reluctance was symptomatic of its lack of real commitment to the principles of Empire settlement. Why should Canada issue bonds, the Minister of Immigration asked pointedly, when the settlers were not even Canadians? Plus, the proposed programme was likely to involve a substantial investment, perhaps as much as $10 million in 'irrecoverable administrative expenditure' according to officials. The pattern was consistent: if Whitehall took the initiative and paid the bills, then Ottawa would go along; otherwise the answer was no. When Amery tried to go around the bureaucrats and press the proposal directly with King, he refused to discuss it.[60] The best that could be managed was a small programme with New Brunswick to settle 500 families on farms provided by the provincial government with the British government advancing $1,500 for stock and equipment.[61]

Ottawa's attitude also reflected renewed misgivings over the results of a successful settlement programme. A few limited demonstrations were one thing; a really large-scale movement quite another.[62] That much was obvious when the United Kingdom attempted to revive the Harvesters Scheme of 1923. The proposal to send 10,000 unemployed miners to the harvest fields of western Canada ran into stiff resistance from immigration officials and provincial governments. Harvesting help should be found in Canada, or at worst in the United States of America, officials argued, to ensure that when threshing was over the migrants went home. After an exchange of cables between Amery and the Prime Minister, the civil servants were forced to yield, but only on the condition of a private understanding that unemployed or unsatisfactory men would be returned at the United Kingdom's expense without going through the formalities of the usual deportation process.[63] Some 25,000 applied, and in late August the 8,500 accepted began to arrive. By September the newspapers carried complaints about the high proportion of 'misfits' and malcontents, unsuited by their lack of industry and proper mental attitude to work rather than by a lack of physical fitness. Reds, agitators and communists, went the reports, were persuading men to refuse work at reasonable wages. In Ottawa, the Minister washed his hands of the scheme, declaring that 'the men were sent out on the entire responsibility of the British Government'; in London, a disappointed Amery admitted that of the 8,500 sent, 6,876 had returned to the United Kingdom, ending hopes that a large number would settle into permanent employment in Canada. 'The experiment of bringing British harvesters to Canada', concluded the *Manitoba Free Press*, 'cannot be put down as anything but a failure.'[64]

Objections

Complaints over the Harvesters Scheme signalled a hardening of Canadian attitudes to assisted settlement. Once again there was talk of 'the immigration problem' and the familiar charges about the quality of Empire settlers surfaced with increasing frequency. The disgruntlement of the harvesters, noted Norman Rogers,

> makes one wonder if the tenacity of the British people has not suffered a relapse since the war. I cannot recall ever having heard similar complaints from any group of foreign immigrants who have to put up with greater difficulties than British settlers coming to this country.[65]

Echoing Rogers's doubts, the Native Sons of Canada complained that Empire settlers had had their personal stamina undermined by doles and their independence destroyed by assisted passages; instead of securing the best stock, Empire settlement promoted the migration of the worst – large numbers of those 'wholly unfit'. According to press reports, Canada was becoming a 'dumping ground' for the United Kingdom's criminals and ne'er-do-wells. Meanwhile organised labour, the political left and Quebec nationalists had become convinced that every assisted immigrant forced a native-born Canadian to emigrate to the United States of America.[66] A few might still be prepared to defend the hapless British immigrant on the grounds that while he might admittedly not be the best, 'he fits in best', but attention focused on what seemed (in the language of Immigration Branch officials) a disproportionate number of 'defectives'. Unquestionably the nature of British immigration had changed: while Empire settlement did not significantly affect total immigration from the United Kingdom, an increasing proportion of the arrivals was made up of assisted classes. Even P. C. Larkin, a convert to Empire settlement, had begun to have second thoughts:

The Salvation Army and many similar organizations derive commission from the steamship companies and they are apt to see imaginary virtues in certain individuals and, when they bring families to the emigration staff here, they have made little or no enquiries about them, with the result that they are found to be no use at all. ... Naturally all thoughtful members of society here are anxious to rid the country of people who are a burden to the community, and I have no doubt think that a new country like Canada will regenerate them, but I am sure you will agree with me that Canadians generally do not want that class; we have enough burdens as it is.[67]

The criticisms and complaints were addressed by a general tightening up of standards and procedures, in particular the establishment of a new medical inspection system; the growing disillusionment prompted the appointment in 1928 of a Select Committee to examine the whole question of immigration. The government justified the replacement of British with Canadian doctors on the grounds that it was a humanitarian measure, undertaken strictly in the interests of the intending immigrant. The claim was disingenuous, as critics pointed out, but their arguments were beside the point. Canadians, including the members of the Select Committee, had become persuaded that a great proportion of Empire settlers were physically and mentally unfit, to the point that large numbers had to be confined to mental institutions on their arrival in Canada; British physicians were either as incompetent as those they examined or part of the conspiracy to dump the United Kingdom's derelicts onto Canada. The new system catered to that belief: taking special precautions was, in the words of the committee's report, a 'serious responsibility' to ensure that emigrants would 'do their share as Canadian citizens'.[68]

Caution, in fact, dominated the committee's final report and recommendations. While the immigration of teenagers and domestics should be continued and efforts made to reunite families, the system of permits should be tightened up. As for the much-praised 3,000 Families Scheme, which had embodied the vision of Empire settlement advocates and on which Whitehall had hoped to base a much-expanded programme, it was to be wound up. 'Time', in the committee's view, was needed to test the results 'before embarking on extended schemes of this character'. In the meantime, the government should 'make an intensive and comprehensive study' of Canada's future development and the role of prospective immigrants. Independent initiatives by the provinces and private organisations were to cease, and the railways' authority to recruit immigrants ended. The committee, in sum, showed little real enthusiasm for immigration of any sort; instead efforts should be made to provide opportunities for 'our own people'.[69] Parliamentary debate on the report was desultory. Although the opposition took the opportunity to attack the Minister and department for alleged inefficiencies, few spoke in favour of expanding immigration or proposed that any effort be made to encourage it. The committee's observation that the government had spent $16.67 for each British immigrant compared with 11 cents for those from the Continent did nothing to encourage initiatives.

Some, including Amery, continued to hope, but for all practical purposes Empire settlement was at an end. Commenting on the committee's report, Amery acknowledged that there had been 'temporary difficulties'; perhaps clearing the air would help ensure 'a far greater measure of co-operation between the Departments at London and Ottawa' and lead to 'important fresh developments'.[70] Putting the best face on the situation, Amery urged Canada to accept the British proposal to negotiate a reduced £10 fare for all British subjects. The Canadians eventually agreed in December, partly on the grounds that a general reduction was preferable to assisted settlement (even though the British government intended to lend prospective migrants the £10 passage money). But the Canadian attitude was unsympathetic: Forke made it clear that Canada was not interested in land settlement schemes and would no longer contribute to the passage of single men.[71] The days for hopes of imperial greatness were gone; the Canadians hardly bothered even to pay lip-service to Amery's dreams.

The mood reflected Canada's changes circumstances. By 1929 the Canadian economy was booming, closely mimicking that of its American neighbour. No longer did Canadians migrate south to find better jobs and higher pay; instead Immigration Branch figures showed that for the first time in many years more Canadians returned from the United States of America than left. 'Everything', in the words of Sir James Woods of the Imperial Bank of Canada, 'seems to be pulling our way.' Canada's small population was proving to be an advantage:

> Unemployment is a problem confronting the nations of the world, and Canada may enjoy comparative freedom in this respect if we exercise prudence in our immigration policy. While the opinion commonly held in Canada is that no effort should be spared to settle our productive farm lands . . . the time has come to go slowly.

Men like Bishop Lloyd and J. F. B. Livesay of the Canadian press might continue to argue that British immigrants were needed to preserve a Protestant Canada, and claim that 'with our Canadian industries expanding on all sides it is absurd for our immigration people to say – and to insist – that there is no opening for British artisans and labourers', but the tide of opinion had turned against them. Mackenzie King congratulated himself that he had 'correctly interpreted Canadian opinion with respect to assisted immigration from the British Isles to Canada'.

The Conservative Party, sensing the shift in the political wind, barely mentioned the subject in House debate and carefully avoided a division over it. The civil servants, equally alert, took the opportunity in January 1929 to notify the railway companies that the movement of farm labourers must be reduced by more than 50 per cent over the next two years; the companies had in any case decided on their own to get out of the immigration business.[72] By the time J. H. Thomas arrived in Ottawa in August 1929 any hope of stimulating Empire settlement had faded. Thomas did what he could to try at least to establish a preference for British over other immigrants, but it was a lost cause.[73]

In March 1930 a new Acting Minister announced that 'assisted settlement is to end'. The onset of the depression and the election of a new government only confirmed what was already a *fait accompli*. When R. B. Bennett and the Conservatives cut off immigration at the end of the summer, the move met with general approval across the country.[74] Although the Empire settlement scheme would be renewed by the British government in 1937 on the ground that the United Kingdom still had 'confidence in its possibilities when conditions improve', Canada's participation was effectively at an end.[75] Attempts to revive the programme in the later 1930s when the rise of fascism again stimulated concern about the 'foreigners in our midst' were short-lived and unsuccessful. While they aroused a flurry of local interest and briefly made the headlines, the schemes proposed by General Hornby and Sir Henry Page Croft got nowhere.[76] The experience of the 1920s had closed the door to assisted migration; Ottawa had had its fill of Empire settlement.

What had the entire effort accomplished? On the face of it, the results between 1922 and 1935 seemed creditable enough. The figures included over 20,000 young women who had come to Canada as domestics, under the house worker programme; almost 10,000 youths as intending farmers; and some 3,500 British farm families (over 60 per cent of whom were still on the land in 1932). In all, the Canadian immigration authorities recorded 107,084 assisted immigrants, excluding a number of agricultural trainees funded entirely by the British government and over 58,000 who took advantage of the lowered £10 fare. But measured against Amery's original vision of millions resettled in a 'Greater Britain' they represented a crushing disappointment. Notwithstanding strenuous efforts coupled with a remarkable degree of patience and flexibility, Whitehall had never managed to expend as much as half of the Empire settlement budget even in the peak year of 1927.[77]

Even more disheartening, perhaps, for those in Canada and the United Kingdom who shared Amery's dream had been the attitude of the Canadian government and the Canadian public. The politicians had exploited the programme when it suited their purposes and scorned it when it did not; the civil servants, never enthusiastic about the idea of assisted settlement, had been at best grudging in administering it. The Canadian public, for its part, had proved a fickle ally: quick to embrace the potential and the promise, as quick to abandon it when the inevitable problems surfaced. For those who clung to the notion of a future Empire united by unbreakable bonds of enduring sentiment and shared affection, this was the cruellest disappointment of all.

Notes

1 So controversial, in fact, that W. D. Scott, the Director of Immigration Branch, found the choice of the word 'settlement' as a substitute for 'immigration' one of the more attractive features of the scheme; W. D. Scott to C. O. Cory, 8 March 1921, Public Archives of Canada (hereafter PAC), Government of Canada, Immigration Branch, RG76/132/30477.

2 Commissioner of Immigration to C. O. Cory, 3 June 1921, RG76/132/30477/1.

3 For the attitude of Immigration Branch officials, see J. A. Schultz, 'White men's country: Canada and the West Indian immigrant, 1900–1969', in Brian Tennyson (ed.), *Canada and the Commonwealth Caribbean*, London, 1988, pp. 257–77; for the problems of soldier resettlement, see Desmond Morton and Glen Wright, *Winning the Second Battle*, Toronto, 1987, *passim*, and J. A. Schultz, 'Finding homes for heroes', *Canadian Journal of History*, 18, 1983, pp. 99–110.

4 Henry Borden (ed.), *Robert Laird Borden: his Memoirs*, 2 vols, Toronto, 1938, vol 2, p. 1038; for Canada's post-war concerns, see J. A. Schultz, 'Canadian attitudes toward Empire Settlement', *Journal of Imperial and Commonwealth History*, 1, 1973, pp. 237–51.

5 An idea much talked about in after-dinner speeches and popular magazine articles: see Carl Berger, 'The true north strong and free', in J. H. Bumsted, *Interpreting Canada's Past*, vol. 2, Oxford, 1986, p. 159.

6 Immigration Branch, Commissioner to Cory, 3 June 1921, RG76/132/30477/1.

7 Immigration Branch, C. O. Cory to R. Greenway, 1 June 1921, RG76/132/30477/1.

8 'Preliminary Memorandum for the Minister of Trade and Commerce', PAC, W. L. M. King Papers, MG26 J1/92/77698.

9 I. M. Drummond, *Imperial Economic Policy 1917–1939*, London, 1974, p. 93, who attributes this unsigned memorandum for the Imperial Economic Conference to O. D. Skelton, one of King's closest advisers and a well-known Anglophobe.

10 Immigration Branch, W. D. Scott to Cory, 8 March 1921, Commissioner to Cory, 3 June 1921, RG76/132/304771/1; Drummond, *Imperial Policy*, pp. 87, 95n.

11 King Papers, P. C. Larkin to King, 28 April 1922, MG 26 J1/76/64307; Larkin to King, 8 August 1922, MG26 J1/76/64501.

12 King Papers, Ernest LaPointe and Charles Murphy to King, 25 October 1922, MG26 J1/79/66783.

13 King Papers, Charles Murphy to King, 16 October 1922, MG26 J1/79/66783.

14 *Ibid.*, Murphy to King, 2 October 1923, MG26 J1/91/77503. King seems to have taken this to heart, marking the last sentence in heavy pencil.

15 Toronto *Globe*, 4 February 1921.

16 King Papers, L. S. Amery to King, 4 July 1923, MG 26 J1/83/70167.

17 *Ibid.*, Amery to King, 14 June 1922, MG26 J1/69/588850.

18 *Ibid.*, Amery to King, 1 May 1922, MG26 J1/69/58836.

19 *Ibid.*, King to Amery, 17 July 1923, MG26 J1/83/70167; Drummond, *Imperial Economic Policy*, pp. 86, 93. In Drummond's phrase, King was 'eager to seem to welcome British migrants' though he refused to move seriously. Even these mild pronouncements to the effect that Canada was prepared to welcome newcomers from

the United Kingdom prompted angry protests from Quebec supporters. See C. Miron, Parti Ouvrier du Canada to King, 4 January 1923, MG26 J1/90/76751.

20 King Papers, J. A. Robb to King, 25 October 1923, MG26 J1/93/78724; *ibid.*, C. L. Burton to King, 16 April 1923, MG26 J1/84/714.

21 *Ibid.*, J. S. Willison to King, 30 September 1922, MG26 J1/83/69946; King to Amery, 16 June 1922, MG26 J1/69/58850; King to Larkin, 22 July 1922, MG26 J1/76/64459.

22 Canada, House of Commons, *Sessional Papers*, 13–14 George V (1923) No. 201: 'Empire Settlement Scheme, Draft Agreements'. After complaints from various social welfare groups, the assisted migration of young children was done away with in 1925.

23 Immigration Branch, F. C. Blair to P. M. Buttley, 27 March 1923, RG76/203/88324; *ibid.*, Charles Stewart to Sir Frederick Williams-Taylor, 7 March 1923, RG76/203/88324. Australia, by contrast, included a loan fund of £34 million among its arrangements.

24 *Ibid.*, W. J. Black to F. C. Blair, 21 March 1923, RG76/203/88324.

25 *Ibid.*, F. C. Blair to Charles Stewart, 22 March 1923, RG 76/203/88324. 'The Imperial Government', Blair sighed, 'seem to be strong on settlement and supervision.'

26 *Ibid.*, Charles Stewart to W. J. Black, 24 March 1923, RG76/203/88324; Albert Buckley, quoted by Drummond, *Imperial Economic Policy*, p. 89.

27 Canada, Department of Immigration and Colonization, *Annual Report* 1923–24, p. 20.

28 Quoted by Drummond, *Imperial Economic Policy*, p. 89.

29 Immigration Branch, F. C. Blair to W. Windham, 10 February 1923, RG76/133/30477/2; *ibid.*, F. C. Blair to W. J. Black, 27 March 1923, RG76/203/88324/1; quoted by Drummond, *Imperial Economic Policy*, p. 93.

30 King Papers, J. A. Robb to King, 9 July 1924, MG26 J1/107/90751.

31 King Papers, Duncan Marshall to King, 5 September 1923, MG26 J1/90/76596; *ibid.*, Charles Magrath to King, 6 November 1923, MG26 J1/90/76408.

32 Montreal *Gazette*, 5 October 1923; King Papers, Herbert Marler to King, 27 July 1923, MG26 J1/90/76561. The *Gazette*, for example, pointed out that Canada had managed to attract only just over 2,000 settlers including those who came under the Ontario government's scheme, while Australia had ten times that many and even New Zealand had received twice as many.

33 Ottawa *Citizen*, 28 February 1923; King Papers, Miller Lash to King, 30 July 1923, MG26 J1/89/75503.

34 *The Times*, 17 April 1923.

35 King Papers, King to Larkin, 10 July 1923, MG26 J1/89/75235.

36 Immigration Branch, W. J. Black to F. C. Blair, 24 March 1923, RG76/203/88324/1; Montreal *Gazette*, 3 October 1923. King added the qualifier, however, that the position of Canada's industries and what they could absorb would have to be considered.

37 King Papers, King to Larkin, 31 May 1924, MG26 J1/103/87102. King grumbled that the provinces had a much greater interest in the settlement scheme than the federal government, but expected the federal authorities to be solicitous of their concerns.

38 *Ibid.*, Lucien Pacaud to F. A. McGregor, 7 February 1924, MG26 J1/102/86755.

39 For the change of heart among western interests, especially the Progressive Party on whom King and the Liberals depended for their hold on power, see Schultz, 'Canadian attitudes', pp. 241–2.

40 King Papers, Miller Lash to King, 30 July 1923, MG26 J1/89/75503; Wallace Nesbitt to King, 31 October 1923, MG26 J1/92/7762.

41 King Papers, Memorandum by F. C. Blair, 'Important Steps in Immigration Since 1921', MG26 J1/171/145864. Immigration Branch officials recognised that the higher wages in the USA were a problem, but noted that there were plenty of unemployed in the United Kingdom; it seemed unlikely that these would be lost to the Americans, since the USA wanted skilled tradesmen whereas Canada aimed to recruit land settlers. *Ibid.*, F. C. Blair to Moyer, 22 November 1926, MG26 J1/128/108811.

42 *Ibid.*, L. Pacaud to King, 3 March 1925, MG26 J1/122/103453.

43 Blair, 'Important Steps in Immigration', p. 8; Immigration Branch, J. Obed Smith to Blair, 24 February 1923, RG76/203/88324; Department of Immigration and Colonization, *Annual Report* 1924–25, p. 24.

44 Department of Immigration and Colonization, *Annual Report* 1924–25, p. 25; Blair, 'Important Steps', p. 6.

45 Toronto *Globe*, 21 August 1926; Schultz, 'Canadian attitudes', p. 242.

46 King Papers, Hewitt Bostock to King, 17 September 1926, MG26 J1/128/108909. A scandal over corruption in the Customs service was threatening to alienate King's support among Progressives and bring down the government.

47 *Ibid.*, Newton Rowell to King, 7 October 1926, MG26 J1/138/117057.

48 *Ibid.*, A. E. Ames to King, 20 October 1926, MG26 J1/27/108183.

49 'Problems of Canada', BBC broadcast address, 19 November 1926, *ibid.*, MG26 J1/139/118658.

50 Ottawa *Citizen*, 23 September 1926.

51 Loans up to the amount of the new rates continued to be available. For comparison, the third-class rate for British paying their own way was approximately $112 while an immigrant from the Continent paid $137. For the new rates, and details of the scheme, see Department of Immigration and Colonization, *Annual Report* 1925–26, p. 24. The encouragement given to charitable organisations to participate in the scheme no doubt helped the work of those organisations, but also shifted the burden of aftercare expenses onto their shoulders, relieving the Canadian government of any obligation to contribute. King Papers, F. C. Blair to O. D. Skelton, 26 January 1927, MG26 J1/127/120071; 'Important Steps in Immigration', p. 3; PAC, Arthur Meighen Papers, F. C. Blair to C. W. Vernon, 16 December 1925, MG26/I/96/055055; Sheila Powell, 'Helping hands: charitable organisations and immigration to Canada', *The Archivist*, November–December 1988, pp. 4–6; Schultz, 'Canadian attitudes', p. 244.

52 Imperial Order of the Daughters of the Empire, *Annual Report*, Meighen Papers, MG 26/I/96/055039.

53 Imperial Conference 1926: 'Confidential Note to the Government of the Dominion of Canada supplemental to the memorandum prepared for the conference', Meighen Papers, MG 26/I/97/055775.

54 The exceptions were Prince Edward Island, Quebec and Alberta. Alberta operated its own 'Hoadley Boys' scheme under a separate agreement with the British government with the Canadian federal government contributing 50 per cent of the fares. The province of Quebec did not participate in Empire settlement, but arranged instead a subsidy from the federal government similar to that given to the other provinces for Empire settlement work but used in the case of Quebec for the repatriation and resettlement of francophones from the USA. (British boy immigration was looked after by the British Immigration and Colonization Association which was active in the Eastern Townships). King Papers, Memorandum by W. J. Egan, 11 January 1930, MG26 J1/173/147646-147855; *Canadian Annual Review*, 1926–1927, p. 180; *ibid.*, 1928–29, p. 162.

55 Salvation Army representatives, it seemed, had been collecting from the boys assisted by the two governments under Empire settlement amounts equal to or in excess of the amount of the grant. The boys were led to believe that they were repaying passage money, not making 'voluntary contributions' to the Army. *Canadian Annual Review*, 1926–27, p. 180.

56 Department of Immigration and Colonization, *Annual Report* 1926–27, p. 7; *Ibid.*, 1927–28, pp. 55, 89; 1929–30, p. 66.

57 Of the $1,000, the British government would contribute $500, the Canadian federal government $250 and the province or organisation the remaining $250. Aside from Ontario, the provincial governments had no interest in the idea. King Papers, W. J. Egan to Charles Steward, 11 January 1930, MG26 J1/173/147646; Department of Immigration and Colonization, *Annual Report* 1928–29, p. 63.

58 Department of Immigration and Colonization, *Annual Report* 1926–27, p. 61; 1929–30, p. 79; 1932–33, pp. 84–5. The balance of the training costs was met by a grant of $15 from the Canadian government and $5 from those provinces which participated. The 'House worker' category represented the single largest class of Empire settlers, with a total of 23,804 assisted arrivals between 1922 and 1931, but whether it met the original goals of the legislation and its supporters seems highly problematical.

59 *Canadian Annual Review*, 1926–27, p. 176.

60 Canada's original proposal presumed that the United Kingdom would continue to pay for the costs of the families' stock and equipment; the British in turn had made it clear that Empire settlement would be 'much more satisfactory if the Dominion Government had some financial interest in the settlement arrangements, apart from administrative expenses'. Ottawa for its part had generally tried to shift even this cost off onto private or provincial sponsors. Imperial Conference 1926, 'Confidential Note to the Government of the Dominion of Canada ...', Meighen Papers, MG26/I/97/055780; Montreal *Gazette*, 6 October 1928; Toronto *Globe*, 20 November 1928; King Papers, R. Forke to King, n.d. [August 1928], MG26 J1/152/129557; W. J. Egan to King, 12 October 1928, MG26 J1/152/129293. Of the families who had come under the original scheme, only some 5 per cent had failed to make good, and Lord Clarendon's remarks were frequently quoted by Canadian officials in defence of Canada's record in encouraging Empire settlement. *Canadian Annual Review*, 1926–27, p. 176; King Papers, F. C. Blair to O. D. Skelton, 26 January 1927, MG26 J1/127/119923.

61 That is, on terms essentially similar to those of the original 3,000 Families Scheme. King Papers, W. J. Egan to Charles Stewart, 11 January 1930, MG26 J1/173/147824; G. C. Creelman to King, 3 December 1926, MG26 J1/130/110543; Canada, House of Commons *Debates*, 25 March 1926; Department of Immigration and Colonization, *Annual Report* 1927–28, p. 65.

62 'Our Administration', King told Sir William Clark candidly in November 1928, 'does not view with favour large settlement schemes.' Quoted by Drummond, *Imperial Economic Policy*, p. 108. The provincial governments had also lost much of their enthusiasm, with Forke reporting that 'I do not find any great inclination on their part to embark on any large Land Settlement Schemes.' King Papers, Forke to King, 30 October 1928, MG26 J1/152/129583.

63 'As we are especially anxious to encourage harvesters movements at the present time', Amery pleaded, 'we should greatly appreciate Forke's and your co-operation.' The 1923 Harvesters Excursion had been organised by the railways, who brought 12,000 men to western Canada for temporary work; the movement in 1928 was an initiative of the British government (apparently at the prompting of the CPR), which negotiated a cheap rate and loaned the passage money from Empire settlement funds. King Papers, Amery to King, 2 July 1928, MG26 J1/157/133966; Forke to King, 1 July 1927, MG26 J1/143/121499; memorandum by F. C. Blair, 'British Harvester Movement – 1928', 14 September 1928, MG 26 J1/171/133206.

64 *Ibid.*, King Papers, W. J. Egan to O. D. Skelton, 4 August 1928; W. J. Egan to L. S. Amery, 30 July 1928, MG26 J1/152/129282; *Canadian Annual Review*, 1928–29, p. 156.

65 King Papers, J. B. Bickersteth to King, 3 July 1928, MG26 J1/150/128228; Forke to King, 30 October 1928, MG26 J1/152/129583; Norman Rogers to Harry Baldwin, 13 September 1928, MG26 J1/156/133201.

66 Meighen Papers, W. H. Wilson to Meighen, 5 March 1926, MG26/I/96/054997; Drummond, *Imperial Economic Policy*, p. 97; petitions submitted by M. Boulanger, MP in Canada, Select Standing Committee on Agriculture and Colonization, *Minutes of Proceedings and Evidence and Report*, (Ottawa, 1928), appendix 8, pp. 813ff.; Toronto *Mail and Empire*, 15 February 1926.

67 King Papers, Larkin to King, 7 December 1928, MG26 J1/154/131021; T. C. Davis to King, 19 October 1929, MG26 J1/161/136962.

68 Notwithstanding his other misgivings, Larkin complained about the 'ever-growing army of officials' blocking would-be emigrants. Out of 6,600 emigrants landed in Canada only six were retained for a second medical examination, he argued, 'so that it looks as though the present method does not need much improvement'. King's anodyne answer, which he thought should pacify 'our ultra-British friends', was that medical inspection had been in operation for years; the only difference now being that examination is held before sailing rather than after arrival'. King Papers, Larkin to King, 29 April 1927, MG26 J1/144/122888; King to G. G. McGeer, 17 April 1928,

MG26 J1/154/131309; Select Committee, *Minutes of Proceedings and Report* . . ., pp. 5, 50ff.

69 Select Committee, *Minutes of Proceedings and Report* . . ., *passim*; Department of Immigration and Colonization, *Annual Report 1927–28*, pp. 8–9; *Canadian Annual Review*, 1927–28, pp. 72ff.

70 King Papers, Amery to King, 14 June 1928, MG26 J1/150/128016.

71 Drummond, *Imperial Economic Policy*, p. 103; details of the programme for 1929 are summarised in the *Canadian Annual Review*, 1928–29, pp. 158–9.

72 King Papers, J. F. B. Livesay to King, 26 February 1929, MG26 J1/164/139373; T. C. Davis to King, 5 October 1929, MG26 J1/161/136962; King to Bickersteth, 30 July 1929, MG26 J1/159/135744; F. C. Blair, 'Important Steps in Immigration' 30 January 1930, MG26 J1/171/195731.

73 Ian Drummond, *British Economic Policy and the Empire 1919–1939*, London, 1972, p. 85; King Papers, J. H. Thomas to Forke, 20 August 1929, MG26 J1/169/144242.

74 *Manitoba Free Press*, 18 March 1930, quoted in *Canadian Annual Review*, 1929–30, p. 180; W. S. Clark to J. H. Thomas, 29 August 1930, DO 35/343/10162/6.

75 King Papers, F. L. C. Floud to O. D. Skelton, 14 November 1936, MG26 J1/216/186657.

76 The Hornby Scheme of 1937 and the Page Croft Scheme of 1938, which proposed to settle British families on Saskatchewan and British Columbia farms respectively with government assistance under the renewed Empire settlement legislation made little headway in Ottawa. While officials promised to give the schemes 'every consideration', the 'Government's attitude was one of caution' given the practical difficulties. Other supporters of renewed immigration included such patriotic groups as the Canadian Corps Association and IODE, the so-called 'Empire Policy Group' of Conservative British MPs, as well as the 'Empire Migration Group' which Vincent Massey organised. Toronto *Globe and Mail*, 22 December and 23 December 1938; Vancouver *Province*, 14 July 1935; *The Times*, 15 June 1937; King Papers, H. B. Donaldson to King, 11 March 1936, MG26 J1/230/ 203035; T. A. Crerar to King, 23 March 1937, MG26 J1/233/200138; PAC, Manion Papers, Sir Henry Page Croft to Manion, 11 February 1939, MG27/III/B7/48.

77 Drummond, *Imperial Economic Policy*, p. 95; Glasgow *Herald*, 12 July 1938.

CHAPTER EIGHT

Empire settlement and South African immigration policy, 1910–1948

Edna Bradlow

Two main motifs emerge from an analysis of South African attitudes and policies towards immigration in the period from the establishment of the Union in 1910 to the election of the Nationalist government in 1948. One perception of immigration was negative, racially determined and therefore exclusionist. It is relevant to this chapter in that it determined the Union's principal immigration legislation, Act 22 of 1913, the Immigrants' Regulation Act; and two important extensions of that legislation, Act 8 of 1930, the Immigration Quota Act, and Act 1 of 1937, the Aliens Act. These enactments were designed to restrict the entry of immigrants regarded at various times as undesirable; respectively 'Asiatics', Eastern and Southern Europeans, and German Jews. The second aspect of immigration policy – the nub of this study – was supposedly more positive: the purported encouragement of white immigration from countries regarded on historic and ethnic grounds as providing suitable additions to the existing mix of the white population of South Africa, namely the United Kingdom and other dominions, or Holland, Germany and Scandinavia.

Attempts by the Imperial government between the wars to encourage British settlement in South Africa were to be largely frustrated, and it is the prime purpose of this chapter to explain the obstacles. To do so it is necessary to examine the period from 1910 to 1948. It will be shown that attitudes and policies towards immigration had been substantially defined in South Africa long before the Imperial government attempted to affect their character. Moreover, the changes which subsequently occurred up to 1948 (and beyond) were to be determined largely by the balance of forces and interests within South Africa, and scarcely at all by imperial lobbying and overtures. Central to the definition of South African immigration policies was, first, the attempt by the white communities to increase their racial dominance by increasing their numbers, but without altering their traditional use of 'ultra exploitable' unskilled black labour;[1] and, secondly, the intense competition for power and status within the white community consequent upon the emergence of an Afrikaner nationalism fearful of British domination. For most of this half century the latter obstructed the former and in the process frustrated the British government's Empire settlement programme.

Smuts's 1947 scheme was the first substantive reversal of traditional South African attitudes, and as such demands inclusion in the present study, although its inception runs slightly beyond the time span of this book. The scheme's abridgement following the Nationalist victory in the 1948 election delayed for over a decade the restoration of a positive policy, during which time Europe passed its emigration peak.

Before the First World War

In 'new' countries population increase was the product both of a higher birth rate and large-scale immigration. Several structural factors, however, militated against any significant influx of the desired settlers to South Africa. Compared to Australia or Canada, the amount of cheap, cultivatable land accessible to transport and markets, necessary for closer settlement, was limited. True, there was marginal land, but this could be made productive only with great capital expenditure, which the modest budget of the Union in its first few decades did not allow. Further, industrialisation was in its infancy, and protection anathema in ruling circles. Consequently, there was insufficient industrial development to create an alternative demand for imported skilled workers.[2] Patrick Duncan, a young administrator in the Transvaal Colony, was therefore being coolly realistic when, in 1909, he warned the newly established White Expansion Society in Johannesburg that 'existing conditions throughout South Africa both on the land and in industries are not such as to attract a large European population who will settle permanently here'.[3]

Moreover, the peculiar socio-economic conditions in South Africa, which swelled the numbers of 'poor whites' after the South African War, were ultimately responsible for diverting from the Union thousands of emigrants who left Europe before and after the First World War. For the mirror image of the dispossessed, indigent white was the poor black. The greatest barrier to South Africa's development on the Australian, let alone the American model envisaged by optimists, was the presence of a vast, apparently tractable, unskilled – and therefore ill-paid – black labour force. Their increasing participation in the white economy reinforced the traditional South African aversion to the employment of white unskilled labour in the same kind of menial work; it reinforced, that is, what a nineteenth-century Cape official, the Attorney-General,

William Porter, had referred to as 'the aristocracy of the skin'. Thus already by the time of Union, the rehabilitation of *déclassé* whites had become a cardinal political objective. Consequently, the inefficiency of South Africa's white inhabitants was protected by the absence of positive encouragement for the immigrant who came with no other capital than his muscles and his determination.[4]

Nevertheless, South Africans of all political persuasions perceived that white dominance was contingent upon increased white numbers. All paid varying degrees of lip-service to this abstract concept. None of the political parties, however, showed a real commitment to encouraging immigration. Louis Botha's South African Party (SAP), a loose coalition of nationalist agrarian groups, which constituted the government in the first decade and a half of Union, subscribed to a policy couched in such contradictory terms that its *bona fides* are doubtful.[5] All that is clear is that its constant goal was the reinforcement of the white elite. While Botha maintained that Dutch South Africa might conceivably welcome as immigrants 'a stream of white labour', he insisted that the settlement on the land of displaced poor whites would necessarily need to precede such a development.[6] This was an attitude even more extremely held by the particularist Orangia Unie wing of the ruling party, led by J. B. M. Hertzog, which wished to postpone the elaboration of positive immigration policies to an indefinite season.[7] The most Botha was prepared to accept was what he described as 'agriculturists', that is yeoman farmers with sufficient capital to buy a farm;[8] ownership and not tenancy was the South African norm.[9] Thus while land policy remained the starting-point of immigration theory, capital was the operative factor. 'It would be a very risky undertaking . . . for anyone to come here with a family without the necessary capital', Botha's secretary informed an Australian enquirer.[10] An aberrant opinion was that of J. C. Smuts, Botha's lieutenant. Smuts recognised the primacy of industrial development in economic growth, a perception he was to retain throughout his political life. In a country short of skilled labour and the facilities to train it, he believed the encouragement of immigration was therefore essential.[11]

The immigration policy of the Unionist opposition – the only fundamentally Empire-orientated political party in South Africa – was theoretically far more positive than the government's, but divisions within the party revealed a good deal of dishonesty on this issue. To wean South Africa from its dependence on black unskilled labour, and to increase the population's English-speaking component, the Unionists called for 'the encouragement of closer settlement coupled with state acquisition of land where necessary, and an active policy having for its aim the attraction and assistance of suitable immigrants'.[12] This was subsequently coupled with the suggestion of a tax on the value of unimproved land, the intention ostensibly being to encourage the 'unlocking' of more land for immigrants. Possibly it was coincidental that the sale of cleared ground was infinitely more profitable than 'raw' ground, and that several of the leading Unionists (such as Percy Fitzpatrick, Patrick Duncan and Thomas Smartt) were involved in land speculation companies. Many of the top Unionists were also mining magnates. In that capacity they tended to oppose the large-scale importation of white skilled workers, lest their *Weltanshauung* included trade unionist ideas, 'pregnant with trouble for the future'.[13] Only Patrick Duncan urged the replacement of indentured black labour by assisting the immigration of unskilled whites.[14] In doing so he postulated the sacrifice of immediate prosperity for the promise of continued white supremacy; a choice, that is, between two major South African aspirations.

The newly established Labour Party's policy was a hybrid based on two principles which reflected its genesis as a white workers' party. It resembled the Unionists in its opposition to the uncontrolled importation of white contract labour, but with the diametrically opposite intention of protecting the bargaining power and wages, and hence the living standards, of white skilled workers. Like Duncan, it urged the importation of white unskilled labour to replace unskilled blacks, but at a wage suitable for 'white living standards'. This was a revolutionary proposal in the context of South African labour relations.[15]

The vapid platitudes characterising immigration discourse before the First World War give the impression that none of these proposals was intended to be put to the test; and indeed in the early years of Union, immigration policy was concerned more with 'Asiatic' restrictions than European entry. In 1913 the differing restrictive immigration laws of South Africa's four components were repealed, and a unified policy was statutorily consolidated under the Immigrants' Regulation Act. 'Asiatic' immigration was henceforth tightly controlled. European 'domestic servants, skilled artizans, mechanics, workmen, or miners' were among those 'not to be deemed prohibited immigrants'; but sluggish industrial growth ensured that there was little demand for imported white labour except in a very limited number of occupations.[16]

Meanwhile a scheme conceived in the heady political atmosphere of the 1911 Imperial Conference proposed to encourage immigration by providing assisted passages for small-scale farmers.[17] It foundered on the rock of Hertzog's rancorous opposition. What Duncan called 'the Hertzog cloud on the horizon' also blocked less-ambitious plans to bring out the families of those Cornish miners (the 'Cousin Jacks') who worked on the Witwatersrand, the intention being to stabilise this highly volatile labour force.[18] The Land Settlement Act of 1912 produced a similar reaction. The Act was intended to remedy the grave deficiencies in agriculture, purportedly as a prior condition for the stimulation of 'commercial development'. The inclusion of immigrants among those deemed 'suitable' to qualify for government-aided land allotment aroused intense emotion in the Hertzogites who constituted a substantial element in the ruling party. Consequently, plans to offer certain lands exclusively to immigrants were dropped. Over the years the proportion of immigrants among those granted land declined drastically. By 1929 the emphasis of the Land Settlement Act had wholly shifted: of 6,000 settlers, only sixty-three were British – or dominion – born. As an immigration stimulant, the Land Settlement Act was a dead-letter.[19]

Before the First World War domestic pressures, including Hertzog's objections and trade union militancy, forced Botha to abandon his 1911 plans and repeat his belief that assisted immigration could only follow the prior settlement of poor whites on the land.[20] Indeed, thereafter the Cabinet and leading parliamentarians constantly assured supporters that the government would never allow 'their own people' to be 'swamped' by strangers.[21] While the government was unable to encourage immigration by providing assisted passages or land grants, there was, however, no obstruction to independent, self-financing white immigration, particularly from the United Kingdom.

It is important to pause and establish what type of immigrants were actually coming to the Union under their own steam in the period before the First World War. Data provided by the conflicting and inadequate records kept before 1924 yield trends rather than definitive information. It is clear, however, that such immigration as took place continued to depend primarily upon conditions in the mining industry, which since the South African War had been going through a period of dislocation caused by labour problems. Thus, despite the fact that while skilled workers on the Rand were in 1914 better off than those similarly employed in Europe or the United States of America,[22] immigration statistics for this class showed, that year, a net deficit.[23] The overwhelming majority of those coming to the Union's shores were from the United Kingdom or its Empire. In 1910 8,314 British settlers arrived in South Africa. In 1913 (one of the few years for which reasonably reliable statistics are available), of the 14,251 new arrivals, 10,009 were British subjects.[24] The significance of these figures can be gauged, however, only when compared to those of Australia (32,725 British immigrants in 1910) and Canada (168,059 entries from the United Kingdom in 1909–10).[25]

Wartime and after

With the outbreak of the First World War, interest in immigration initially languished, apart from an enthusiastic but impractical scheme to bring in Belgian peasants. Local interest revived, however, in 1916, as a result of developments in the United Kingdom during the previous year. In March 1915, when there were still high expectations that the war would be won quickly, the Royal Colonial Institute established a committee to investigate the settlement of ex-servicemen on the land, both at home and abroad. Sir H. Rider Haggard, who as a member of the Dominions Royal Commission had visited the Union in 1914, returned in early 1916 to investigate the availability of land for British settlers.

Hertzog's newly formed National Party rather than the government now dictated immigration policy. The National Party arose out of the Northern Republics' defeat in the South African War, probably the most divisive and traumatic experience in Afrikaner history. Immigration restriction was an important aspect of what Professor Rodney Davenport has called the Afrikaner 'Risorgimento', with its interlocking social, financial and political structures, intended initially to protect the Afrikaner and subsequently to ensure his dominance. Those who advocated state-aided immigration, particularly for British settlers, were therefore suspected of being motivated by a desire to destroy the Afrikaner identity – in some cases a not unfounded accusation.[26] Consequently, as Rider Haggard travelled through South Africa on his imperial business, Afrikaners were warned against allowing land purchase to achieve what conquest had failed to do.[27]

Emotionally and politically vulnerable to this challenge, Botha's government persisted in its apathetic approach to immigration. The South African High Commissioner in London was a member of the Tennyson Committee set up in 1917 to broach the question of ex-servicemen settlement in the dominions; but Nationalist opposition ensured that the South African government, unlike the governments of the other dominions, refused to commit itself to the provision of cheap land to such ex-servicemen. The most the government would do was to waive the health restrictions in the Immigrants' Regulation Act, thereby allowing the untrammelled entry of shell-shocked or wounded men.[28] Moreover, the Union government evaded responsibility for making a future decision by emphasising that the South African Parliament would be the final arbiter in accepting any state-aided scheme. Immediately after the war the government, now led by Smuts, again tentatively raised the topic of imperial immigration;[29] but the Nationalists predictably continued to perceive this as a frontal attack on their vision of ultimate South African sovereign independence.

As Nationalist anti-British sentiment and Republican propaganda increased, government inertia therefore persisted. In response to, and mindful of, Canadian and Australian determinations to get 'a large influx of good English blood',[30] the Unionists consequently redoubled their efforts to acquire post-war British emigrants for South Africa. Wartime imperial sentiment and simultaneous prosperity within the country were not commodities lightly to be squandered.[31] In mid-1916 therefore the Unionist hierarchy established an organisation to attract prospective settlers, at first by initiating small land schemes and later in the industrial field.[32] The Unionists consulted the high priest of British imperialism, Lord Milner, as to how South Africa might acquire 'desirable immigrants . . . considering the attractions offered by the various dominions'.[33] Subsequently, in 1919 at its first post-war congress, the party jettisoned its former anodyne phrases, and came down firmly in favour of British immigration through 'the systematic and continuous introduction of suitable white British subjects and by helping their settlement on the land'.[34] The establishment of the 1820 Memorial, Settlers' Association was the outcome of this resolution. Its founder was Charles Crewe, a leading Unionist.

This, then, was the political background in the Union when the British government's post-war emigration plans began to emerge. As described earlier in this book, one consequence of the Haggard mission, of the Dominions Royal Commission and of the Tennyson Committee report[35] was, ultimately, the establishment at the Colonial Office of the Oversea Settlement Committee.[36] An immediate task for the committee was to ensure a flow of British ex-servicemen and women and their dependents to the Empire by negotiating settlement schemes with the governments of the dominions.[37]

National Party opposition to such proposals was, again, predictable. It fluctuated between vituperation (such as Hertzog's claim that the proposed emigration of Poor Law and reform school children would make South Africa 'the dirt heap of the Empire'[38]) and economic arguments (that unemployment and the plight of the predominantly Afrikaans-speaking poor whites precluded 'any kind of immigration'[39]). Consequently, the Smuts government dared show only minimal enthusiasm for the British plans, as the statistics indicate. By the end of 1922 a mere 5,894 settlers had come to South Africa and Rhodesia (compared to the 74,000 who went to Canada and Australasia).[40] Ex-servicemen were positively welcomed to South Africa only if they were financially well endowed or had offers of guaranteed employment.

Meanwhile the onslaught of depression and high unemployment from the winter of 1920 had led the British government to seek a more permanent arrangement with the dominions, one which would siphon off these unemployed thousands and redistribute them in the Empire, while at the same time encouraging the exploitation of under-developed imperial resources.[41] Amery's concept of state-aided Empire migration and land settlement, adumbrated at a conference in London early in 1921, was therefore basically a scheme of overseas relief for the United Kingdom's unemployed, clothed in the vocabulary of enlightened imperial self-interest and the still attractive appeal of imperial sentiment. The details of the subsequent Empire Settlement Act of 1922 have been dealt with elsewhere in this volume. What is germane here is the reaction of the South African government.

At the Imperial Conference of June 1921, South Africa publicly 'dissociated herself rather sharply' from the draft proposals which were later embodied in the Act,[42] on the usual ground that 'the limited field for white labour in South Africa [would] preclude co-operation by the Union government on the lines contemplated by the other Dominions'.[43] Privately, however, the South African delegation sent by Smuts did agree to some alternative form of co-operation, possibly for example using the newly formed 1820 Memorial, Settlers' Association.[44]

The ambiguities of the South African government's reaction can be explained only in terms of the country's domestic politics, which limited imperial powers of persuasion. In November 1920 Smuts and the SAP had been forced to seek an alliance with the Unionists after his party's disastrous showing in the March election.[45] The coalition fought another election in February 1921. In his opening campaign salvo on 3 December 1920, Smuts made a statement on immigration which clearly reflected Unionist pressure upon him. His remarks were significant, not only as a departure from the traditional South African emphasis on agricultural development but also as an earnest less of present exigencies than of future projections. Smuts reiterated his earlier conviction that agricultural development alone was insufficient for South Africa; the poor white and unemployment problems would be solved and the 'white basis of the future South Africa' ensured by industrialisation and urbanisation. He therefore accepted as a corollary the immigration of skilled European artisans. These hopes of economic diversification were, however, immediately aborted when recession (and subsequent depression) hit South Africa late in 1921. Unprofitable mines closed, nascent industry languished, and unemployed rural whites vainly pounded the streets of the larger towns in search of work.[46]

The Nationalists in opposition naturally made enormous political mileage out of this concatenation of SAP/Unionist merger, the depression and the discussions in London at the 1921 state-aided immigration conference.[47] Consequently the government was forced to administer the Immigrants' Regulation Act more stringently, and publicly to disclaim that any form of immigration 'for political purposes' was being implemented.[48]

While this disavowal was strictly speaking true, the Smuts government, influenced particularly by its ex-Unionist wing, did not entirely abandon its attempts to induce British immigrants to come to South Africa. It continued to use the High Commissioner's London office for screening prospective settlers, as it had been doing for several years. In November 1920 the publicity department of the South African Railways, with the High Commissioner's co-operation, inaugurated a campaign designed ostensibly to advertise the country's tourist attractions and resources but also directed at well-to-do British emigrants.[49] Subsequently the government established a settlement department in the High Commissioner's Office, under a Department of Lands official. His function was to advise those (primarily British) settlers in the 'small beginner' category, who had already decided to emigrate. Between 1921 and 1923 1,030 such settlers arrived, bringing something like £4 million in assets.[50] Once in South Africa they were further assisted by the Lands and Agriculture Departments and *The Farmer's Weekly* at whose disposal the government had placed its advisers and officials.[51] This was hardly the type of emigration envisaged by the British government, emigration which would 'siphon off' and 'redistribute' the United Kingdom's unemployed. But by mid-1923 the consonance of increasing white fears that their 'civilisation' would be swamped by black numbers and white hopes that the country was emerging from the depression encouraged the Smuts government to go further. It openly announced its intention of acquiring – under the Empire Settlement Act – British settlers and the British government subsidy for assisted passages and land purchase, using the Union's own Land Settlement Act as bait.[52]

The move, though modest, was a milestone in the South African context. Its target, despite Smuts's personal enthusiasm for skilled industrial workers, was still that *rara avis*, the comfortable yeoman farmer, the guardian of social peace and stability – and also, alas, the man who had seldom been available in the United Kingdom or any other Western European country, as an export commodity. ('The happy and powerful', as de Tocqueville remarked, 'do not go into exile.') The type of unskilled immigrant the Australian states were prepared to pay simply to arrive was still not included in the South African plans, which therefore aroused criticism both locally and in certain quarters in the United Kingdom.[53]

The National and Labour Parties went into the 1924 election as allies (the Pact) against the Smuts government. Labour was still opposed to encouraging the importation of contract labour, whether white or black.[54] This attitude conformed with a strand of Nationalist thinking which was reinforced as ever-increasing numbers of migrant rural Afrikaners sought to enter industry. The fact, however, that the membership of the Labour Party was still predominantly English-speaking now curbed conventional Nationalist invective against British settlers. Immigration therefore played a small role in the election which resulted in Smut's defeat.

As a result of that election the hesitant steps towards the first, positive, official immigration policy in Union history were halted; Smuts had to wait over twenty years for another chance. Between 1924 and 1933 official policy virtually reverted to the obstructive lack of interest which had characterised the period before the First World War. Even though the country experienced an outward seepage of British-born and South African subjects, the Pact government abandoned all pretence of fostering immigration, however feebly.[55] The British were a particular anathema to the dominant political partner, not least because they were accused of bringing in with their cultural baggage 'ideas of the equality of all civilised men and women'.[56] Further, the Pact government preferred settlers from the other two *stamlande* (Germany and Holland). Consequently, immigration from the United Kingdom was discouraged in various ways. The advice bureaux in London and Cape Town were closed; the assisted-family operation (aborted by Hertzog in 1911 and resuscitated after the war) was terminated;[57] and bilingualism in certain public employment was strictly enforced.[58]

Nevertheless the British continued to make up the largest group of immigrants; 27,813 persons out of over 52,000 arrivals. Their numbers were still negligible, however, compared to the many more thousands accepted by the other dominions.[59] 'I look out of the window at groups of English immigrants coming ashore from a ship just in, on its way to Australia', Patrick Duncan regretfully observed. 'They pass our doors but do not stay here.'[60]

The Hertzog government's segregationist and Afrikaner Nationalist rhetoric in other spheres was far less extensively implemented than previous historiography has suggested.[61] A similar conclusion can be inferred in the case of immigration policy. While Smuts theoretically aspired to increase white numbers, and Hertzog opposed British settlement particularly, in practice the volume and type of white immigration remained unchanged; all immigrants came voluntarily and at no expense to the state. Both SAP and Pact governments ultimately represented the belief 'that it is practicable and desirable to preserve a national and cultural entity, however much the expansion of populations is restricted in that preservation'.[62]

Land companies and the 1820 Association

In the absence of state enterprise, two non-governmental sources filled the vacuum. These were the land companies, concerned with profits, and the 1820 Memorial, Settlers' Association mentioned earlier. Already by 1910 most of the best land in South Africa was privately owned,[63] and South African demand alone would have taken up any arable land which came on the market. There were, however, large empty tracts either crown or company owned in the Transvaal, Eastern Orange Free State, Zululand and the Eastern Cape, on which settlers might be successfully placed, though initially not in the closer settlement pattern favoured by the government.[64]

Under the 1912 Land Settlement Act, the way was opened for private land schemes. Whereas in the other dominions governments and land companies had sometimes gone a long way towards attracting settlers by offering cleared or partly cleared land at reasonable prices,[65] in South Africa developed land was expensive, and the settler himself was expected to do the pioneering work, on the assumption that eventually his land would prove profitable. This put South Africa at a disadvantage compared to the other dominions. Consequently, the land companies came to realise that while they had a potentially profitable investment, the provision of certain basic facilities was essential for ultimate success.

One such scheme was Sir Percy Fitzpatrick's Cape Sundays River Settlement, 21 miles from Port Elizabeth. This had been established in 1913 as a combined business and patriotic venture when the shortcomings of the Land Settlement Act were already becoming apparent.[66] One-third of the land was reserved for British immigrants who would be sandwiched between the local settlers to encourage acculturation. There were also the Transvaal companies, such as the Transvaal Consolidated and Land Exploration Company founded in 1893, but they attracted fewer settlers than those in the Cape. These companies owned vast remote tracts deemed suitable for large-scale ranching or maize cultivation. Consequently, their problems were more concerned with transport and marketing facilities than with the water shortage which handicapped schemes like the Sundays River project.

European *émigrés* and demobilised British ex-servicemen with a little capital and no experience provided the land companies with potential customers.[67] By 1922 at least twenty new companies were operating out of London alone.[68] At worst many of these 'mushroom' companies were 'unadulterated swindles';[69] at best they neglected to make even the most elementary but essential soil and water analyses. The establishment by the Smuts government of a settlement department in the

High Commissioner's office in London was intended as much to protect as to encourage would-be settlers. The ineffectiveness of its supervision can be gauged from the failure of the Sundays River Company. Few of those British ex-officers who purchased its land in the expectation of developing viable citrus orchards would have risked their meagre capital had the High Commission office not supposedly vetted the company's information. Yet far from the well-irrigated plots promised in the company's brochure, the settlers came – in all ignorance of South African conditions – to a searing drought which made of their allotments a treeless, sun-baked waste. Many lost their capital before the crucial ingredient, water, could be provided.[70]

Unlike the land companies, the 1820 Memorial, Settlers' Association[71] was concerned less with profits than people. Its roots lay in the establishment of the White Expansion Society in May 1909 by enthusiasts in London and Johannesburg.[72] Among the latter were Unionists such as Patrick Duncan who carried their intentions a step further in 1916 with the land settlement scheme mentioned before. In 1919 Unionist immigration proposals were dovetailed with the plans of the descendants of the 1820 British settlers to commemorate their illustrious ancestors. Thus, when the 1820 Association was formed in April 1920, several months before the SAP/Unionist merger, it had influential Unionist support for its decision to encourage and aid the settlement of carefully selected and preferably British immigrants in the Union and Rhodesia.[73]

The new association, as already noted, was led in South Africa by Sir Charles Crewe, a leading Unionist immigration enthusiast. At its other operational centre in London, a committee was established which had strong support from men whose names read like a roll-call of imperial South African history: Lords Milner, Methuen and Selborne; Otto Beit, Geoffrey Dawson, Philip Kerr, Rudyard Kipling and many others. They provided the means and the determination to assist the type of immigrants the Smuts government preferred – but whose entry in considerable numbers it could not publicly espouse.[74]

The 1820 Association's aims – the strengthening of the white races in South Africa by the introduction of primary producers and the strengthening of the ideology of Empire by the introduction of British settlers – were endowed with a quasi-religious significance reminiscent of the objectives of Afrikaner nationalism.[75] The replacement of the Union's war losses of English South Africans was a related if short-term intention.[76]

'Character' was emphasised as the criterion of acceptance for support by the 1820 Association;[77] but 'character' seems to have been a class attribute, equated with an elitist education and adequate means, which

[185]

meant the possession of £1,500 and £2,000 capital for single and married men, respectively. Thus, the admission of working-class settlers was initially rejected as 'fatal, wrong and economically unsound'; only by admitting 'a high class of immigrants' could a high standard of civilisation be maintained. 'We want masters not men', Crewe told a London audience.[78] But many of that class lay among the poppies in Flanders fields. Moreover, fund-raising was a strain, for the 1820 Association never enjoyed mass support either in the United Kingdom or South Africa. In 1923, however, the Imperial government recognised the organisation. Under the Empire Settlement Act it contributed a per capita grant for every settler, thus strengthening the ties between the 1820 Association and the official British emigration scheme.

After the First World War it was believed that the United Kingdom had a surplus of women and the dominions an abnormal shortage. There already existed in South Africa an organisation, the South African Colonisation Society, dedicated to bringing 'suitable' British women to South Africa. This was absorbed in 1919 by the Society for the Oversea Settlement of British Women (SOSBW), which aimed to co-ordinate British supply with dominion demand. The SOSBW was officially recognised in 1920 when it was designated the Women's Branch of the Oversea Settlement Department, and from 1924 it worked closely with the 1820 Association.

The attitude of the Smuts government was inevitably ambivalent, for while the 1820 Association was bringing in the 'right' type of settler,[79] its conspicuous imperial ideology was an embarrassment. Thus, the government played a very minor role in the 1820 Association's affairs. Nevertheless the National Party, observing the composition of the London committee, labelled it 'an anti-Afrikaner conspiracy' and a government front, designed to make South Africa subservient to British interests.[80] The inception of the Pact government in 1924 terminated even the unenthusiastic support the 1820 Association had received from government circles. This, together with the 1927 controversy over the South African national flag, discouraged British immigration to the Union, compounding an apparent reluctance to leave the United Kingdom; what Lady Milner described as 'a general stick in all classes to emigrate.'[81]

South Africa avoided a net migration loss in the last years of the 1920s only through the entry of Eastern Europeans, although they were the least desirable immigrants from the viewpoint of the Hertzog government. British farmers and men with enough capital to live off the income were being diverted to Southern Rhodesia. As a result, the 1820 Association was forced to modify its original middle-class orientation. By 1929 the emphasis was on merely personal attributes such as good health, a capacity for hard work and an adaptability to local conditions.[82] Consequently, the 1820 Association began casting around for candidates from 'all classes', including working-class boys.[83] Paradoxically the Pact government's colour bar employment policy, with its insistence on a 'living wage' for unskilled white labour, favoured these very immigrants. Canada and Australia had already absorbed them in thousands as agricultural labourers who would ultimately work their own farms. In the Union the 1820 Association helped these young men to obtain land. Under the conditions which obtained in South Africa's agricultural system, however, the possession of even a modicum of capital after the farm had been acquired was still important, and the 1820 Association erred in failing to stress this point.[84]

The advent in 1931 of a three-year depression and its effect on primary producers, coupled with a punishing drought in the Transvaal, and the over-valuation of the South African pound, sharply contracted the 1820 Association's activities. Only 101 settlers arrived under its aegis between September 1931 and September 1932, while 126 left.[85] Then in 1934 the end of drought and depression, the formation by Hertzog and Smuts of a Fusion government, and a rise in the price of gold and wool, broke South Africa's cycle of disasters. Money became cheaper and land prices eased, while burgeoning industrialisation increased the demand for skilled artisans, upon whom the 1820 Association now focused the main thrust of its endeavours.[86] Moreover, with the shortage of suitable British applicants (even from India where the Government of India Act of 1935 caused many early retirements), its activities were extended to Scandinavians, Dutch and even German Jews.[87] As a result 1937–38 was a record year. Over 1,000 immigrants (88 per cent of whom were wage-earners) came to the Union under the 1820 Association's aegis. The highest accolade was received in 1939 when the British government showed its satisfaction by increasing the 1820 Association's grant from the Oversea Settlement Department.

While immigration into the Union was drastically and unavoidably reduced during the war years, the 1820 Association continued to prepare itself for an anticipated post-hostilities British influx.[88] In the interim period between the end of the war and the inauguration of Smut's scheme, it was virtually the only organisation doing anything about immigration, with its London and Cape Town offices acting as unofficial conduits.[89]

By January 1946, after exactly twenty-five years of existence, the 1820 Association had sponsored 10,000 settlers, overwhelmingly British in origin. Its policy over those years had been predominantly elitist, ethnocentric and land-orientated, defined as it was both by the preferences of successive South African governments and by its founders' conviction of the excellence of British 'blood' and institutions. As such, it was a microcosm of the whole range of experience in South African immigration history – with the crucial difference that the 1820 Association kept alive and coherently implemented a real commitment to both the existing and the potential value of immigration. Thus, while the organisation never really fulfilled the expectations of its founders, it was important for its positive approach to immigration at a time when official South African policy was characterised by platitudes or ritual incantations.

Pre-war and post-war

The fusion of the National and South African Parties in June 1934 produced in December the United South African Nationalist Party, which, shorn of its radical 'jingoes' and its Purified Nationalists under D. F. Malan, represented the indeterminate middle ground of white South African politics. On the immigration question, the new party indicated that while it supported 'acceptable' European immigration, 'a state-financed scheme . . . under existing conditions is not desirable'.[90]

This doctrine of 'no change' implied 'do nothing', but economic requirements immediately made this an untenable policy. Between 1934 and 1939 the quickening tempo of economic growth, particularly on the Rand, inaugurated a period of almost uninterrupted prosperity which virtually solved the poor white problem, sucked into the economy great numbers of black workers and raised the living standards of the total population.[91] Economic factors therefore made this period the most propitious moment since Union for instituting an active and rationalised immigration policy. Consequently, employers began to appeal for a more-positive approach, as the local labour supply proved inadequate, particularly in the mining, construction and manufacturing sectors.

The United Party government was, however, collectively confused on this issue primarily because – despite the prevailing climate of reconciliation – the old SAP/Nationalist divergences persisted, as they did on other emotionally divisive questions.[92] Immigration impinged on matters about which South Africans were not invariably rational; the imperial connection, a broad South African nationalism, and the relationship between black and white and white and white.[93] The ambivalences implicit in government immigration policy were no more surely revealed than during the passing of the 1937 Aliens Act. Designed to exclude German Jews, although they were ideal immigrants, its rationale was purely political.[94]

By comparison, the two main opposition parties were able to adopt unequivocal (though contradictory) stances. As heirs to the Unionists, the Dominion Party favoured mass, preferably British, immigration. At the centre of Nationalist opposition there was still an obsession with the 'swamping' of the Afrikaner both physically and culturally. When the National Party did occasionally support immigration, it was as a ritualistic act, based on the slogan 'assimilability'. Examined more closely, this meant welcoming those who would identify totally with the Afrikaners at a time when Nationalist ideology was increasingly expressing itself through separatist cultural and economic organisations. It meant the total exclusion of Jews and limitations on the hitherto unrestricted entry of British settlers who could fulfil the requirements of the Union immigration legislation.

Between 1933 and 1939 the net migration gain was about 27,174, an undoubted increase on the 16,443 for 1924–33[95] but hardly dramatic in view of the government's political strength and the country's prosperity. The demographic trend present at the time of unification continued; white population growth was achieved overwhelmingly by natural increase.[96] The one major change in the immigration pattern in the half decade before the Second World War was the shift away from the predominantly British orientation of earlier migrations. This was the result of a conjunction of particular political and socio-economic conditions in the United Kingdom,[97] the inception of an attractive government-assisted Southern Rhodesian scheme which siphoned off potential British settlement in South Africa[98] and a net gain in South Africa of foreign-born (particularly Dutch) immigrants.[99]

The 1939–45 war was the midwife of profound changes in South African society. Though the Herenigde National Party (HNP)[100] strongly opposed South Africa's participation on the Allied side, a great sense of national purpose was aroused among government supporters. Wartime needs diversified and strengthened the economy even further, making heavy demands on the country's manpower and material resources. The isolation of thousands of South Africans was broken by their experiences abroad as members of the armed forces. By the end of 1945, when a devastated Europe was ready for renewed mass emigration on a large scale, the Union was also prepared economically, politically and psychologically for the inception of an immigration scheme which would go far beyond Smuts's tentative essays in that direction after the First World War. It is important to emphasise that the scheme was not a response to Imperial government encouragement.

Even before the end of hostilities the formulation of a post-war policy had become a much-canvassed topic. Those in favour based their support on economic assumptions, which tended to be more-sophisticated repetitions of old arguments tailored to the changed circumstances of wartime growth. Put succinctly, the discussion postulated that greater productivity, increased earning capacity and a rise in the living standards of the whole population would be an immediate and spectacular consequence of immigration and its concomitant, an inflow of capital.[101]

As in the past, fear was the *raison d'être* for a subsidiary 'emotional/moral' argument favouring immigration. White population growth had failed to keep pace with that of blacks, and this was purportedly creating an insecurity which prevented whites from acting in a wholly just fashion.[102] Stripped of its verbal finery, this was the old white domination credo, modernised to suit the new morality of the Atlantic Charter. An also-ran was a cultural proposition: immigration would benefit the arts and sciences.[103]

In spite of this propaganda barrage emanating from private individuals, the institutionalised political response was predictable. The government still prevaricated, and supported by the Labour Party insisted that demobilisation was the country's most pressing need. Smuts was indebted to the volunteer servicemen whose vote had given him a resounding victory in the 1943 election. But this was also a deceptive victory. The HNP had cut into Afrikaner support for the United Party through an electoral campaign which concentrated on domestic issues, particularly race relations.[104] The most positive approach to mass post-war immigration came – not unexpectedly in view of its Unionist ancestry and 1820 Association connections – from the Dominion Party, which regarded a much enlarged white population as essential to both security and industrial expansion.[105]

HNP opposition reflected the xenophobia and its corollary, the exploitation of group identity and group sentiment as political instruments, which had characterised Nationalist discourse since 1914. Large-scale (and particularly British) immigration continued to be perceived as an anti-Afrikaner political ploy, *tout court*.[106] From the other end of the political spectrum the liberal voice was alone in proposing improved economic opportunities for blacks as the best expedient for maintaining industrial expansion. Consequently, the liberals were prepared to offer their support for a more-vigorous policy only if immigration were not used to perpetuate the exploitation of blacks in a racially determined social structure.

Meanwhile in Europe the war was entering its final stage. In view of the United Kingdom's slower rate of population growth and post-war requirements, the British government was reluctant to lose skilled manpower through uncontrolled and unassisted emigration. It still, however, regarded emigration to the dominions 'as a contribution to the best interests of the Commonwealth'.[107] The United Kingdom therefore began to sound out the dominions on the possibilities of a combined assisted migration scheme. All the Prime Ministers at the 1944 Commonwealth Conference gave precedence to demobilisation. In the South African case, there were the two additional constraints which had attended all immigration proposals since Union: the presence of a large, indigenous, unskilled labouring class; and the likelihood of arousing 'acute political controversy' through the apparent endorsement of a British-orientated scheme.[108] In the light of the HNP's 1943 electioneering campaign, practical considerations such as the shortage of white housing and employment opportunities were also used to reinforce these arguments.[109] Consequently, in February and June 1945 and again the following year at the Commonwealth Conference, the South African government rejected any such immigration scheme.[110]

However, early in 1946, the South African economy was, as noted before, in a very strong position, and the government was encouraging the decentralisation of industry, a policy designed to redress the imbalance between mining, agriculture and still lagging industrial development, but one which placed a severe strain on across-the-board manpower resources.[111] Moreover, the preliminary report of the 1946 census was published on 13 August, against a background of African industrial unrest on the Rand and Indian opposition to the 'Ghetto' Act, leading to a radicalisation of black politics and the concomitant fears of whites that they and their 'civilisation' were about to be submerged. The report indicated that out of a total population of 11.5 million, under 2.5 million were whites, and that blacks were increasing at four times the white rate. These figures could hardly have surprised the government, but their 'cold, merciful logic' was the lever which finally got things moving after months of indecision and paralysis.[112] For while the HNP interpreted the combination of census figures and unrest as confirming the need for their segregation policy, Smuts used them to persuade white South Africans that a 'bold and positive' immigration policy was imperative so as to 'strengthen our European basis'. 'The present world situation', he added 'gives me a good chance to obtain suitable immigrants.'[113] This faith in immigration as the solution to many of the country's most pressing economic and racial problems was perhaps the most consistent of Smut's political beliefs. In 1946 circumstances enabled him to initiate a policy which he regarded as his greatest contribution to South Africa's well-being.

Parliament was in recess when Smuts announced his government-sponsored scheme on 14 August 1946 – the day after the publication of the census report. 'Let us not be afraid', he announced to the party faithful in the Transvaal, 'let them come to the industry which is clamouring for them. I look on this . . . as a God-given chance.'[114] The reasons for the inception of this 'New Immigration Policy' were issued the following day in a statement to the press; to the manpower requirements and the demographic evidence were added South Africa's 'exposed geographical position' and its enhanced strategic importance.

The rationale for white opposition to immigration has frequently been mentioned in this chapter; what was new was the black reaction. The announcement of the scheme coincided with the moment when the moderate Native Representative Council joined the more militant African National Congress and Indian National Congress in taking 'an extreme line against colour discrimination'.[115] Thus, the acclaimed intention of strengthening white numbers aroused 'the very deepest resentment', reinforcing a conviction that whites could never envisage peacefully sharing political power and economic opportunity with blacks.

The primary aim of the Smuts scheme was to attract immigrants to the Union's shores quickly in order to pre-empt the other dominions. North-Western Europeans in general were traditionally regarded in South Africa as suitable immigrants; but for sentimental and administrative reasons the United Kingdom remained under Smuts's scheme the main source of supply. All natural-born British subjects were entitled to unrestricted admission, provided they complied with the requirements – mainly health and financial – of existing immigration legislation. Though South Africa offered no tangible benefits (such as assisted passages) compared to the other dominions, it was claimed that some quarter of a million British citizens almost immediately indicated a desire to emigrate to the Union.[116] The question immediately arises: what provoked such interest? There was patently a multiplicity of reasons ranging from employment opportunities to the climate and the ease of life for whites which many British servicemen had observed during brief wartime visits.

Despite Smuts's original hyperbolic intention of 'letting them all come', the emphasis fell heavily on skills.[117] An order of occupational preference was drawn up, headed by skilled workers (particularly builders) with specific job offers who could pay their own passages.[118] Initially the British government demurred on the grounds that only South Africa among the dominions insisted on trained artisans, whom the United Kingdom could not spare. But soon British Labour Exchanges were put at the Union government's disposal, subject to recruitment being dispersed around the country in order not to disrupt British industry unduly.

All too slowly administrative machinery creaked into action.[119] This comprised an Immigration Council in South Africa to co-ordinate all aspects of Union immigration policy, three oversea selection committees operating in Europe, and voluntary local committees to liaise between the council and employers.[120] The Smuts scheme was well under way, however, before accurate advice on local industrial conditions in South Africa was obtained by accepting the aid of employers and overcoming the scruples of a trade union structure dedicated to the closed-shop principle.[121] The confusion caused by delays in establishing the scheme's working parts was exacerbated by the system of allocating sea passages. After protracted negotiations, the Union Castle Company agreed in March 1947 to set aside two former troopships to serve primarily as immigrant carriers.[122] Moreover, despite Smuts's emphasis on the dissemination of accurate information, a brochure publicising the country was issued only in May 1947, when the first immigrants were already arriving. Thus, the advantages of the scheme's snap announcement were dissipated for want of prior planning. This was typical of Smuts. Once he had conceived an idea, he neglected the details, and failed efficiently to delegate authority or supervise implementation himself.

This gave the opposition the maximum opportunity to deride the scheme – often viciously – both in Parliament and in newspapers (particularly *Die Burger* and *Die Transvaler*) which had a close relationship with the National Party. While social issues such as the chronic housing shortage were assiduously canvassed, the old mysticism associated with the survival of Afrikanerdom still dominated Nationalist rhetoric; it was now, however, coupled with the charge that immigrants would be 'wrongly orientated' in their attitudes to the colour 'question'. Moreover, by 1947 the HNP was making a determined bid to establish a separate Afrikaner trade union movement and an important and new aspect of its attack on the scheme harped on the noxious effect it would have on white working-class interests.

The more than 60,000 immigrants (two-thirds of whom were British) who entered South Africa in 1947–48, mainly as a result of Smuts's initiative (which can at best be described as state-encouraged immigration), represented a dramatic increase, far exceeding the volume in any other period since Union and to be surpassed only in 1963–64 as a result of Dr H. F. Verwoerd's immigration legislation. This figure did not, however, match Smuts's annual target of 50,000, which was equivalent to about 2 per cent of the existing white group and regarded by experts as 'a safe absorption rate'. Nor did it remotely begin to reduce the black/white numerical disparity (and hence reassure whites), which was substantially the scheme's *raison d'être*. It did not even approach the gain from natural increase; in 1948, immigration's *annus mirabilis*, the net migration gain of 20,922, represented an 11.2 per cent increase, compared to 17.6 per cent by natural growth.[123]

Nevertheless much was achieved. Just over half the immigrants came as family units. This, together with the strong technical bias evinced in the occupations of males, gave the Smuts scheme a qualitative advantage over the pattern of previous years. The 25–34 age group predominated so that the country benefited by the acquisition of people whose productive capacity would span several more decades.[124] Most of the Smuts settlers were satisfied with their move; less than 1 per cent returned to the United Kingdom during the scheme's operation. Furthermore, the cost was comparatively low. By the end of September 1948, £235,630 had been spent, which covered the capital expenditure on two transit camps in South Africa and the monthly running costs of the scheme abroad.[125] By January 1948 a trifling sum of £10 had been advanced in recoverable loans, an effective riposte to the HNP accusation that the Smuts state-sponsored scheme was in fact a state-aided one.[126]

Above all the Smuts policy was a major breakthrough psychologically. Smuts finally abandoned the equivocations of earlier years by rejecting the claims traditionally made by Afrikaner Nationalists: that immigration had the conscious and sinister intention of destroying the Afrikaner. Letters to his wife – surely the most truthful on the subject – indicate, on the contrary, that from the standpoint of white South Africa, the scheme was conceived in a conciliatory spirit, removed from political expediency. Far from 'ploughing under' the Afrikaner, Smuts wrote, 'my doel is om hulle to red en die land van gewisse ondergang in die verre toekoms te red. Nou is ons kans – wat ons miskien nie gou weer in so 'n mate sal kry nie.'[127]

The HNP had made it plain that if successful in the 1948 election, one of their first acts would be to dismantle this 'dangerous' scheme.[128] To some extent this intention was facilitated by the adverse reaction in the United Kingdom to the Nationalist victory, thus reducing would-be settler numbers significantly. The scheme's *ad hoc* machinery was retained only long enough to settle immigrants already given permission to enter. Soon after D. F. Malan's government assumed power, more-rigorous selective criteria were instituted, ostensibly to protect the country 'against an outlook on life or world outlook generally foreign to that current in South Africa'.[129] Thereafter, until 1961, the National Party deliberately translated the traditional conservative perceptions of the dangers of immigration into a coherent system of exclusion, motivated by hostility.

Immigration is an experience which South Africa has shared with many other countries. The majority of whites in the Republic today are either Europeans, in the strict sense of the word, who came mainly in the great post-war immigration of 1948–50, and the even greater 1960s and 1970s waves (the latter after the neighbouring Portuguese colonies achieved independence); or they are descendants of Europeans who arrived intermittently between the seventeenth century and the early twentieth century. Yet paradoxically the existential fact of South Africa's geographical isolation and attendant transport problems reinforced the predisposition prevalent before about 1943 to disregard immigration as a potential stimulus to the growth of the white population.

The pace and size of human migrations are always subject to a number of delicately balanced push and pull factors: geo-political, economic, social and psychological. The 1820 British settlers, for example, migrated to the purportedly 'empty' Eastern Cape frontier because of the pressure of the post-Napoleonic economic recession on a country which was already perceiving emigration as a socio-economic safety valve. Many of the thousands who went to South Africa in the last quarter of the nineteenth century were drawn by the pull of the mineral discoveries, but an equally large proportion were Eastern European Jews propelled by the hardships of life in Tsarist Russia.

Compared to North America or Australia, however, the pull factors operating in South Africa were, and in the period under consideration largely remained, limited, primarily comprising the country's physical beauty, its moderate climate and the presence of a vast, black, untrained labour force. The United States of America had attracted unskilled millions by its inexhaustible need for labour. In South Africa de-tribalisation and the creation of an indigenous black urban proletariat dependent upon white entrepreneurial skills, were the most decisive factors inhibiting large-scale immigration. And the parallel internal migration of unskilled rural whites (mostly Afrikaners), who were perceived as needing state protection from social displacement, simply reinforced this trend.

The discourse of the main political parties in the two decades after Union emphasised the need for sound rural development as the precursor to industrial growth. Structural imperfections in South African agriculture, however, made its products uncompetitive in world markets. Economic growth was therefore in practice contingent upon prior industrialisation accompanied by considerable immigration. But industrial diversification, which had begun in the Pact period and burgeoned during Fusion, took off substantially only as a result of wartime requirements. Yet even in the late 1940s the manufacturing industry was not fully mature, and many immigrant artisans still found their skills too specialised for South African conditions.

In sum, South African circumstances, and consequently attitudes and policies concerning immigration, differed qualitatively from those of the other dominions, and ensured that the Union would not emulate their far more positive policies. While in the first twenty years of unification issues such as South Africa's constitutional status within the Commonwealth enjoyed a centrality in political debate denied to immigration, the latter was nevertheless frequently a gauge of prevailing public sentiment.

Initially the main opposition to state-sponsored immigration was a function of the hostility between the two white communities; virtually from the time of Union the voting strength of the Afrikaners effectively vetoed any such policy. This struggle for power within the white electorate accordingly frustrated the Imperial government's inter-war Empire settlement plan. Put another way, imperial considerations played a minimal role in influencing South African policy; and when such considerations were mooted (as for example, during the First World War) their effect was counter-productive.

Subsequent to the 1924 Pact victory, immigration policy became an important adjunct of what was increasingly identified as the crucial question in politics: the ordering of the black/white relationship. Thus, Smuts's serious attempts to encourage white immigration a few months before the 1924 election, and more especially from 1946 to 1948, were inspired by fears of black domination rather than by imperial ideology.

Similarly, Verwoerd's 1961 legislation was intended ultimately to address this issue. In reversing all previous political orthodoxy on the desirability of state-aided immigration, Verwoerd's policy was an extraordinary one which went far beyond Smuts's tentative essay. In developing it, the Nationalists were forced to free themselves from the prejudices and fears which had characterised their party's outlook since its inception. The old perception of British immigrants as 'stemvee' – 'voting cattle' who threatened indigenous Afrikaner institutions – or competitors who took the bread from 'die volk's' collective mouth, had to be jettisoned. Fears that immigrants would prove as 'unassimilable' to Afrikaner cultural norms as blacks were deemed to be, or have the 'wrong' attitudes on colour, had to give way, in the defence of white supremacy, to a recognition of cultural pluralism. The historically engendered spiritual withdrawal, the feelings of insecurity and inadequacy compounded by physical isolation, had to be reversed.

Notes

1 F. A. Johnstone, *Class, Race and Gold*, London, 1976, pp. 57 ff. deals with the complementary internal 'protective measures' taken by the state to moderate the 'structural insecurity' of white workers; E. Bradlow, 'Immigration into the Union 1910–1948: Policies and Attitudes', Ph.D. diss., University of Cape Town, 1978.
2 UG 12–14, *Report of the Economic Commission, January 1914*, p. 26.

3 *The Star*, 20 October 1909.

4 TG 13–08, *Report of the Transvaal Indigency Commission 1906–08*, pp. 126–7; *The Cape Times*, 23 August 1911, H. Burton; *House of Assembly Debates* (hereafter *H of A Debs*) 1912, vol. II, 12 April 1912, F. Creswell.

5 Jagger Library, University of Cape Town, *Duncan Papers*, I.D. 5(d) Duncan to Lady Selborne, 11 September 1910.

6 *The Cape Times*, 13 July 1910, 29 July 1910.

7 *Ibid.*, 20 August 1910.

8 British Parliamentary Papers, *Imperial Conference 1911, Dominions No. 7, Minutes of Proceedings of the Imperial Conference, 1911*, Cd. 5745, LIV, 1911.

9 *Royal Commission on the Natural Resources, Trade and Legislation of Certain Portions of His Majesty's Dominions, Part I. Migration, Land Settlement, and Immigration*, Cd. 7706, XIII, 1914–6; *Third Interim Report of the Royal Commission on the Natural Resources etc.*, Cd. 7505, XVIII, 1914.

10 Central Archives, Pretoria, Prime Minister's Office, 1/1/237,110/1/1913, 14 January 1913.

11 *The Cape Times*, 10 May 1910.

12 East London Museum, *Charles Crewe Papers*, Minutes, Progressive Party Conference; Library of the University of Witwatersrand, A.602, *Unionist Party Scrapbook and Press Clippings, The Transvaal Leader*, 17 March 1913, R. Feetham.

13 South African Political Archives, Pamphlet Collection, P1–22.

14 *Duncan Papers*, I.D.5(g), Duncan to Lady Selborne, 11 June 1913.

15 Central Archives, Prime Minister's Office, 1/1/105,20/21/1913, Contract Immigrants Bill, AB 3–13; H of A Debs vol. II 21 May 1912, vol. III 12 February 1913, vol. IV 10 March 1914, vol. XIII 11 February 1929.

16 On the Transvaal mines; tailors, cabinetmakers, upholsterers and saddlemakers at the Cape; and throughout the Union, domestics.

17 *Imperial Conference 1911, Dominions, No. 7, Minutes*, Cd. 5745.

18 *Duncan Papers*, I.D.5(g), Duncan to Lady Selborne, 11 June 1913; *The Cape Times*, 26 June 1911, 27 July 1911, 31 July 1911; *Royal Commission on the Natural Resources etc, Part II. Minutes of Evidence taken in London in June and July 1914, and Papers Laid before the Commission*, Cd. 7710, XIII, 1914–16; *Royal Commission on the Natural Resources etc. Minutes taken in London during October and November 1912*, Cd. 6516, XVI, 1912–13, pp. 233–4.

19 SC 6-1910-1911, *Report from the Select Committee on Closer Land Settlement*; *H of A Debs* vol. II, April 1912, *passim*; *The Cape Times*, 13 April 1912, 16 April 1912, 1 November 1913; UG 8–22, *Annual Departmental Reports (Abridged)* No. 1; *Royal Commission on the Natural Resources etc., Part I*, Cd. 7706.

20 *The Cape Times*, 26 September 1911, Botha; *H of A Debs* 1913, Hertzog.

21 See, for example, *The Cape Times*, 21 September 1912, A. Fischer at Reitz (OFS); 7 December 1912, Botha at Grahamstown; 8 November 1912, Smuts in Pretoria; 30 November 1912, Burton at Grahamstown; 31 October 1912, J. X. Merriman at Worcester; 20 October 1913, T. Watt in Johannesburg declared that to bring in immigrants under similar conditions to those in Canada and Australia would be 'a criminal act'.

22 U.G. 12–14, *Report of the Economic Commission*.

23 *Royal Commission on the Natural Resources etc., Part II, Mining, Mining Conditions, Trade, Legislation*, Cd. 7707, XIII, 1914–16.

24 UG 24–14, *Department of the Interior, Annual Report for the Calendar Year 1913*; UG 4–31, *Fourth Census of the Population of the Union of South Africa, 4 May 1926 (Enumeration of Europeans only). Report with Summaries and Analysis.*

25 *Imperial Conference 1911. Dominions. No. 8. Papers laid before the Conference*, Cd. 5746, LIV, 1911; Australian figures included troop movements.

26 *Duncan Papers*, I.D.5(n) undated paper by Duncan entitled 'Political Parties'; *De Burger*, 30 September 1916 on 'politieke immigratie'.

27 *De (later Die) Burger*, 28 January 1916.

28 *De Burger*, 11 December 1918; *H of A Debs* 13 February 1919, Minister of the

Interior.

29 *De Burger*, 6 November 1919, 2 December 1919, Smuts.

30 *Crewe Papers*, W. Long to Crewe, 11 October 1917.

31 *H of A Debs* 5 March 1919, W. D. Baxter. Primary products were being exported at high prices.

32 *Duncan Papers*, I.C.20, J. A. Moodie to Duncan 18 January 1919; *De Burger*, 6 June 1916.

33 *Duncan Papers*, I.D.15 (1), 23 August 1916. Copies of this communication went to Lord Selborne and Rider Haggard.

34 *Crewe Papers*, Minutes of Unionist Conference, October 1919.

35 *Final Report of the Royal Commission on the Natural Resources etc.*, Cd. 8462, X, 1917–18; *Extracts from Minutes of Proceedings and Papers Laid before the Conference, 1917–1918*, Cd. 9177, XVI, 1918. See also I. M. Drummond, *Imperial Economic Policy 1917–1939*, London, 1974; I. M. Drummond, *British Economic Policy and the Empire 1919–1939*, London, 1972.

36 *Report of the Oversea Settlement Committee for the Year Ended 31st December 1928*, Cmd. 3308, VIII, 1928.

37 *Report of the Oversea Settlement Committee for the Year Ended 31st December 1919*, Cmd. 573, XXII, 1920; *Report of the Oversea Settlement Committee for the Year Ended 31st December 1920*, Cmd. 1134, XV, 1921.

38 *The Cape Times*, 21 October 1920.

39 *Ibid.*, 25 November 1920.

40 G. F. Plant, *Oversea Settlement*, London, 1951, p. 74; *De Burger*, 5 November 1921, quoting Col. Wood, Under Secretary for Colonies, gave a figure of 5,000 who had come to South Africa by the end of 1921.

41 *United Empire*, vol. XIII, April 1922.

42 *H of A Debs* 23 June 1923, Smuts.

43 *Conference of Prime Ministers and Representatives of the United Kingdom, the Dominions and India, held in June, July and August, 1921*, Cmd. 1474, XIV, 1921 Session 1, p. 8.

44 Jagger Library, University of Cape Town (microfilm), *Smuts Papers*, vol. XXV, 2, 1 July 1921, notes on the discussion; Drummond, *Imperial Economic Policy*, p. 73.

45 W. K. Hancock, *Smuts, II, The Fields of Force 1919–1950*, Cambridge, 1968, ch. 2.

46 *Duncan Papers*, I.D. 5 (n), Duncan to Lady Selborne, 29 September 1920, 13 October 1920; I.D. 5(o), 4 May 1921.

47 *De Burger*, 10 March 1921, 26 March 1921, 2 November 1921, etc.; *H of A Debs* 23 May 1921, Malan; 1 July 1921, 15 June 1922, Hertzog. *De Burger* gave good coverage to British reports on migration, including a special column entitled 'Imperial questions' dealing with 'Empaaier' politics.

48 *H of A Debs* 19 June 1921, 10 June 1921, Duncan, then Minister of the Interior, who was forced to implement this fainéant policy; 14 June 1922, Smuts.

49 A. Eames-Perkins, 'The coming of the settler', *The Cape Times Annual*, 1921; *H of A Debs* 11 July 1922, J. W. Jagger, Minister of Railways.

50 *H of A Debs* 23 June 1923, Smuts; *The Cape Times*, 14 May 1923.

51 *The Farmer's Weekly*, 28 September 1921.

52 *H of A Debs* 23 June 1923. This being the last day of the session, debate was precluded.

53 *Die Burger*, 18 July 1923, report of British Empire Service League Congress, London, 16 July 1923; *The Cape Times*, 3 July 1923; *The Rand Daily Mail*, 15 November 1923.

54 *H of A Debs* 20 June 1922, R. B. Waterston, 20 April 1923, A. Barlow; *Die Burger*, 4 January 1924.

55 The Nationalist press continually referred to immigrants as 'these importations'.

56 *The Cape Times*, 9 July 1930, quoting a correspondent in *Die Burger*.

57 *H of A Debs* vol. X, 8 November 1927, Minister of the Interior; *H of A Debs* vol. XII, 6 February 1929, R. H. Struben; *Crewe Papers*, Lady Milner to Crewe, 23 January 1929.

58 *H of A Debs* vol. XIV, 10 February 1930, M. Kentridge, 12 February 1930, L. Blackwell.

59 See UG 19–30, UG 37–30, UG 29–31, UG 31–32, UG 32–33, and UG 42–34, *Statistics of Migration*, 1928–33.

60 *Duncan Papers*, I.D.5(t), to Lady Selborne, 19 February 1926.

61 T. R. H. Davenport, *South Africa: a Modern History*, pt 2, Johannesburg, third ed, 1987.

62 A. Chester, 'Expanding the population', *South African Business Efficiency*, October 1946, p. 8.

63 *Royal Commission on the Natural Resources etc.*, pt 1, Cd. 7706, pp. 3, 8; *The Cape Times*, 7 June 1911.

64 *Royal Commission on the Natural Resources etc.*, pt 1, Cd. 7706, Secretary, Department of Agriculture.

65 'A decade of colonisation: retrospect and prospect of land settlement schemes', *The African World Annual*, 1915.

66 J. P. R. Wallis, *Fitz: the Story of Sir Percy Fitzpatrick*, London, 1955, gives Fitzpatrick's version of the venture; D. Duminy and Bill Guest, *Interfering in Politics: a Biography of Sir Percy Fitzpatrick*, Johannesburg, 1987.

67 *Duncan Papers*, I.C.20, Chairman, Maldwyn Estates to Duncan (a director), 18 January 1919, 25 January 1919, 8 March 1919, 21 April 1919.

68 UG 14–26, *Report of the Economic and Wage Commission*, pp. 365 ff.

69 *The Cape Times*, 13 October 1920.

70 *Duncan Papers*, I.D. 5(bb), Duncan to Lady Selborne, 7 July 1936; *The Cape Times*, 6 November 1920, 26 July 1921, 7 September 1923. The scheme was 'rescued' by the government in 1924 and prospered.

71 Hereafter referred to as the 1820 Association.

72 *Duncan Papers*, vol. II, 41 (a and b), Duncan to Frank Fletcher, Marlborough College, 17 May 1909.

73 J. Stone, *Colonist or Uitlander? A Study of the British Immigrant in South Africa*, Oxford, 1973, p. 125, n. 21, constitution of the Association article (i). The practical aid was in the form of training facilities, help with the purchase of land and stock, etc.

74 *The Cape Times*, 13 October 1920, Crewe.

75 *Ibid.*, 11 April 1921, 29 June 1923; *The Times*, 31 May 1921.

76 *De Burger*, 12 January 1920, 17 September 1920.

77 *The Cape Times*, 9 September 1925, 20 November 1925, 12 March 1927, various leading Association figures.

78 *Ibid.*, 26 October 1921, 29 June 1923, 9 August 1923.

79 *H of A Debs* 7 July 1921; *Smuts Papers*, vol. XXVI, no. 63, 5 April 1923, vol. XXVII, no. 204, 29 March 1923.

80 *De Burger*, 23 September 1920, 11 April 1921, 5 December 1922, 4 January 1923; *Senate Debates* 27 March 1922.

81 *Crewe Papers*, to Crewe, 23 January 1929; J. A. Manson, 'Settlement in South Africa', *The 1820*, vol. I, no. 1.

82 *South Africa*, vol. CLXIV, 6 December 1929.

83 *South Africa*, vol. CLXVI, 18 July 1930, 26 September 1930; *The 1820*, vol. I, no. 5, November 1929.

84 *The Farmer's Weekly*, 20 June 1928, 11 July 1928, 1 August 1928, 3 April 1929.

85 *The Cape Times*, 28 September 1932, 1820 Association, Annual Meeting; *The 1820*, vol. III, no. 9, March 1932; no. 12, June 1932; vol. VII, no. 1, July 1935.

86 *South Africa*, vol. CLXXXIII, 6 July 1934; vol. CXCI, 26 September 1936.

87 *The 1820*, vol. VIII, no. 5, November 1936, p. 5.

88 *Smuts Papers*, vol. LXV, no. 36, R. A. Hockley to Smuts, 18 December 1941; Stone, *Colonist*, p. 129.

89 *The Cape Times*, 11 December 1945; *South Africa*, vol. CCXVI, 3 November 1945; vol. CCXVII, 5 January 1946.

90 *Duncan Papers*, I.A.5(j); *The Cape Times*, 6 June 1934.

91 *Union Statistics for Fifty Years: Jubilee Issue 1910–1960*, tables G-4, G-6; S. H. Frankel, 'An analysis of the growth of the national income', *South African Journal of Economics*, vol. XII, June 1944, pp. 112–38.

92 Hancock, *Smuts*, vol. ii, ch. 16.

93 *The Cape Times*, 6 November 1935, Smuts; *Die Vaderland*, 10 August 1936; *The Sunday Times*, 11 October 1936.

94 *H of A Debs* vol. XXVIII, January 1937, *passim*.

95 Report No. 286, *Statistics of Immigrants and Emigrants 1924–1964*, 1965, Table 13.

96 J. F. Loedolff, *Nederlandse Immigrante: 'n Sosiologiese ondersoek van hul inskakeling in die Gemeenskaplewe van Pretoria*, Cape Town, 1960, p. 18, Table 4.

97 A. J. P. Taylor, *English History 1914–1945*, Oxford, 1965, pp. 409–13; *Smuts Papers*, vol. CXXII, no. 24, Secretary of State for Dominion Affairs to Minister of External Affairs, 16 December 1935; *Union Statistics for Fifty Years*, Table C-7; *The 1820*, vol. VIII, no. 3, September 1936.

98 *South Africa*, vol. CXCIX, 3 September 1938; vol. CC, 3 December 1938.

99 Special Reports, 119, 128, 141, *Statistics of Migration 1937–1939 (abridged)*.

100 *Herenigde* is the Afrikaans equivalent of 'reunited'. Hertzog and Malan were reconciled in September 1939.

101 A. G. Thomson, 'The scramble for manpower', *South African Business Efficiency*, January 1946; P.H.G. and E.K., 'Post war immigration', *Commercial Opinion*, vol. XXI, no. 246, July 1943; J. Keddie, 'South Africa needs more manpower', *South African Industry and Trade*, vol. XXXIX, March 1943; S. H. Frankel, 'World economic welfare', *South African Journal of Economics*, vol. XI, September 1943; L. Bethlehem, 'Give us more people' *The Forum*, vol. V, no. 42, 16 January 1943; etc.

102 E. Kahn, 'Immigration and the future of the non-European', *Race Relations*, vol. X, no. 2, 1943.

103 E. J. Burford, 'Thoughts on immigration', *Trek*, vol. X, 17 May 1946; also Bethlehem, 'Give us more people'.

104 Davenport, *South Africa*, p. 337.

105 *The Natal Witness*, 8 January 1945, C. F. Stallard, the party leader; *H of A Debs* vol. XLVII, 19 February 1944, F. H. Acutt, C. Neate.

106 See *Die Transvaler* (whose editor was Dr H. F. Verwoerd), 26 November 1941, 3 November 1942, 6 October 1945 etc; *H of A Debs* vol. XLVII 1944 *passim*.

107 Public Record Office (PRO), DO 35/325, M822/65, C. W. Dixon, 6 June 1944; DO 35/1324,M822/54 undd. memorandum, about July 1944; *Migration within the British Commonwealth*, 1945, Cmd. 6658, X, 1944–45, p. 3; *The Cape Times*, 29 April 1946; *South Africa*, vol. CCXIV, 1 July 1944.

108 PRO, DO 35/1324,M822/54, telegram no. 100, South African Acting High Commissioner to Dominions Office, 9 September 1944: DO 35/1325, M822/65, C. W. Dixon, 6 June 1944.

109 *South Africa*, vol. CCXVII, 16 March 1946; *Senate Debates*, 1946, 2 May 1946; *H of A Debs* vol. LVII, 6 May 1946.

110 PRO, DO 35/1324,M822/54, War Cabinet memorandum on migration, 26 March 1945; *ibid.*, Union High Commissioner to Permanent Under-Secretary of State, Dominions Office, 13 June 1945; *Senate Debates*, 3rd Session, 9th Parliament, 1946–47, 2 May 1946; *H of A Debs* vol. LVII, 6 May 1946; G. Heaton Nicholls, *South Africa in My Time*, London, 1961, p. 410.

111 *Smuts Papers*, vol. CLXV, no. 37, memorandum of D. D. Forsyth, Chairman of the Immigration Selection Board, 14 July 1946.

112 *The Times*, 16 August 1946.

113 *Smuts Papers*, vol. LXXXIV, no. 193, 27 January 1947.

114 *South Africa*, vol. CCXVIII, 17 August 1946.

115 Hancock, *Smuts*, II, p. 485, quoting J. H. Hofmeyr.

116 *Smuts Papers*, vol. LXXX, Smuts to Mrs Smuts, 7 September 1946, quoting the Union High Commissioner.

117 Unprinted annexures to the Votes and Proceedings of the House of Assembly, An. 302/1949, Schedule of occupations of immigrants, 1946–48.

118 *Smuts Papers*, vol. CLXVI, no. 115, unsigned, about September 1946.
119 *Smuts Papers*, vol. CLXVI, Hofmeyr Memorandum, 9 December 1946; Jagger Library, University of Cape Town, *Lawrence Papers*, Immigration File 1946–47, Minutes of emergency meeting of Immigration Council, 10 December 1946.
120 *Government Gazette*, 3801, 25 April 1947, Notce 826, dd. 16 April 1947.
121 South African Federated Chamber of Industries Archives, Pretoria, Secretary, Immigration Council to Secretary, SAFCI, 30 July 1947; *Lawrence Papers*, Immigration File 1946–47, Minutes of meeting of Immigration Council, 24 December 1946; National Union of Distributive Workers, Cape Town, Minutes of Annual Conference, 1947; South African Trades and Labour Council Report, 1946.
122 *Lawrence Papers*, Immigration File 1946–47; *The Times*, 26 March 1947; M. Murray, *Union Castle Chronicle 1853–1953*, London, 1953, p. 339.
123 *Union Statistics for Fifty Years*, Table C-3; 28, 839 came in 1947, 36, 631 in 1948.
124 UG19–1950, Statistics of Migration, 1950, Table 7c.
125 *Senate Debates*, 5th Session, 9th Parliament, 1948, 10 September 1948.
126 *H of A Debs* vol. LXII, 27 January 1948, Minister of the Interior.
127 *Smuts Papers*, vol. LXXX, 7 September 1946, Smuts to Mrs Smuts. 'My goal is to save them and save the country from certain downfall. Now is our chance which perhaps we won't get again to such an extent.'
128 *The Cape Times*, 18 May 1948, Swart, the OFS leader.
129 H of A Debs vol. LXIV, 16 August 1948, vol. LXV, 16 September 1948.

INDEX